PERGAMON INTERNATIONAL LIBRARY
of Science, Technology, Engineering and Social Studies
The 1000-volume original paperback library in aid of education,
industrial training and the enjoyment of leisure
Publisher: Robert Maxwell, M.C.

A Complete Defence to 1P-K4

SECOND EDITION

THE PERGAMON TEXTBOOK
INSPECTION COPY SERVICE

An inspection copy of any book published in the Pergamon International Library
will gladly be sent to academic staff without obligation for their consideration for
course adoption or recommendation. Copies may be retained for a period of 60 days
from receipt and returned if not suitable. When a particular title is adopted or
recommended for adoption for class use and the recommendation results in a sale
of 12 or more copies, the inspection copy may be retained with our compliments,
The Publishers will be pleased to receive suggestions for revised editions and new
titles to be published in this important International Library.

PERGAMON CHESS SERIES

General Editor
David N. L. Levy

Some other books in the series:

ALEXANDER, C. H. O'D. & BEACH, T. J.
Learn Chess: A New Way for All
Volume 1: First Principles
Volume 2: Winning Methods

AVERBAKH, Y.
Chess Endings: Essential Knowledge

BARDEN, L. W.
The Ruy Lopez: Winning Chess with 1P-K4

BELL, A.
The Machine Plays Chess

BOTVINNIK, M.
Anatoly Karpov: His Road to the World Championship

ESTRIN, J. & PANOV, V.
Comprehensive Chess Openings

KARPOV & ROSHAL
Anatoly Karpov: Chess is My Life

KEENE, R.
The Chess Combination from Philidor to Karpov

LEVY, D. N. L.
Learn Chess from the World Champions

SUETIN, A. S.
Modern Chess Opening Theory

VUKOVIC
The Art of Attack in Chess

A Complete Defence to 1P-K4

A STUDY OF PETROFF'S DEFENCE

by

BERNARD CAFFERTY

and

DAVID HOOPER

SECOND EDITION

PERGAMON PRESS

OXFORD · NEW YORK · TORONTO · SYDNEY
PARIS · FRANKFURT

U.K.	Pergamon Press Ltd., Headington Hill Hall, Oxford OX3 0BW, England
U.S.A.	Pergamon Press Inc., Maxwell House, Fairview Park, Elmsford, New York 10523, U.S.A.
CANADA	Pergamon of Canada Suite 104, 150 Consumers Road, Willowdale, Ontario M2J. 1P9, Canada
AUSTRALIA	Pergamon Press (Aust.) Pty. Ltd., P.O. Box 544, Potts Point, N.S.W. 2011, Australia
FRANCE	Pergamon Press SARL, 24 rue des Ecoles, 75240 Paris, Cedex 05, France
FEDERAL REPUBLIC OF GERMANY	Pergamon Press GmbH, 6242 Kronberg-Taunus, Pferdstrasse 1, Federal Republic of Germany

First edition 1967
Second edition 1979

British Library Cataloguing in Publication Data

Cafferty, Bernard
A complete defence to 1P-K4. — 2nd ed. —
(Pergamon chess series). — (Pergamon international library).
1. Chess — Openings
I. Title II. Hooper, David
794.1'22   GV1450.2   78-40919

ISBN 0-08-024089-5 (Hardcover)
ISBN 0-08-024088-7 (Flexicover)

Printed in Hungary by Franklin Printing House

Contents

PREFACE TO THE SECOND EDITION   vii

PREFACE TO THE FIRST EDITION   ix

INTRODUCTION   xi

A BIOGRAPHICAL NOTE   xiii

Part I. Petroff's Defence

The Modern Attack	3
The Classical Attack	44
The Cozio Attack	67
The Nimzowitsch Attack	76
The Kaufmann Attack	81
The French Attack	84
The Paulsen Attack	87
Cochrane's and Other Variations	91
The Three Knight's Game	97
The Barcza Opening	102
The Bishop's Opening	105
Philidor's Defence	113

Part II. Other King's Pawn Openings

The Four Knights Opening	123
The Vienna Opening	128
The Scotch Opening	131
The Centre Opening	135
The King's Gambit	138
The Bishop's Opening	146

INDEX OF GAMES   148

Preface to the Second Edition

THIS book has been revised and expanded to take account of the immense amount of serious competitive play in the decade since the first edition was completed in 1966. During this period the Petroff has gained a new supporter in the person of the former world champion Petrosian. Some commentators even attribute the loss of his title in 1969 to his failure to carry on playing the Petroff after it had brought him two comfortable draws late in the match against Spassky. Meanwhile, older supporters of the defence such as Smyslov and Bronstein have not lost faith in it. Even the current world title holder Karpov has adopted it occasionally.

The layout is similar to that of the first edition so that new lines of play may be easily identified. Philidor's Defence, however, has been expanded from a page to a chapter of its own.

The authors wish to acknowledge the help provided by many readers of the first edition who sent in comments, queries and recommendations.

Birmingham
Whitchurch, Hants
March 1978

BERNARD CAFFERTY
DAVID HOOPER

Preface to the First Edition

I AM advocating in this book a defensive system to the king's pawn opening based on the open game (1 P–K4 P–K4), yet avoiding the Ruy Lopez by playing instead Petroff's Defence (2 N–KB3 N–KB3).

This way of avoiding the Lopez has been regularly used in the past and present by Mason, Pillsbury, Marshall, Rabinovich, Kan, Kashdan, Alexander, Trifunovich, Mikenas, Kholmov, and Rossetto. Others, from Morphy to Alekhine, and more recently Smyslov, Lilienthal, and Bronstein, have used Petroff's Defence from time to time.

Part I deals with Petroff's Defence both from Black's point of view and from White's. I hope this will be useful to all players who play or defend the king's pawn opening. I have endeavoured not only to show the currently popular variations, but also to deal with all old and forgotten lines which, as we sometimes find to our cost, may at any moment be resuscitated. Altogether my research has covered more than a hundred years of tournament chess.

Some opponents may avoid Petroff's Defence altogether, and you will need to know good defences against the Vienna Opening, King's Gambit, etc. This is dealt with in Part II, but with a difference, only from Black's point of view. The two parts of the book together make a complete answer to 1 P–K4.

I have used the sign + to indicate a fairly substantial advantage, for White if after a White move, or for Black if after a Black move. The sign ± indicates that White stands better, and the sign ∓ that Black stands better. These signs should not be too precisely interpreted. In making some hundreds of assessments there will be inconsistencies, not to say errors. The sign = means a balanced game, offering equal chances to Black and White.

Some games are included, not too well known, but otherwise chosen for no special reason; some to illustrate opening strategy; some because they are short, piquant, or curious; some positional; and some for the cut and thrust of tactical play, that is for pleasure, perhaps the best reason of all.

Petroff's Defence was mentioned in Part II of the first known textbook of the modern game, *Repeticion: de Amores: E Arte de Axedrez con el juegos de Partido...*, Lucena, c. 1497. Part I of this book concerns love, but not love of chess. Other early works (before 1830) which added new ideas to the defence are *Libro da Imparare Giocare a Scachi, Et de belissimi Partiti...*, Damiano, 1512; *Libro de la Invencion liberal y arte del juego del Axedrez...*, Ruy Lopez, 1561; *Il Giuoco degli Scacchi*, Cozio, 1766; *Il Giuoco Incomparabile degli Scacchi*, Ponziani, 1769. The further history of this defence may be traced from the Biographical Note (p. xiii), and from notes here and there in the text.

It would be a tedious task to make a complete bibliography. Besides searching most of the world's chess magazines and openings books I checked records of several hundred tournaments up to about 1950. Leonard Barden kindly supplied me with information collected from several hundred tournaments after this date, without which I could hardly have finished the task. I am also grateful to Mr. B. H. Wood, Mr. K. Whyld, and Miss E. Tranmer for the privilege of using their libraries.

Finally, I must again thank Leonard Barden, whose authority in the realm of openings theory is unquestioned, for kindly consenting to write an Introduction to this book.

Chertsey, Surrey   DAVID HOOPER
May, 1966

Introduction

THE practice of many chess masters has shown that a thorough knowledge of a small field in the openings is a better guarantee of success than a wide smattering of variations. The difficulty for the practical player is that the openings which are generally recognized as best, like the Sicilian, the King's Indian, and the Ruy Lopez, cannot be grasped and assimilated easily. If you play them in tournament chess against a strong opponent, you run the risk of being surprised by a recent novelty. Club chessplayers and amateurs also find the sophisticated strategy of the fashionable openings a barrier to handling them successfully.

The increasing complexity of the openings has naturally led to a search for attacks and defences where the ideas are easily grasped and which reduce the possibility of surprise innovations. There has been a fashion for gambits like the Scotch and King's Gambit for White, and for defences like the Caro–Kann (1...P–QB3) and the Robatsch (1...P–KN3) for Black. These defences, however, imply closed strategical play, which does not appeal to every taste.

The Petroff Defence, the subject of this book, has recently attracted a growing interest from leading players wanting an all-purpose defence to 1 P–K4. The success of the Petroff in stopping White from winning—and in tournament chess it is half the battle to draw with Black against your stronger rivals—is shown by the reputation of grandmaster Trifunovich of Yugoslavia, its leading exponent today. He would certainly be included in any grandmaster's list of the half-dozen players in the world most difficult to beat.

Nor should it be thought that the Petroff is just a negative defence aiming at half a point. Its attraction for the player who is interested in a counter-attacking weapon is shown by the names of its other leading present-day exponents. Rossetto of Argentina, and Kholmov and Mikenas of the Soviet Union, are all inventive and imaginative players alert for novel strategy. A generation ago Frank Marshall, one of the most gifted tacticians of all time, favoured the Petroff above other defences to 1 P–K4.

In club chess the Petroff has practically been forgotten. Hence anyone who knows it thoroughly can use it to aim for the full point. The tournament and match player can rely on it as a method of reaching a sound position from the opening with little risk, and of achieving still more if White tries too hard to carry out his obligation to refute a supposedly second-rate opening.

I believe that we shall be seeing a lot more of the Petroff during the next few years, and that this book will become an essential reference tool for anyone using the defence or playing against it. David Hooper relied on the system regularly when competing with success in international events and in the British Championship. The book is both the fruit of his years of study of the nuances of the defence and a survey of the latest up-to-the-minute developments. Included here is every significant Petroff Defence of the last ten to fifteen years, taken from my own virtually complete library of tournament bulletins and magazines of this period. Chess theory changes constantly, even in a stable opening like the Petroff, so that you will find many references here right up to the latest events of 1966.

The book is intended to enable anyone who reads it to meet 1 P–K4, the most common opening move in chess, with confidence. It therefore includes a full analysis of other king's pawn openings by which White may choose to sidestep the Petroff. When you study the book you will find many new openings ideas, and several new assessments of old positions. So many variations in the Petroff have had little analysis and practice that fresh approaches are more likely than in the fashionable openings of the moment.

Like others in the Pergamon Chess Series, this is meant basically as a practical book to help you win more games. David Hooper shares my own view that the real test of the success of *A Complete Defence to 1 P–K4* is whether, after reading and absorbing it, you do better than before in your tournament, match, club, or postal chess. In writing an earlier book in the series, on the Ruy Lopez, I had a similar philosophy. That book did indeed have some value for practical players, and was used by Boris Spassky in preparation for his successful world title eliminators against Keres and Tal. Likewise, I expect *A Complete Defence to 1 P–K4* to be useful for ambitious players at all levels of the game.

May, 1966   LEONARD BURDEN

A Biographical Note

ALEXANDER DMITRIEVICH PETROFF was born in the village of Viserovo near Pskov on 12 February 1794 o.s. When a child of 4 he learnt the moves, and as a boy of 10 he played chess at St. Petersburg. As a young man he soon became Russia's strongest player. He went into the civil service but did not achieve much success there; perhaps opportunities were not open to him. As to his chess he said he had neither the time nor the means to travel. He played and bettered the leading amateurs of St. Petersburg and Warsaw, but never played a master from any other country. Nor did he play what we should today call a serious game of chess. His few surviving games show combinative talent and a fondness for direct play and the open game. We can only guess at his strength, and he was amongst the leading players of his generation; but it is doubtful whether he was as strong as either La Bourdonnais or his celebrated rival M'Donnel.

Outside of Russia not much was known about Petroff. The German master Anderssen was fond of a little joke: "Who has ever seen Petroff? The Russians have invented him so that they can have a master." Upon retirement, however, in 1863, Petroff made his first and only trip abroad, visiting Berlin, Vienna, and Paris. He met, but did not play, some of the leading masters of a younger generation. In Paris he met Morphy "more than once" but "that immortal refused serious talk about the game"—so Petroff noted in his diary. He ended his tour at Dieppe playing the Rev. D. M. Salter at various odds. Several times, after losing a game, Salter would telegraph Loewenthal in London to find out how he should have played! Loewenthal extended a welcome to Petroff, endeavouring to persuade him to visit London, then the chess capital of the world. Petroff declined, on account, he said, of pressing business. Returning to Warsaw he gave up playing. He died on 22 April 1867 aged 73.

It is difficult to imagine that Petroff had any strong chess ambitions. Unlike the Ourousoff brothers and Jaenisch he seemed reluctant to put his reputation to the test outside his own country. He lived in Warsaw for the last twenty-seven years of his life, and it would not have been so difficult for him during this time to have met some of the famous Berlin players. He kept few if any scores of his games, and sent no analyses to the chess press. He was content to let Jaenisch sing his praises. He met Morphy and Kolisch, probably in private, and showed a curious reluctance to visit the London Clubs where he might have met Bird, Blackburne, Boden, Loewenthal, G. A. MacDonnell, Staunton, and Steinitz. He preferred to spend some time at Dieppe playing odds games. He wrote one chess book, the second in the Russian language, in 1824. In it he condemned the defence later named after him. Perhaps he would have been an even more forgotten player than he is had he not met Jaenisch in 1837.

Carl Andreyevich Jaenisch (1813–72), a Major in the Engineers, Knight of the Order of St. Anne and St. Stanislav, resigned his commission at the age of 27 because he "loved chess so much". He travelled around Europe, residing some time in Paris. With great industry he set about writing his *magnum opus*, published in two parts, *Analyse Nouvelle des Ouvertures de Jeu des Echecs* (1842–3)—an English edition followed a year or so later. This book fairly launched Petroff's Defence, hitherto considered almost unplayable. He gave numerous new variations many of which are still considered playable. He did of course work on this book with Petroff, who was probably the abler analyst. Even so, Petroff's Defence would in all probability never have been so called had Jaenisch not written his book, and had he not been so generous in giving praise and credit to Petroff whom he greatly admired. It might as well have been called Jaenisch's Defence. Jaenisch himself never wrote another book of lasting value, nor was he particularly successful as a player, and in the later years of his life he more or less faded from the chess scene.

PART I

Petroff's Defence

1 P-K4 P-K4
2 N-KB3 N-KB3

Chapter 1

The Modern Attack

1 P–K4	P–K4
2 N–KB3	N–KB3
3 P–Q4	

Introduced by Petroff in 1837. Played by Steinitz (as early as his first match with Black-burne, 1862), and advocated by him in his Modern Chess Instructor (1889). It has become popular since 1958 and was given a great impetus by its adoption by Fischer in 1962. At first, as is the case with all new attacks, practical results tended to favour White a little, but better defensive lines have since been found. Although fashionable, 3 P–Q4 is not necessarily stronger than 3 N×P.

3 ...	P×P

For sound alternatives see the Symmetrical Variation, and also Philidor's Defence (Chapter 12).

4 P–K5

The best move, but White may also play 4 B–QB4 leading to the Ourousoff Gambit.

4 ...	N–K5

By **4...Q–K2** Black wins a pawn, but at the expense of a cramped game, **5 B–K2 N–K5** (if 5 ... N–N5 6 0–0 N×KP 7 R–K1 K–Q1 8 N×P±, or here 6 ... N–QB3 7 R–K1! and not 7 N×P KN×KP 8 R–K1 Q–Q1 9 B–QN5 B–K2 10 N–B5 0–0 11 N×B ch Q×N 12 B×N QP×B 13 P–KB4—as given by Steinitz—13 ... B–N5 +) **6 0–0 N–QB3 7 R–K1** and now 7 ... P–KR3 8 B–QB4 N–N4 9 N×N P×N 10 N–Q2 P–N5 11 N–K4 N×P 12 N–N5 P–KB3 13 B–B4 P–Q3 14 Q×QP B–Q2 15 QR–Q1± (Napier–Marshall, Monte Carlo, 1902). If White does not want to play a gambi the may proceed simply **6 Q×P Q–N5 ch** 7 Q×Q B×Q ch 8 P–B3, or 7 QN–Q2 N×N 8 B×N Q×Q 9 N×P–QR3 10 B–KB4 N–B3 11 N×N± (Mieses–Grob, Zurich, 1934).

5 Q×P

The Normal Variation. For 5 Q–K2 see the Steinitz Variation.

| 5 ... | P–Q4 |
| 6 P×P e.p. | N×QP |

See Diagram 1.

1

This apparently simple position is deceptive. Active piece play follows, attended by sudden dangers for Black as is often the case in open positions. As a result of the unusual placing of his king's knight Black's Q4 square is less well guarded than usual; also he cannot so effectively harass White's queen which, if driven, can move to a good position at KB4 or QR4.

Yet Black has no weaknesses; his development is not backwards; and if he keeps it so he can hope for equality.

THE NORMAL VARIATION

LINE 1 (*from Diagram 1*)

7 B–Q3

Showalter's move (1896), and probably best. **7 B–KB4** comes into consideration, **7 ... N–B3** 8 Q–Q2 ch Q–K2? (8 ... B–K2! The point of White's idea is seen after 8 ... P–KN3 9 B–K2 B–N2 10 B–KR6) 9 B–K2 N–K5 10 Q–K3 N–N5 11 Q–B1 Q–B4 12 0–0! Schmid–Kinzel, Siegen, 1970. Now if 12 ... Q×P 13 Q–K1. It is clear that Black's premature attempt to take the initiative has dislocated his position.

| 7 ... | N–B3 |

7 ... Q–K2 ch is not wholly satisfactory. The idea is to oppose White's KB, **8 B–K3** (8 K–Q1? N–B3 9 Q–QR4 Q–Q2 10 N–B3 B–K2 11 N–Q5 0–0 12 N×B ch Q×N∓, Bronstein–Ragozin, Moscow, 1957) **8 ... B–B4** (8 ... N–B4 9 B×N B×B 10 N–B3, while 8 ... N–B3 also comes into consideration, with probable transposition) **9 N–B3 N–B3** and now (1) 10 Q–QR4 B×B 11 P×B Q–Q2 12 P–Q4 B–K2 13 P–Q5 N–N1 14 Q–N3, Black has the worst of it, but he drew the game (Bronstein–Kholmov, U.S.S.R. Team Championship, 1958), or (2) 10 Q–KB4 B×B 11 P×B Q–K3 12 0–0–0 B–K2 13 P–Q4 Q–B4 14 PQ5± (Spassky–Kholmov, Rostov, 1960).

Black may at once oppose bishops, **7 . . . B–B4** and White should reply 8 0–0. This has not been tested. If 8 B×B Q–K2 ch!

8 Q–KB4

See Diagram 2.

2

LINE 1 (A) (*from Diagram 2*)

8...   **P–KN3**

At the present time masters prefer this move. Black gets a strong post for his bishop. The fianchetto was introduced by Alatortsev in 1945 (though after 7 N–B3) and in this position (after 7 B–Q3) it was pioneered by Milner-Barry.

White often attacks by KN–KN5 and N×B(K6), or by B–QB5 and B(QB5)×N(Q6). Black may well then be left with an isolated centre pawn, but it is not hard to defend. As is well known an isolated centre pawn commanding strong points on an adjacent file can often be a strength rather than a weakness—compare with Tarrasch's views on the isolated pawn resulting from his defence to the Queen's Gambit.

White may also attack by advancing his KRP, which is not very effective if Black plays his moves in the right order, in particular not castling too soon on the king's side.

The strength of Black's game is his KB, and attempts are often made to exchange it. Black must not permit this too easily, but if it is unavoidable must seek compensation in the time which White expends on the exchanging operation.

9 N–B3

The earliest attempts to refute Black's 8th move went as follows: **9 0–0 B–N2 10 R–K1 ch B–K3 11 N–N5** (11 Q–QR4 0–0 12 B–KN5 Q–Q2 13 N–B3 P–KR3 14 B–R4 P–R3∓, Milich–Trifunovich, Yugoslav Championship, 1958) **11 . . . 0–0 12 N×B P×N**, and now:

(1) 13 Q–KN4 B–Q5 (13 . . . Q–B3 is also good, since if 14 Q×P ch Q×Q 15 R×Q B–Q5 16 R–K2 QR–K1, or 14 R–B1 N–K4, or 14 Q–N3 N–N5 15 R–B1 N–B4 16 Q×BP QR–B1 17 Q×P N×B 18 P×N N–N6! 19 RP×N R×B +, Hubner–Segal, Dresden, 1969) 14 Q×KP ch K–R1 15 R–K2 Q–R5 16 P–KN3 Q–R4.

(2) 13 Q–N3 B–Q5 14 R–B1 N–B4 (14 ... N–K4 intending 15 ... N×B and then 16 ... Q–Q–B3 is even better) 15 Q–R3 N–K4 (Broadbent–Milner-Barry, Buxton, 1950).

In all cases Black has excellent attacking chances.

Euwe's suggestion **9 N–Q4** can well be met by 9 ... Q–K2 ch 10 B–K3 N–K4=, or 9 ... N–N5 10 0–0 N×B 11 P×N B–K2=.

The idea of opposing bishops on the long diagonal can also be satisfactorily met by Black:

(1) **9 0–0 B–N2 10 B–Q2** 0–0 (10 ... Q–B3 is sound 11 R–K1 + B–K3 12 Q–QR4? Q×P 13 N–R3 0–0 14 P–B3 N–K4∓, Heusler–Kozlov, European Postal Cup, 1971–2, but not 10 ... B×P 11 B–B3 B×B 12 N×B B–K3 13 KR–K1 0–0 14 N–KN5 N–K1 15 Q–KR4 N–B3 16 Q–R6 +, Neumann–Spala, postal, 1958) 11 B–B3 B–B4 12 B(B3)×B K×B 13 B×B N×B 14 N–B3 Q–Q3= (Robatsch–Kolarov, Kecskemét, 1962), or

(2) **9 B–Q2 Q–K2 ch 10 B–K2 N–K5 11 N–B3 N×B 12 0–0–0 B–K3 13 N–Q4 N×N 14 Q×N N–N6 ch 15 RP×N B–R3 ch 16 K–N1 0–0=** (Kotkov–Vistanetskis, Vilna, 1961).

9 ...	**B–N2**

See Diagram 3.

3

10 B–K3

10 B–Q2 is the alternative, but is not stronger than the text move, **10 ... B–K3** (10 ... Q–K2 ch is also good, perhaps better, since if 11 K–B1 B–K3 12 R–K1 0–0 13 P–KR4 Q–B3 14 Q–R2 B–B5∓, Yudovich–Gusakov, Perm, 1960) **11 0–0–0** and now:

(1) 11 ... Q–B3 12 Q×Q (for 12 N–KN5 Q×Q see the main line) 12 ... B×Q 13 N–KN5 0–0–0 (better than 13 ... B–B5 as in Furman–Lengyel, Leningrad, 1962) 14 N×B P×N 15 KR–K1 KR–K1 16 N–K4 N×N 17 R×N R–Q5 and White has no significant advantage (Tal–Rossetto, Amsterdam, 1964).

(2) 11 ... 0–0 12 P–KR4 Q–B3 (or 12 ... P–KR3 13 KR–K1 R–K1! 14 P–R3 Q–B3 15 Q×Q B×Q 16 B×RP B×N 17 P×B B–N5, Boleslavsky–Trifunovich, Zagreb, 1958. Black drew, having enough for the pawn) 13 Q–R2 (13 Q×Q B×Q 14 N–KN5 N–N5=, Steiner–Bisguier, Omaha, 1959; or 13 Q–N3 N–N5 14 B–KN5 N×P ch 15 K–Q2 N×N +) 13 ... N–K4 14 N×N (14 B–KN5 N×N 15 P×N Q×P∓, Krogius–Kholmov, U.S.S.R. Championship, 1959) 14 ... Q×N 15 P–B4 (15 Q×Q B×Q 16 P–R5 KR–K1 17 P–QN3 **B–B4**= as in the stem game Boleslavsky–Alatortsev, Moscow, 1945, or 15 B–KB4 Q–QR4

16 P–R5 P–KN4) 15 ... Q–KR4 (15 ... Q–B3 16 P–R5±) 16 B–K2 (16 N–K2 N–B5!∓ as given by Mikenas) 16 ... B–N5 17 B×B Q×B 18 P–R5 KR–K1. The exchanges have rendered White's attack ineffective.

10 P–KR4 is premature, as Black has not castled yet. 10 ... B–K3 11 P–R5 Q–K2 12 B–K3 0–0–0 13 0–0–0 B×N 14 P×B N–N4∓ (Klavin–Maslov, Lithuania–Latvia, 1959).

10 ...   **B–K3**

See Diagram 4.

4

10 ... 0–0 probably transposes, (1) 11 0–0–0 B–K3 12 P–KR4 (A recent idea. If 12 B–QB5 R–K1, and not 12 ... Q–B3 13 Q×Q B×Q 14 N–QN5±) 12 ... Q–B3 (A timely response. Not 12 ... P–QR4? 13 P–R5 Q–B3 when a Birmingham League game Ingram–Rowley, 1975 had the drastic finish 14 Q–R2 N–N5 15 B–Q4! N×B ch 16 R×N Q–B4 17 P×P Q×P 18 N–K5 Q–B4 19 P–KN4 B×N 20 P×Q B×Q 21 R–N1 ch mating) 13 Q×Q (13 Q–R2 N–K4 14 B–KN5 N×N 15 P×N Q×P 16 P–R5 Q×RP∓, Medina–Mjagmarsuren, Skopje, 1972. Not 13 Q–N3 N–N5 14 B–KN5 because of 14 ... N×P ch 15 K–Q2 N×N+) 13 ... B×Q 14 N–K4 (14 N–KN5 B×QN 15 P×B B×P 16 P–R5 P–B3 17 N×P K×N 18 P×P ch K–N1 19 R–R7 N–K4 20 B–KR6 KR–K1=, Bannik–Nikolich, postal, 1966) 14 ... B–N2 15 N×N P×N 16 B–K4 KR–Q1= (Kholmov–Parma, Sukhumi, 1966). (2) 11 0–0 B–K3, and not 11 ... Q–B3 12 N–Q5±.

11 0–0–0

This is more often played nowadays than **11 0–0** and if then **11 ... 0–0** there follows:

(1) 12 N–KN5 R–K1 13 QR–Q1 Q–B3 14 Q×Q B×Q 15 N×B P×N 16 N–N5 N×N (QR–B1 is better) 17 B×N B×P 18 R–Q7±, Larsen–Trifunovich, Dortmund, 1961.

(2) 12 B–QB5 R–K1 (12 ... Q–B3 13 Q×Q B×Q 14 N–QN5±, Unzicker–Jimenez, Leipzig, 1960; or 12 ... P–N3 13 B–R3 N–K2 14 QR–Q1±, Yanofsky–German, Stockholm, 1962) 13 QR–Q1 Q–B3 and after 14 B×N P×B 15 Q×P KR–Q1 Black has two bishops and an active game for his pawn.

(3) 12 QR–Q1 Q–B3 (or 12 ... Q–B1 13 N–KN5 B–B4 14 KN–K4 B–K4 15 N×N B×Q=, Ivkov–Beni, Tel-Aviv, 1964) 13 Q–QR4 (13 Q–N3 N–K4=) 13 ... N–K4 14 N×N Q×N 15 KR–K1 KR–K1 16 B–KB4 Q–QB4= (Unzicker–Alexander, Hastings, 1954–5).

(4) 12 KR–K1 R–K1 13 QR–Q1 (Simagin–Vesovich, postal, 1963–6) 13 ... Q–B3=.

After **11 0–0** Black can also play 11 ... Q–B3 and meet 12 Q–QR4 by 12 ... Q–K2 saving his queen.

If **11 N–Q4** N×N 12 B×N P–KN4! 13 Q–K3 N–B5 14 B×N Q×B∓ (Mihajlchisin–Trifunovich, Zagreb, 1961).

11 . . .	**Q–B3**

See Diagram 5. For 11 . . . 0–0 see preceding notes.

5

As the following variations show, White has no appreciable advantage:

12 Q×Q B×Q 13 N–K4 B–N2 (13 . . . N×N 14 B×N 0–0 15 N–N5, Tringov–Sumov, Tel-Aviv, 1964) 14 KN–N5 (14 N×N P×N 15 P–QR3=, Gligorich–Trifunovich, Ljubljana, 1960) 14 . . . 0–0 15 N×B P×N 16 N–N5 KR–K1 17 KR–K1 N–K4 18 K–N1 N×B= (Parma–Trifunovich, Bled, 1961).

12 Q–QR4 P–KR3 (White threatened to win the queen) 13 N–Q4 0–0 (13 . . . B–Q2 14 KN–N5 N×N 15 B×N R–Q1 16 Q–R3±, Bogdanovich–Dely, Sarajevo, 1964) 14 N×N (14 N×B P×N with chances for both sides according to Mikenas) 14 . . . P×N=, since if 15 Q×BP B×P! Of course when White castles on the queen's side he cannot so easily get an advantage by breaking up his opponent's pawns on that side, for this opens up lines bearing upon his own king position.

12 N–KN5, a recent idea is White's best try. Then 12 . . . Q×Q 13 B×Q B×N (Double-edged. 13 . . . 0–0–0 may well be sounder) 14 P×B (14 N×B B×P ch) 14 . . . B×P 15 KR–K1 ch K–B1 16 P–B4! N×BP 17 N–K4 N(5)–K4 18 N–B3! N×B ch 19 R×N B–K3 20 B–R6 ch followed by N–Q5 and according to Keres White has a strong initiative.

LINE 1 (B) (*Continue from Diagram 2*)

8 . . .	**B–K3**

See Diagram 6.

6

This line is probably a little inferior to 1(A). **8 ... B–K2** is playable, probably transposing. One independent line is **9 0–0 0–0 10 B–Q2 B–B3 11 N–B3 B–K3 12 KR–K1 Q–Q2 13 QR–Q1 B–B4=**, Murey–Vasyukov, Moscow, 1967.

9 N–B3

Polugaevsky gives **9 N–N5!±**, but quotes no analysis to back up the judgement. Black may still play 9 ... P–KN3 or 9 ... Q–Q2 intending 0–0–0.

9 B–Q2 is sometimes played here, with the idea of deterring Black from playing a king's fianchetto, and also seems strong, e.g. **9 ... Q–Q2 10 N–B3 B–K2** (not 10 ... 0–0–0 11 0–0 P–KR3 12 Q–QR4 K–N1 13 B–K3 with an attacking position for White, Evans–Rossetto, Amsterdam, 1964) **11 0–0–0 0–0** (11 ... 0–0–0 12 B–K3 Q–K1 13 Q–QR4±, Matanovich–Krivech, Yugoslav Championship, 1952; or 11 ... P–QR3 12 N–KN5 B×N 13 Q×B P–B3 14 Q–QB5 P–QN3 15 Q–R5 ch K–B1 16 P–KR3, Jazek–Batik, postal, 1957; but 11 ... B–B4 is playable) **12 KR–K1** (12 P–KR4 P–B3 13 KR–K1 B–B4 14 B×B Q×B 15 Q×Q N×Q 16 P–KN4, Mednis–Horowitz, New York, 1955, 16 ... N–Q3 17 N–Q5 with some pressure for White) **12 ... B–B4=**, and not 12 ... B–B3 13 N–K4 N×N 14 Q×N P–KN3 15 B–KR6 KR–K1 16 Q–KB4±, Friedgood–Roux, Tel-Aviv, 1964.

9 ...   B–K2

The oldest move, no longer fashionable.

9 ... P–KN3 is the modern preference with the great likelihood of transposing to Line 1(A). If **10 N–Q4** then 10 ... Q–Q2, or 10 ... N–N5, but not 10 ... B–N2 11 N×N (11 N×B P×N 12 0–0 Q–B3 13 Q–N3 0–0 14 N–N5 N×N 15 B×N N–Q5=, Buljovchich–Ilijevsky, Jugoslav Championship, 1965) 11 ... P×N 12 B–K3 0–0 13 0–0 Q–B3 (Mikenas suggests 13 ... R–N1) 14 Q–QR4±, Pietzsch–Vistaneskis, Riga, 1961.

10 0–0

10 P–QN3 0–0 11 B–N2 B–B3 12 0–0 N–K2 13 QR–Q1 Q–B1=, Gunston–MacDonald, postal, 1927.

White could try **10 B–K3** followed by 0–0–0.

10 ...   Q–Q2

10 ... 0–0 is also sound, 11 B–K3 B–B3 (it would be somewhat better to transpose back to the main line by 11 ... Q–Q2) 12 QR–Q1 N–K2 (12 ... Q–B1 13 B–QB5 R–Q1 14 N–KN5, Unzicker–Keller, Lugano, 1959) 13 B–QB5 N–N3 14 Q–N3 (better than giving up both bishops to win a pawn) 14 ... B×N 15 P×B Q–B3 16 N–N5 (Nezhmetdinov–Damsky, Kazan, 1964), and White has a slight advantage; his pieces are active, but his pawns are weak, so that Black has counter-chances. The game ended in a draw.

11 B–K3

11 N–K4 N×N **12 B×N** 0–0–0= (Milich–Rabar, Novi Sad, 1945).

11 ...		0–0	
12 QR–Q1		QR–Q1	

See Diagram 7.

7

The chances are even.

13 N–KN5 B×N **14** Q×B P–B3 **15** Q–R4 B–B4 **16** B–B5 B×B **17** R×B Q–K3 **18** N–Q5 R–B2 **19** KR–Q1 KR–Q2 **20** N×P R×N **21** B×N R(B2)–Q2 **22** Q–N3 Q×P= (Smyslov–Kan, Leningrad–Moscow, 1939).

13 B–QB5 Q–B1 **14** N–KN5 B×N **15** Q×B KR–K1 **16** B×N (16 N–QN5 is an improvement) **16 ...** R×B! **17** N–K4 Q–Q1 **18** Q–R5 R–Q4 **19** Q–K2 Q–R5 with good play for Black (Broadbent–Hooper, Club game, London, 1954).

LINE 1 (C) (*Continue from Diagram 2*)

8 ...		Q–K2 ch	

This too is not a good line. The original idea was to block the K file, forestalling the variation 8 ... P–KN3 9 0–0 B–N2 10 R–K1 ch, but it is now known that this is not necessary, since Black has nothing to fear in this line.

9 B–K3		P–KN3	

9 ... P–KR3, intending an extended fianchetto, is an interesting idea, 10 N–B3 B–K3 (or 10 ... P–KN4 at once, 11 Q–QR4 B–Q2 12 N–Q5 Q–Q1) 11 0–0 P–KN4 12 Q–QR4 B–N2 13 B–Q4 0–0 14 B×B K×B with chances for both sides (Pavlov–Breazu, Stalin, Roumania, 1959).

10 N–B3		B–K3	

This move does seem really satisfactory. Konstantinopolsky suggests **10 ... B–N2 11 N–Q5 Q–Q1** and now **12** 0–0 B–K3 **13** N–B3 transposes to Line 1(A), both players having lost two tempi, whilst 12 0–0–0 0–0 13 B–QB5 B–K3 14 N×P Q×N 15 B×N Q–N3! gives Black a good attack.

11 N–Q4

The older 11 0–0 B–N2 12 KR–K1 0–0 13 B–QB5 is less effective.

11 ...	**B–N2**
12 N×N	

Better than 12 N×B

12 ...	**P×N**
13 0–0	**0–0**
14 B–Q4	

See Diagram 8.

8

White succeeds in exchanging Black's powerful KB, after which Black is at some disadvantage because of his broken pawns on the queen's side—which is not the same thing as saying that Black has a lost game.

See Game 3.

Both the following games favoured White, but were ultimately drawn:

14 ... QR–N1 15 B×B K×B 16 P–QN3 (16 Q–Q4 ch Q–B3 17 Q×P R×P=) 16 ... Q–B3 17 Q×Q ch (Spassky–Rossetto, Amsterdam, 1964, see Game 3).

14 ... B×B 15 Q×B N–B4 16 Q–K5 Q–Q3 17 Q–QR5 QR–N1 18 QR–Q1 N–Q5 19 KR–K1 KR–Q1 (Minich–Djurovich, 20th Yugoslav Championship, 1965).

LINE 2 (*Continue from Diagram 1*)

7 N–B3	**N–B3**

7 ... B–KB4 is playable, but leaves White with some pressure in most cases, 8 B–N5 (8 Q–K5 ch Q–K2 9 N–Q5 Q×Q ch 10 N×Q P–KB3 11 N–KB3 K–Q2 12 B–KB4 N–B3 13 0–0–0 R–Q1 14 B–QN5 K–B1, Bronstein–Borisenko, Moscow, 1946, and now Schwarz continues 15 KB×N P×B 16 N–K3 B–K5 17 N–Q4±) 8 ... P–KB3 (8 N–B3 is better, if 9 Q–K3 ch B–K2 10 N–Q5 B–K3, or if 9 B×Q N×Q 10 N×N R×B) 9 B–KB4 N–B3 (9 ... B×P? 10 R–B1 B–B4 11 B–N5 ch P–B3 12 0–0 N×B 13 KR–K1 ch +) 10 Q–QR4 B–K2 11 0–0–0 0–0 12 N–Q5 K–R1 13 P–R4 B–Q2 14 Q–N3 B–KN5 15 P–R5 B×N 16 P×B± (Stein–Sakharov, match, 1960).

8 Q–KB4

If 8 B–QN5 Q–K2 ch 9 Q–K3 B–Q2 10 0–0 Q×Q= (Sooer–Estrada, Varna Olympiad, 1962).

See Diagram 9.

9

LINE 2 (A) (*Continue from Diagram 9*)

8 ...   B–K3

For the most part we shall now consider those lines in which White does not play B–Q3 transposing to Line 1.

8 ... **P–KN3** at once is rather less precise:

(1) **9 B–N5!** B–N2 (Black can avoid broken pawns only by foregoing castling, 9 ... B–Q2 10 B×N B×B 11 0–0 B–N2 12 R–K1 ch K–B1) 10 B×N ch P×B 11 0–0 0–0 12 B–K3 P–QR4 13 B–Q4 R–K1 14 B×B± (Bronstein–Maslov, Spartakiad, 1959).

(2) **9 B–K3** B–N2 10 0–0–0 and if 10 ... 0–0 (10 ... B–K3 is correct) 11 P–KR4 (after 11 B–N5 Q–B3 12 B×N P×B 13 Q×Q B×Q 14 B–Q4 B×B, Bertok–Rabar, Yugoslav Championship, 1962, Black was able to defend successfully) 11 ... P–KR3 12 B–B4 B–B4 13 B–N3 R–K1 14 N–Q4 N×N 15 B×N B–K3 16 KR–K1 P–KN4 17 Q–B3 P×P 18 N–K4 N×N 19 R×N Q–N4 ch 20 B–K3 Q–B3 21 Q×Q and White won the endgame (Gligorich–German, Stockholm, 1962).

(3) **9 B–Q2** B–N2 (9 ... Q–K2 ch also equalizes, 10 B–K2 B–K3 11 0–0–0 B–N2 12 P–KR4 P–KR3 13 KR–K1 Q–B3 14 B–Q3 Q×Q 15 B×Q 0–0–0 16 N–K5 N×N 17 B×N B×B 18 R×B B–B5=, Keres–Trifunovich, Bled, 1961. If here 11 N–KN5? B–R3 12 0–0–0 P–B3+, Geller–Trifunovich, Bled, 1961, or 11 N–Q4 B–R3! 12 N×N B×Q 13 N×Q B×B ch with a dead draw, Geller–Smyslov, Leningrad, 1971. White cannot improve since if 12 Q×B N×N 13 Q–N7 N×P ch 14 K–Q1 0–0–0 15 K×N N–B4 with a powerful attack for Black) 10 0–0–0 0–0 (now White gets an attack which is not, however, decisive. 10 ... B–K3! transposes to the text) 11 P–KR4 P–KR3 12 N–Q5 B–K3 13 B–B3 B×N

14 R×B Q–K2 15 B×B K×B 16 P–R5 P–KN4 (if 16 ... R–R1 17 P×P, Gufeld–Rabar, Moscow, 1961) and the sacrifice 17 N×P P×N 18 R×P ch K–R1 19 B–Q3 K–R1 leaves Black with the better of it.

(4) **9 N–Q4** B–N2 (9 ... B–Q2! is satisfactory for Black) 10 N×N P×N 11 B–K2 0–0 12 0–0 B–B4 13 Q–QR4 P–QR4 14 B–B3 R–R3 15 N–Q1 B–Q2 16 B–K3 Q–N1 (Maslov–Mikenas, Vilnius, 1959), Black's pawns are weak, but he has fighting chances.

Finally, from the position of Diagram 9 Black may try for the extended fianchetto **8 ... P–KR3** and then if 9 P–KR4 (9 B–K3!) 9 ... B–K3 10 B–Q2 P–KN3 11 0–0–0 B–N2 12 B–Q3 Q–B3= (Suetin–Mikenas, U.S.S.R. Team Championship, 1953).

For the position after 8 ... B–K3, i.e. Line 2(A), see Diagram 10 and continue as follows:

10

9 B–Q2

White develops his bishop here because after **9 B–K3** Black has the excellent reply 9 ... **N–B4,** and now (1) 10 B–Q3 B–Q3, 11 Q–K4 N×B 12 Q×N=, if 12 ... Q–B3 13 N–K4 Q×P 14 0–0 Q–N3 15 Q–N5 (Simagin–Vistanetskis, Spartakiad, 1962) White scarcely has enough for his pawn; Black might continue 15 ... N–Q5. (2) N–QN5 B–N5 ch 11 B–Q2 B×B ch 12 N×B 0–0 13 0–0–0 R–B1 14 N–KB3 Q–K2 15 B–Q3 P–QR3= (Fuderer–Bronstein, Kiev, 1959). (3) 10 R–Q1 B–Q3 11 Q–K4 N×B 12 Q×N Q–B3 13 B–Q3= (Shiyanovsky–Vistanetskis, Vilnius, 1958).

9 B–N5 is not effective here, 9 ... N×B 10 N×N B–Q3 11 Q–K4 Q–Q2 12 B–B4 B×B 13 Q×B 0–0–0 14 0–0 N–K2 15 P–QR4 P–QR3 16 N–Q4 N–N3= (Boleslavsky–Maslov, Spartakiad, 1963).

9 ...   **P–KN3**
10 0–0–0

10 N–Q4 Q–Q2 11 Q–B6 R–KN1 12 N×B P×N 13 0–0–0 B–K2 14 Q–B4 R–KB1 15 Q–N3 B–B3 with good play for Black (Gipslis–Vistanetskis, Tallinn, 1959).

10 ...   **B–N2**
11 N–QN5

This is part of White's plan: to exchange bishops on the long diagonal, and then to attack the K-side; but the plan miscarries.

For **11 B–Q3** see Line 1(A).

White could attack at once by **11 P–KR4** Q–B3 12 Q–QR4 P–KR3 13 B–R6 0–0 14 B×NP N×B 15 Q×N winning a pawn but opening lines towards his own king, 15 ... N–R4 with a promising position for Black (Mnatsakanyan–Maslov, Spartakiad, 1963).

11 N–KN5 0–0 12 P–KR4 P–KR3 13 N(N5)–K4 (13 N×B P×N 14 Q–N4 Q–B3 15 B–Q3 N–K4 16 Q–R3 P–QN4! 17 QR–K1 QR–K1 18 N–Q1 N(4)–B5 with attacking chances, Pinchuk–Chesnaukas, U.S.S.R. Team Championship, 1969) 13 ... Q–K2 (13 ... N×N 14 N×N Q–K2 15 B–B3 P–B4 16 B×B±, Sakharov–Maslov, Spartakiad, 1959) 14 N×N P×N 15 B–B4 QR–B1= (Nikolayevsky–Vistanetskis, Spartakiad, 1959). The open lines available to Black easily compensate him for the isolated pawn.

11 ...   **P–QR3**

Instead Black can easily equalize by **11 ... Q–K2** 12 B–B3 B×B 13 N×B 0–0–0, when there is little point in White's attacking the K-side, the bird having flown; and now 14 P–QR3 N–B4= (Sakharov–Maslov, Vilnius, 1959), or 14 B–Q3 P–B3 (not 14 ... KR–K1 15 KR–K1!, Boleslavsky–Chukayev, Spartakiad, 1959) 15 KR–K1 Q–B2=.

12 B–B3

See Diagram 11.

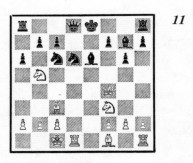

11

There may follow:

12 ... B×B 13 N×B Q–K2 14 B–Q3 0–0–0 15 KR–K1 Q–B1= (Krogius–Trifunovich, Varna, 1960).

12 ... P×N! 13 B×B R×P 14 R×N P×R 15 B×R Q–R4 and Black has a strong attack for his piece (Konstantinopolsky).

Line 2 (B) *(Continue from Diagram 9)*

8 ...   **B–B4**
9 B–N5

Chigorin's idea, which occurred in the stem-game (for 7 N–B3) Chigorin–Pillsbury, St. Petersburg, 1895–6.

9 ...   **Q–K2 ch**

See Diagram 12.

12

After the older continuation **9 ... B–K2** 10 N–Q4 B–Q2 as played (with success) by Pillsbury, Black's pawns are weakened on the Q side (a familiar, but not fatal, situation) 11 B×N (11 N×N P×N) 11 ... B×B 12 N×B P×N 13 0–0 (13 Q–QR4! is better, with some advantage to White, Gligorich–Bajec, Yugoslav Championship, 1951) 13 ... 0–0 14 B–K3 R–N1 15 QR–N1 and now 15 ... N–B1 16 Q–B3 Q–Q2 17 QR–Q1 B–Q3 18 P–QN3 Q–K3 as in the stem-game Chigorin–Pillsbury mentioned above, or 15 ... P–QR4 16 KR–Q1 R–N5 with fighting chances for Black (Kopayev–Shiffman, correspondence, 1953).

9 ... B×P? 10 N–K5 P–KN4 11 Q–K3 B–K2 12 N×N+ (Geller–Nahlik, Szczawno-Zdroj, 1958).

10 B–K3

10 K–B1 B–K5 and now:

(1) 11 B×N ch B×B 12 N–K5 0–0–0 13 N×B P×N 14 Q–QR4 (Mikenas suggests 14 B–K3 and Euwe continues 14 ... Q–K3 15 B×P N–B5 16 B–K3 B–N5 with counterplay for Black) 14 ... N–N4 15 B–K3 Q–N5 16 Q–R6 ch K–N1 17 Q×P N–Q5 18 B×N Q×B 19 R–Q1 Q×R ch= (Suetin-Kholmov, Moscow, 1964).

(2) 11 B–Q2 N×B 12 N×N 0–0–0 13 R–K1 P–B4 14 N–B3 (14 N–N5 Q–Q2 15 N–K6 P–N4 16 N×NP B–R3∓) 14 ... Q–B4 15 N×B P×N 16 Q×P Q–N4 ch (16 ... B–Q3 17 B–B3 R–N1 18 P–KR4±, Szabó–Strand, Budapest–Stockholm, 1966) 17 K–N1 (17 P–B4 Q×NP 18 B–N5 B–N5 19 R–N1 Q×P 20 B×R R×B 21 R–B1 Q–N7 22 Q–N1 Q×Q 23 R×Q P–QR4=, Mukhin–Borisenko, U.S.S.R., 1968) 17 ... Q×P 18 B–N5 R–Q2 19 Q–K8 ch N–Q1 20 N–K5 R–Q4 21 B×N R×B 22 Q–K6 ch K–N1 23 N–B7 B–N5+ (Szabó).

(3) 11 B–R4 0–0–0 12 B–K3 P–B3 13 N×B (13 P–R4 B×N 14 P×B N–K4 15 B–N3 K–N1 16 R–Q1 N–B1=, or 14 Q×B N–K4 15 Q–B4 N(3)–B5= according to Suetin) 13 ... Q×N 14 R–Q1± (Keres).

10 ...	**N×B**
11 N×N	**Q–N5 ch**
12 Q×Q	**B×Q ch**
13 P–B3	

See Diagram 13.

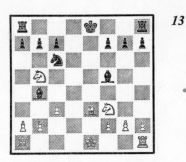

13

13 ... B–Q3 14 N×B ch (14 0–0–0 0–0–0 15 N×B ch R×N=) 14 ... P×N 15 N–Q4 (15 0–0–0 B–K3! 16 R×P B×P 17 N–Q4 N×N 18 B×N 0–0 19 R–Q7 KR–N1 20 R–K1 P–QR4 21 R–K5 B–B5 22 P–KR4 P–QN4 23 R–KN5 P–N3 24 P–R5 R–Q1=, Gurgenidze–Kholmov, Grozny, 1969) 15 ... N×N 16 B×N 0–0 17 P–QR4 KR–K1 ch 18 K–Q2 P–Q4= (Szabó–Kholmov, Budapest, 1964).

13...B–R4 is less good, 14 P–QN4 B–Q6 15 P–QR4 P–QR3 16 N(N5)–Q4 (better than 16 0–0–0 B–K7!) 16...N×N 17 B×N B–QN3 18 0–0–0 B×B 19 R×B B–B3 20 KR–K1 ch K–B1 21 R–Q7+ (Parma–Trifunovich, Amsterdam, 1965). 16...B–QN3 is an improvement, but after 17 N×N P×N 18 B×B P×B 19 0–0–0 0–0–0 (19...B–K5 20 KR–K1 P–KB4 21 N–K5±) 20 N–K5 B–K5 21 N×KBP! B×P 22 N×QR B×R 23 N–K6 White wins a pawn and has some winning chances in the endgame.

LINE 3 (*Continue from Diagram 1*)

7 B–N5

Recommended by Steinitz, and first played in one of his games against Pillsbury at St. Petersburg, 1895–6. The move is no longer feared.

See Diagram 14.

14

7 ...   N–B3

This reply, introduced in 1924 in the game quoted below, equalizes without difficulty. Even so, the older 7 ... P–KB3 is also satisfactory for Black, and possibly offers more chances of complicating the game.

There follows **8 B–KB4** (Hartlaub's 8 N–B3 is too speculative) **8 ... N–B3** and now:
(1) 9 Q–K3 ch Q–K2 10 N–B3 (10 Q×Q ch B×Q 11 N–B3 B–B4 12 0–0–0 0–0–0 13 N–Q4 N×N 14 R×N N–B2=, Zubarev–Marshall, Moscow, 1925) 10 ... B–N5 11 B–K2 Q×Q 12 B×Q N–B4 13 N–Q5 0–0–0 14 0–0–0 N×B with good play for Black (Stoltz–Alekhine, Munich, 1941).

(2) 9 Q–Q2 B–B4 10 B–K2 Q–K2 11 0–0 0–0–0 12 R–K1 (Steinitz–Pillsbury, St. Petersburg, 1895–6) and Black could have safely played 12 ... Q–B2 with good prospects. Instead he continued 12 ... N–K5 13 Q–B1 P–KN4 14 B–Q3 B–R3! with chances for both sides. If 15 N–B3 P×B, or if 15 N–R4 P×N 16 B×B KR–N1 17 Q–B4 R×P ch!

(3) 9 Q–Q1 Q–K2 ch 10 B–K2 B–N5 11 0–0 0–0–0 12 R–K1 P–KN4 13 B–Q2 Q–N2 14 N–B3 B–B4 with about level chances (Smyslov–Mats, Spartakiad, 1963).

(4) 9 Q–QR4 is also to be considered.
Finally, even **7 ... Q–Q2** is playable here—see Game 5.

8 Q–K3 ch

A confession of failure, but other moves hand over the initiative to Black:
8 Q–Q2 B–K2 9 N–B3 N–K4!   *10...P–QB3*
8 B×Q N×Q 9 N×N K×B 10 N–QB3 11 0–0–0 K–B2 (Butcher–Hooper, Clubgame, London, 1954). Black, having the bishop-pair, won.
8 Q–B3 P–B3 9 B–KB4 Q–K2 ch 10 B–K2 B–K3 11 QN–Q2 0–0–0 12 0–0 Q–B2∓ (Bogolyubov, Ilyin-Genevsky and Rabinovich–Levenfish, Kubbel and Romanovsky, Leningrad, 1924). Black won after 13 P–QR3 P–KN4 14 B×P P×B 15 Q×R B–N2 16 Q×P B–B4.

8 ...	**B–K2**
9 B×B	**Q×B**
10 Q×Q ch=	

10 ... N×Q (10 ... K×Q is also good, 11 N–B3 B–K3 12 N–KN5 K–Q2 13 N×B QR–K1) **11 N–B3 B–N5 12 B–K2 0–0–0=** (Kostich–Kashdan, Bled, 1931).

The Normal Variation has been shorn of its terrors from Black's point of view. Euwe remarks, "It is not easy for White to maintain the initiative... he has some preponderance in space, but the absence of centre pawns, and the tensions resulting from it, have a levelling effect."

The king's fianchetto is now firmly established and variations 1 (A) and 2 (A) are interlinked, for many transpositions are possible. Black should follow two rules: firstly to develop as quickly as possible and secondly to delay castling—which is not to say he shouldn't be ready to castle. Generally, Black castles queen's side only after queens are exchanged. He should try to keep his fianchettoed bishop, his strongest piece; but in a general way may exchange this piece (perhaps to weaken White's queen's side pawns) after the queens are off the board, that is when he is no longer in danger of being attacked on the king's side. Or he may exchange his KB after castling on the queen's side when the holes on the king's side are not likely to be disadvantageous to him.

Another general rule for Black is not himself lightly to initiate exchanges of minor pieces in the centre, but rather to leave upon White the onus of forcing open lines. As Euwe remarks, White has rather more space, and premature exchanges will tend to enhance this advantage.

Finally a word about the queen's side pawns. In several different contexts situations arise in which Black's pawns on this side become doubled and isolated. Perhaps, naturally, he may not seek out these lines. Even so masters have been willing enough to defend such pawns, and their weakness cannot, on the evidence of practical examples, be called decisive. The first time this happened (in 1895!) Pillsbury won as Black. He used the doubled QBPs to support pieces in the centre, and gained a king's side initiative whilst Chigorin chased the weak pawns. In general such pawns will not be fatal if Black can keep his fianchettoed bishop bearing down on White's queen's side, or if Black can make active use of the open lines.

To some, Games 1 and 3 may seem dull; but they demonstrate that this defence stands up to attack from two of the very strongest masters in the world. Game 4 shows a successful attack against the fianchetto, possible because of inaccurate play by Black.

Line 1 (B) is safe enough for Black as an occasional alternative. Very often if White tries too hard to make too much out of too little Black gains the initiative as in the Broadbent game quoted. However, this line is not very well tested. Line 2 (B) is good enough for a draw, if Black seeks a peaceful game. On the other hand, if Black seeks new paths he will find a number of unusual ideas, such as the "extended fianchetto", scattered in the text.

Game 1   Tal–Rossetto, Amsterdam, 1964. 1 P–K4 P–K4 2 N–KB3 N–KB3 3 P–Q4 P×P 4 P–K5 N–K5 5 Q×P P–Q4 6 P×P e.p. N×QP 7 B–Q3 N–B3 8 Q–KB4 P–KN3 9 N–B3 B–N2 10 B–Q2 B–K3 11 0–0–0 Q–B3 12 Q×Q B×Q 13 N–KN5 0–0–0 14 N×B P×N 15 KR–K1 KR–K1 16 N–K4 N×N 17 R×N R–Q5 18 QR–K1 R×R 19 R×R P–QR3 20 P–KN3 K–Q2 21 P–KR4 B–Q5 22 R–K2 R–KB1 23 B–K1 B–N2 24 B–K4 B–R3 ch 25 B–Q2 N–Q5 26 R–K1 B×B ch 27 K×B N–B6 ch 28 B×N R×B 29 K–K2 R–B4 30 R–Q1 ch R–Q4 31 R–Q3 K–K2 32 R–QB3 K–Q3 33 R–N3 R–K4 ch 34 K–B3 R–B4 ch 35 K–N2 P–N3 36 P–N4 R–B4 37 R–Q3 ch R–Q4 38 R–K3 R–Q5 39 K–N3 P–K4 40 P–N5 P–QR4 41 R–KB3 K–K2 42 R–B3 K–Q3 43 P–N3 K–Q2 44 R–B3 K–K2 45 R–B6 R–Q3. ½ : ½ Black showed his isolated pawn to be no serious weakness, and played well to neutralize White's bishop-pair.

Game 2   Pavlov–Breazu, Stalin, Roumania, 1959. 1 P–K4 P–K4 2 N–KB3 N–KB3 3 P–Q4 P×P 4 P–K5 N–K5 5 Q×P P–Q4 6 P×P e.p. N×QP 7 B–Q3 N–B3 8 Q–KB4 Q–K2 ch 9 B–K3 P–KR3 10 N–B3 B–K3 11 0–0 P–KN4 12 Q–QR4 B–N2 13 B–Q4 0–0 14 B×B K×B 15 QR–K1 Q–B3 16 N–N5 (better 16 N–K4) 16 ... B–Q4 17 N(B3)–Q4 N(B3)×N 18 N×N(Q4) P–R3 19 N–K2 P–KR4 20 N–N3 R–R1 21 P–KB4 Q×NP 22 P×P P–R5 23 N–B5 ch N×N 24 R×N Q–N3 ch 25 K–R1 P–R6! 26 B–B1 (if 26 R×B P×P ch 27 K×P and Black mates in 7) 26...QR–K1 27 R×B P×P ch 28 K×P R×P ch. 0: 1

Game 3   Spassky–Rossetto, Amsterdam, 1964. 1 P–K4 P–K4 2 N–KB3 N–KB3 3 P–Q4 P×P 4 P–K5 N–K5 5 Q×P P–Q4 6 P×P e.p. N×QP 7 B–Q3 N–B3 8 Q–KB4 Q–K2 ch 9 B–K3 P–KN3 10 N–B3 B–K3 11 N–Q4 B–N2 12 N×N P×N 13 0–0 0–0 14 B–Q4 QR–N1 15 B×B K×B 16 P–QN3 Q–B3 17 Q×Q ch K×Q 18 N–R4 KR–K1 19 KR–Q1 B–N5 20 P–KB3 B–B4 21 K–B2 R–K4 22 B×B R×B 23 R–K1 R–QR4 24 QR–Q1 P–R4 25 R–Q3

R(N1)–N4 26 R–B3 P–B4 27 R(B3)–K3 P–B5 28 R–K7 R–N2 29 R(K1)–K2 P–B3 30 R(K7)–K3 R–Q4 31 N–B3 R–Q5 32 R–K5 N–N4 33 N–R4 P×P 34 RP×P R–Q4 35 R(K5)–K3 N–Q5 36 N–B3 N×R 37 N×R ch P×N 38 K×N P–R4 39 K–Q2 R–N5 40 R–K1 P–QR5 41 K–B3 R–B5 42 R–QR1 P×P 43 P×P K–K4 44 R–R6 P–N4 45 R–R6 P–R5 46 P–R3 R–B4 47 R–QB6 P–N5. ½ : ½ Black cleverly prevented a blockade of his isolated pawns, and duly advanced and eliminated them. The game was surely drawn after Black's 27th move.

Game 4 Zhilin–Gusakov, Perm, 1960. 1 P–K4 P–K4 2 N–KB3 N–KB3 3 P–Q4 P×P 4 P–K5 N–K5 5 Q×P P–Q4 6 P×P e.p. N×QP 7 N–B3 N–B3 8 Q–KB4 P–KN3 9 B–Q2 B–N2 10 0–0–0 0–0 11 P–KR4 B–K3 12 P–R5 R–K1 13 Q–R2 B–B4 14 P×P RP×P 15 B–KN5 Q–Q2 16 Q–R7 ch K–B1 17 N–Q5 P–B3 18 Q–R8 ch! B×Q (if 18 ... K–B2 White mates in 4) 19 R×B ch K–B2 20 R–R7 ch. 1 : 0 If 20 ... K–K3 21 N–B4 mate, else Black loses a piece or more.

Game 5 Bardeleben–Hartlaub, Cologne, 1905. 1 P–K4 P–K4 2 N–KB3 N–KB3 3 P–Q4 P×P 4 P–K5 N–K5 5 Q×P P–Q4 6 P×P e.p. N×QP 7 B–N5 Q–Q2 8 N–B3 N–B3 9 Q–Q2 Q–K3 ch 10 B–K2 P–B3 11 N–Q5 Q–B2 12 0–0–0 B–K3 13 P–B4 0–0–0 14 B–B4 P–KN4 15 B–K3 B–B4 16 Q–B3 N–K5 17 Q–N3 N–R4 18 Q–R4 P–N3 19 P–QN4? R×N! 20 P×R N–B6 21 B–R6 ch K–N1 22 Q–R3 B×P! 23 Q–N2 Q–K2 24 P–Q6 Q–K3 25 K–Q2 (better 25 R–Q4) 25 ... N–B5 ch 26 B×N Q×B 27 P×P ch K–B1 28 K–K1 N–R5 ch. 0 : 1

THE STEINITZ VARIATION

1 P–K4	P–K4
2 N–KB3	N–KB3
3 P–Q4	P×P
4 P–K5	N–K5
5 Q–K2	

5 N×P is feasible, but tame: 5 ... P–Q4 6 B–K3 P–QB4 7 N–KB3 N–QB3 8 QN–Q2 B–KN5 9 B–K2 Q–B2= (Pilnik–Piazzini, Buenos Aires, 1953).

5 B–QN5 is a tricky move to meet. 5 ... P–QR3 and 5 ... P–QB3 are both met by 6 Q×P when the desperado move 6 ... N×P only opens the KB file for White. 5 ... B–N5 ch is solid if Black does not greedily take all the pawns offered, 6 P–QB3 P×P 7 0–0 N–QB3! 8 P×P B–K2 9 Q–Q5 N–B4 10 B–K3 N–K3 with a solid position (Cafferty–B. H. Wood, Birmingham, 1969).

The soundest reply is 5 ... N–QB3 with likely transposition to an old and tried variation of the Ruy Lopez, 6 0–0 B–K2 (6 ... P–QR3 is also good, 7 Q–K2 N–B4 8 B–QB4 B–K2 9 R–Q1 P–Q4!=, Shamkovich–Smyslov, Leningrad, 1971, or 7 B×N QP×B 8 R–K1 N–B4 9 N×P N–K3 10 N–B5 Q×Q 11 R×Q P–KR4! 12 N–B3? P–R5∓ in view of the coming P–KN3, Voronov–Maslov, Uzbekistan, 1970) 7 R–K1 (Tal–Darga, Havana, 1963) 7 ... N–B4 8 N×P N×N 9 Q×N 0–0=, since Black can now freely advance his QP. If 10 B–QB4 P–Q3 11 N–B3 P×P 12 Q×P B–Q3 13 Q–KR5 B–K3 14 B–KN5 Q–Q2, or if 10 B–K3 P–Q4 11 N–B3 P–QB3.

See Diagram 15.

15

The move 5 Q–K2 was strongly advocated by Steinitz in 1889. A few years later it fell out of use, because Pillsbury defended against it so well. It was revived in 1962 by Fischer, and because of the extremely sharp nature of the tactical variations arising from it no final judgement can be given, though Black has good practical chances.

LINE 1 (*Continue from Diagram 15*)

5 ...   **N–B4**

Although known for many years this move first occurred in master play in 1959. It should give Black a satisfactory game.

6 N×P   **N–B3**

The best move, given by Bardeleben as long ago as 1889.

7 N×N

The almost invariable reply, but since the variations that follow leave Black with no problems, White should probably prefer Tal's **7 B–K3.** Now 7 ... N×P gives White a strong initiative, but probably no more, after 8 N–N5 N–K3 9 P–KB4. The safer play is 7 ... N×N **8 B×N N–K3** 9 B–B3 P–Q4 10 P×P Q×P=, or 8 ... Q–R5 9 B–K3 Q–QN5 ch 10 P–QB3 Q–K5 11 P–KB4 P–Q4 12 N–Q2 Q–N3 13 N–B3 P–QB3 14 0–0–0 (Tal–Kholmov, Alma-Ata, 1969) when Kholmov recommended 14 ... P–QR4 intending to advance this pawn still further.

7 ...   **QP×N**

The soundest move. White gets a wing majority; but his KP is if anything weak rather than strong, whilst Black gets freedom of action for his pieces and the prospects of rapid development. (The idea may be compared with a variation of the Caro-Kann favoured by Nimzowitsch: 1 P–K4 P–QB3 2 P–Q4 P–Q4 3 N–QB3 P×P 4 N×P N–B3 5 N×N ch KP×N.)

Results after **7 ... NP×N** have rather favoured White. If 8 B–K3 Q–R5 9 Q–B4 (White seeks a small advantage for the endgame) 9 ... Q×Q 10 B×Q N–R5 11 B–N3 N–N3 (Spassky–Vistanetskis, Tallinn, 1959). **8 N–B3** is more usual, and now:

(1) 8 ... B–K2 9 Q–N4 N–K3 (Trifunovich).

(2) 8 ... B–R3 9 Q–N4 (9 Q–K3 B×B 10 R×B Q–R5!) 9 ... B×B 10 R×B and now Boleslavsky and Euwe give 10 ... P–Q3 11 B–K3 Q–Q2 12 Q–N3 P×P 13 Q×P ch N–K3, but it is doubtful whether Black has sufficient compensation for his broken pawns.

(3) 8 ... R–QN1 9 P–QR3 (9 P–B4 B–K2 10 Q–B2 P–Q4 11 B–K3 N–Q2 12 0–0–0 0–0, Fischer–German, Stockholm, 1962. White should now play 13 N–R4—instead of Fischer's 13 P–KN4—after which Euwe suggests 13 ... R–N5 14 P–QR3 R×N, with at all events fighting play for Black) 9 ... B–K2 10 B–K3 P–Q4 (10 ... R×P? 11 B×N B×B 12 N–R4+) 11 P×P e.p. P×P 12 B×N P×B 13 Q–K5 Q–Q3 14 Q×NP Q–Q5 15 Q×Q P×Q 16 N–Q1± (Keres–Bolbochan, Buenos Aires, 1964).

8 N–B3	**B–B4**
9 B–K3	

9 P–KN3 N–K3 10 B–K3 N–Q5 11 B×N Q×B= (Tal–Szabó, Havana, 1966), or 9 P–KN4 B–K3 10 B–N2 Q–R5! 11 P–KR3 P–KR4 12 P–N4 N–Q2 13 P–R3 P×P 14 P×P Q×R ch 15 B×Q R×B ch 16 K–Q2 0–0–0 and White's wild play has left Black with a winning attack (Figler–Borisenko, Ivano-Frankovsk, 1971).

9 ...	**P–KR4**

To restrain White's K-side pawns, since if 9 ... B–K2 10 P–KN4! B–N3 11 R–Q1 Q–B1 12 B–N2, but 9 ... Q–K2 10 P–KN4 B–Q2 11 B–Q2 P–KR4 to break White's pawns up is playable, 12 P×P Q–R5 13 0–0–0 0–0–0= (Ney–Mikenas, Baltic Championship, 1965).

10 R–Q1	**Q–K2**
11 R–Q2	

Indirectly defending his KP.

11 ...	**N–Q2**
12 P–B4	**0–0–0**

With a good game for Black according to Mikenas. If now 13 B×P Q–N5! with many threats.

LINE 2 (*Continue from Diagram 15*)

5 ...	**B–N5 ch**
6 K–Q1	

This was the move recommended by Steinitz (originally indicated in Cook's Synopsis). It fitted **in** with his concept of the king as a strong piece, even in the middle game, over

3*

whose protection one should not be too worried. The majority of theoreticians hold that Black gets too strong an attack for the pawn, but the variations are very complex, Black often has to give up more material, and the final word has not yet been spoken.

6 QN–Q2 is safe, but untested, so it is uncertain whether Boleslavsky is right in claiming that it gives White a slight advantage. He only gives 6 ... N×N 7 B×N B×B ch 8 Q×B P–Q3 9 Q×P N–B3 10 B–N5 B–Q2 11 B×N B×B 12 0–0–0. Improvements for Black may be sought, e.g. 6 ... N–N4, or later 8 ... P–QB4, or even 8 ... N–B3 9 B–N5 Q–K2! 10 0–0 0–0 11 QR–K1 Q–B4 12 B×N QP×B 12 N×P B–K3= (Cafferty–Cameron, Leicester, 1966).

6 ...	**P–Q4**
7 P×P e.p.	**P–KB4**
8 N–N5	

After **8 P×P Q×P 9 N×P** "White gains a clear pawn" (Steinitz). However, after **9 ... N–B3** Black has a great deal of compensation, **10 P–QB3** (10 N×N P×N 11 B–K3 P–QR4 12 P–QB3 B–R3 13 Q–K1 0–0–0 ch 14 K–B2 B×B 15 Q×B B–B4 +, or 11 P–KB3 B–R3 12 Q×B N–B7 ch 13 K–K2 Q–K4 ch 14 B–K3 P–B5 15 Q×P ch K–K2 16 Q–N7 ch K–B3 17 Q–B6 ch B–Q3 18 Q–B3 P×B +; it is not so clear after 11 P–QB3! since now 11 ... B–R3 12 Q×B N×KBP ch 13 K–K2 Q–K4 ch 14 B–K3 P–B5 15 Q×P ch K–K2 16 Q–N7 ch K–B3 17 Q–B6 ch K–K2, draw by perpetual check, Muffang–Pape, Compiègne, 1923, the point being that after 17 ... B–Q3 18 Q×B ch Q×Q 19 B–Q4 ch and 20 K×N, White has three minor pieces and a pawn for the queen; or 11 P–QB3 B–B4 12 P–B3 B–R3 13 Q×B N–B7 ch 14 K–B2! N×R 15 B–KB4 Q–Q2—15 ... B–Q3 would be only a slight improvement—16 B–B4 and now Black's king comes under fire, e.g. 16 ... B–Q3 17 B×B Q×B 18 Q–N7 QR–N1 19 Q–B7 ch K–Q1 20 N–R3 N–B7 21 Q×RP P–B4 22 N–N5 +, Gleeson–Ms Rowley, correspondence, 1971) **10 ... N×N 11 P×N B–Q2 12 B–K3** (12 P–B3 or 12 QN–Q2, 12 ... 0–0–0) **12 ... R–QB1 13 P–B3 0–0 14 Q–B4 ch Q×Q 15 B×Q ch R×B +.**

8 ...	**0–0**
9 Q–B4 ch	**K–R1**

See Diagram 16.

16

The following continuations favour Black in the main:

10 Q×B N–QB3 11 Q–R3 N×P ch 12 K–K1 N×R 13 P×P Q–K1 ch 14 B–K2 P–B5 15 K–B1 B–Q2 16 N–Q2 N–K4 17 QN–B3 N–N5 18 B–Q3 (Steinitz–Pillsbury, St. Petersburg, 1895–6) **18 ... P–KR3**∓.

10 N×N P×N **11 Q×B** (11 P×P B–N5 ch 12 B–K2 B×B ch 13 K×B Q–R5, or 11 ... Q–B3 12 P×N=Q Q×P, Kharus–Gurevich, Riga, 1975 when White can hold the position by 13 Q–KN3 Q–KN3) ¦11 ... B–N5 ch 12 B–K2 B×B ch 13 K×B N–B3 14 Q–K1 (14 P×P R×P ch, or 14 Q×N PQ–R5) 14 ... Q×P (14 ... Q–R5 is also good)15 K–Q1 QR–K1 16 P–QN3 P–K6 17 B–R3 Q–B5 18 B×R P–K7 ch and wins (Lipschutz–Showalter, match, 1896).

10 P×P N×P ch **11 K–K2** Q–K2 ch **12 K×N** Q–K8 ch+.

10 N–B7 ch R×N **11 Q×R** N×P ch **12 K–K2** N×R **13 P×P** Q–Q2 **14 P×N=Q** Q×Q **15 Q–B4** B–Q2 Q–R4 ch + (Steinitz).

It is clear from the above analyses that Black has more than one way of getting good play against the Steinitz Attack.

Game 6 Fischer–German, Stockholm, 1962. 1 P–K4 P–K4 2 N–KB3 N–KB3 3 P–Q4 P×P 4 P–K5 N–K5 5 Q–K2 N–B4 6 N×P N–B3 7 N×N NP×N 8 N–B3 R–QN1 9 P–B4 B–K2 10 Q–B2 P–Q4 11 B–K3 N–Q2 12 0–0–0 0–0 13 P–KN4 B–N5 14 N–K2 N–N3 15 N–Q4 Q–K1 16 P–B3 B–K2 17 P–B5 P–B4 18 N–N5 P–Q5 19 B–KB4 P×P? (19 ... B–N2 20 R–N1 P–QR3 is better) 20 N×P(B3) N–R5 21 B–QN5! R×B 22 N×N R–N5 23 N–B3 B–N2 24 KR–K1 K–R1 25 P–B6! B–Q1 26 B–N5 R–Q5 27 P×P ch K×P 28 B–B6 ch K–N1 29 Q–R4 R×R 30 N×R. 1 : 0 Black had a satisfactory position till move 19 when he overestimated his chances on the QN file.

THE OUROUSOFF VARIATION

1 P–K4	P–K4
2 N–KB3	N–KB3
3 P–Q4	P×P
4 B–QB4	

See Diagram 17.

17

This gambit was first analysed by the Russian master Prince S. Ourousoff in 1857. It is not as strong as 4 P–K5 but offers scope to players who like the unbalanced struggles that arise from gambits.

4 ...	N×P

It is sound play to accept the gambit, but you must be prepared to defend against a very strong attack. Neither Lasker nor Rubinstein was successful in the defence in the games quoted below.

Fortunately there are three good ways of declining the gambit:

4 ... P–Q4 5 P×P B–N5 ch 6 P–B3 (6 B–Q2 B×B ch 7 Q×B 0–0) 6 ... Q–K2 ch 7 B–K2 P×P 8 P×P B–QB4 9 0–0 0–0 10 P–B4 R–K1 11 B–Q3 B–KN5=.

4 ... B–B4 5 0–0 (5 P–K5 P–Q4 6 P×N P×B 7 Q–K2 ch B–K3 8 P×P R–N1 9 B–N5 B–K2 10 B×B K×B 11 N–R4 K–Q2∓) 5 ... P–Q3 (5 ... N–B3 transposing to the Max Lange Attack is of course sound, but no less complicated than the main line of this gambit; not 5 ... N×P 6 R–K1 P–Q4 7 B×P Q×B 8 N–B3 Q–R4, since unlike a similar line in the Two Knights Defence—with N at QB3 instead of B at QB4—the queen becomes an easy object of attack, 9 R×N ch B–K3 10 R–K5 Q–N3 11 N–Q5 B–Q3 12 N–R4± according to Sozin) 6 P–B3 P–Q6 (not 6 ... P×P 7 N×P 0–0 8 B–KN5 B–K3 9 B×B P×B 10 Q–N3 Q–B1 11 P–K5 N–N5 12 N–K4±, Hartlaub–Leonhardt, Hamburg, 1906) 7 Q×P N–B3=. Now 8 P–QN4 B–N3 9 P–N5 N–QR4 10 P–K5 P×P 11 Q×Q ch K×Q 12 B×P P–K5 13 N–K5 B–QB4 with good play for Black (Spielmann–Alekhine, Stockholm, 1912), or 8 B–KN5 P–KR3 9 B–R4 B–KN5 10 QN–Q2 N–K4=.

4 ... N–B3—see Scotch Opening.

5 Q×P   N–KB3

5 ... N–B4? (5 ... N–Q3? 6 0–0) 6 B–KN5 (6 N–K5? N–K3 7 0–0 N–B3 8 B×N BP×B 9 N×N NP×N 10 N–Q2 Q–B3∓) 6 ... P–KB3 7 B–K3±, and now 7 ... P–B3 8 N–B3 P–Q4 9 0–0–0 B–K2 10 Q–R4 QN–Q2 11 N×P P×N 12 Q–R5 ch P–N3 13 Q×QP + (Estrin–Taimanov, Leningrad, 1949), or 7 ... N–B3 8 Q–Q5.

6 B–KN5

6 N–B3 N–B3 7 Q–R4 B–N5 8 0–0 B×N 9 P×B 0–0 10 B–Q3 N–K2 11 B–KN5 N–N3∓ (Marshall–Torre, New York, 1925).

6 ...   B–K2

Black may now return the pawn and break White's attack, 6 ... N–B3 7 Q–R4 P–Q4 8 B×N P×B 9 B–N3 B–K3 10 N–B3 B–QN5 11 0–0–0 B×N 12 P×B Q–K2 13 B×P 0–0–0, with about level chances.

7 N–B3

See Diagram 18.

18

LINE 1 (*Continue from Diagram 18*)

7 ...   N–B3

Probably Black's best move, though he can also go for the simple life by the move that is the antidote to so many gambits, viz. 7 ... P–Q4 8 N×P N×N 9 Q×N Q×Q 10 B×Q P–QB3= (Gibbs–J. Littlewood, Ilford, 1961).

8 Q–R4   P–Q3

8 ... P–Q4 opens the game too much now, 9 0–0–0 B–K3 10 KR–K1 0–0 (10 ... P–KR3 11 B×N B×B 12 Q–R5 B×N 13 R×B ch K–B1 14 R×QP Q–B1 15 R×N P–KN3 16 R×NP P×R 17 Q×NP. 1 : 0 Tereschenko–Rotlewi, St. Petersburg, 1909, Game 7) 11 B–Q3 P–KR3 12 K–N1! (12 B×P N–K5 13 Q–B4 B–Q3 14 Q–K3 B–QB4 15 Q–B4 B–Q3=) 12 ... Q–Q2 13 B×P N–K5 14 B–KN5 B×B 15 N×B+ (Khmeldnipsky–Eventov, U.S.S.R., 1956).

9 0–0–0   B–K3

9 ... B–B4 10 KR–K1 0–0 and now: (1) 11 Q–B4 B–N3 12 P–KN4 N–QR4 13 B–Q3 Q–Q2 14 B×N B×B 15 N–Q5 B–Q1 16 B–B5 B×B 17 P×B P–KB3 18 P–KR4 P–QN4 10 N–Q4 N–B5 20 Q–K4+ (an offhand game, Keidanski–Lasker, Berlin, 1891). (2) 11 R×B N×R 12 B×N P×B 13 R–K1 N–N3 14 Q–R6 P–B3 15 P–KN4 B×NP 16 R–N1 P–Q4 17 B–Q3=.

10 B–Q3

10 KR–K1 B×B 11 Q×B 0–0 12 R–K3 N–Q2 13 P–KR4 (13 R×B N×R 14 R–K1 R–K1 15 N–Q5 N–N3+ Richter) 13 ... KR–K1 14 B×B R×B 15 R×R N×R 16 N–N5 N–K4 17 Q–K4 N(K2)–N3∓ (Berlin–Budapest, correspondence, 1937–8).

10 ...   P–QR3

10 ... Q–Q2 is not altogether satisfactory because Black is forced to castle into an attack, 11 B–N5 0–0 12 N–K5 (12 N–Q4 P–QR3 13 B–Q3, Mieses–Rubinstein, Breslau, 1912,

13 ... P–R3 14 N×N P×N 15 B×P N–N5∓) 12 ... Q–K1 13 N×N P×N 14 B–Q3 P–KR3 15 P–B4± (R. C. Griffith).

11 KR–K1

Practical experience of this position is lacking. Black could try 11 ... P–KR3 here. If 11 ... Q–Q2 12 N–K4 N×N 13 B×N 0–0–0 14 B×N B×B ch 15 N×B Q×B (15 ... P×B 16 Q–R4 is too risky) 16 N×B P×N 17 Q–KN4=. This shows at all events that acceptance of the gambit is not unsound; Black can at least draw.

LINE 2 (*Continue from Diagram 18*)

7 ...	P–B3

Black extends his centre, but retards his development. It is, however, just possible that he can equalize. See note to Black's 10th move.

8 0–0–0	P–Q4
9 KR–K1	

9 Q–R4 Q–R4? (9 ... B–K3! 10 B–Q3 QN–Q2 11 N–Q4 N–B4 12 P–B4 N–N1=) 10 KR–K1 B–K3 11 N–Q4 with excellent attacking prospects (Heikinheimo–Crepeaux, Dubrovnik, 1950).

9 ...	B–K3

9 ... 0–0 10 Q–R4 P–KR3? (if 10 ... QN–Q2 11 B–Q3 P–KN3 12 R–K2 according to Keres, but 10 ... B–K3 is better, as shown later) 11 B×QP! QN–Q2 (11 ... BP×B 12 R×B+, or 12 N×P+) 12 B–QB4 P–N4 13 B–Q3 P×B 14 N×P R–K1 15 B–R7 ch K–B1 16 B–B5 K–N1 17 N×BP+ (Schlechter–Neustadtl and Tietz, Carlsbad, 1901).

10 B–Q3

Or **10 Q–R4 QN–Q2 11 B–Q3** when Black cannot avoid transposition to the main line, 11 ... P–B4? 12 N–K5 N×N 13 R×N P–Q5 14 P–B4 N–Q2 15 B–N5 B×B 16 P×B Q–B2 17 B×N ch K×B 18 Q–K4 Q–B3? (18 ... QR–K1 with an uncomfortable position) 19 R×BP! and won (Timoshenko–Karpov, Moscow, 1967).

10 ...	QN–Q2

10...0–0! is to be considered, 11 Q–KR4 P–KR3 (11 ... P–KN3 12 N–Q4±) and now if 12 B×P N–K5 13 Q–B4 B–Q3 14 Q–K3 B–B4 15 N–Q4 Q–B3 16 B×N Q×B=.

11 Q–KR4	Q–R4

11 ... **N–B4** 12 N–Q4 N(B3)–Q2 (12 ... N–N1 13 P–B4 B×B 14 P×B N–K2 as suggested by Bykhovsky is a stubborn defence, but where will the Black king be safe?) 13 B×B Q×B 14 Q×Q ch K×Q 15 P–B4 P–KN3 16 P–KN4+.

12 N–Q4

White maintains the advantage, 12 ... 0–0–0 13 N×B P×N 14 R×P B–N5 15 N–K2 P–KR3 16 B×N N×B 17 K–N1 B–Q3 18 N–Q4± (Estrin–Klaman, Semi-final, U.S.S.R. Championship, 1946).

THE SYMMETRICAL VARIATION

1 P–K4	P–K4
2 N–KB3	N–KB3
3 P–Q4	

See Diagram 19, and continue as follows:

19

3 ...	N×P

Some theorists consider that this reply is not as correct as 3 ... P×P. Tarrasch, on the other hand, condemned the latter move since it gives up the centre. Whoever is right, or whether the moves are equally good, 3 ... N×P brings fair results in practice, offers Black a varied choice of continuations, and has often been Black's preference in the master play of the last decade, especially in view of the popularity and good results of Line 1(B).

Black can instead reply 3 ... **P–Q3**, transposing to Philidor's Defence, for which see Chapter 12.

3 ... **P–Q4** is possible. It has no independent value, since 4 N×P N×P transposes back to the text, but seems dubious:

4 P×QP P×QP 5 B–N5 ch! (5 Q×P Q×P 6 N–B3 Q×Q 7 N×Q B–QB4=) **P–B3 6 P×P!** (6 Q–K2 ch B–K2 7 P×P P×P 8 B–QB4 0–0 9 0–0 P–B4 10 R–K1 B–Q3 11 B–KN5 B–N2=) 6 ... **Q–R4 ch 7 N–B3 P×P 8 N×P P×B 9 Q–B3 Q–B2** and now 10 0–0 B–N2 11 R–K1 ch with an attack, or even stronger 10 B–B4 Q–N2 11 Q×Q B×Q 12 KN×P N–R3 13 0–0–0 B–K2 14 KR–K1 K–B1 15 N–Q6 with great pressure. In the only master game played in this variation Black refused the piece sacrifice, but after 6 ... P×P 7 B–K2!

(7 B–QB4 B–N5 ch 8 P–B3 Q–K2 ch 9 B–K2 P×P 10 N×P 0–0=) 7 ... B–QB4 8 P–B3! (Stein–Bronstein, U.S.S.R. Championship, 1967) Black was forced to exchange queens and go into an ending in which he had no compensation for the weak Q- side pawns.

4 B–Q3

4 P×P is less effective for White:

(1) 4 ... P–Q4 (simple and safe) 5 QN–Q2 and now 5 ... B–KB4=, or 5 ... N–B4 6 N–N3 N×N 7 RP×N B–K2 (7 ... N–B3 8 P–R3 B–K2=, Thalkhasuren–Espinoza, Tel-Aviv, 1964) 8 B–KB4 B–KN5 9 P–KR3 B–R4 (Sokolsky–Lilienthal, U.S.S.R., 1938).

(2) 4 ... B–B4 5 B–QB4 (5 Q–Q5 B×P ch 6 K–Q1 P–KB4 7 B–QB4 R–B1 8 QN–Q2 P–B3; or 6 K–K2 P–KB4 7 P×P e.p. N×P 8 Q–K5 ch K–B1, if here 7 QN–Q2 P–B3 8 Q–Q3 P–Q4 9 P×P e.p. 0–0) 5 ... N×P 6 B×P ch K–B1 (6 ... K×B 7 Q–Q5 ch K–K1 8 Q×B? N×R, but 8 0–0 is unclear, e.g. 8 ... N–K5 ch? 9 K–R1 N–B7 ch 10 R×N B×R 11 B–N5 P–B3 12 Q–Q6+) 7 Q–Q5 N×R 8 B–R5 (8 Q×B ch K×B 9 Q–Q5 ch K–B1 10 N–B3 P–Q3 11 B–N5 P–B3 12 Q–B4 Q–K1 13 N–K4, Simagin–Khachaturov, Moscow, 1959) 8 ... Q–K2 9 B–N5 B–B7 ch 10 K–K2 Q–K3 11 N–B3 with a good attack (Khachaturov). The whole variation is speculative and unclear.

Note the unusual move order **4 N×P P–Q3 5 N–KB3 P–Q4 6 B–Q3** leading to the other main subdivision of the opening, the Classical Attack (Chapter 2).

4 ...	**P–Q4**
5 N×P	

See Diagram 20.

20

Here too the capture with the pawn makes things easier for Black who can equalize in more than one way: **5 P×P** and now:

(1) 5 ... N–QB3 6 B–KB4 (6 B×N P×B 7 Q×Q ch K×Q 8 N–N5 N×P 9 B–KB4 P–KR3=, or 6 Q–K2 B–KB4, or 6 0–0 B–KB4 7 P–B3 B–B4=, Crowl–Milner-Barry, Radio match, 1947, or here 6 ... B–KN5=) 6 ... B–KN5 7 QN–Q2 (or 7 0–0 N–Q5 8 P–B3 N–K3 9 B–N3 B–K2=) 7 ... N–B4 8 B–K2 N–K3 9 B–N3 B–QB4 10 P–B3 0–0= (Milich–Trifunovich, Beverwijk, 1963).

(2) 5 ... B–K2 6 0–0 0–0 7 P–B4 B–K3 (simpler than 7 ... P–QB3 8 Q–B2 B–KB4 9 N–B3 N–R3 when Black loses a pawn but gets some counter-attack) 8 B–KR3 N–QB3 9 P–QR3 N–B4=.

(3) 5 ... N–B4 6 0–0 B–K2 7 N–B3 P–QB3 8 N–Q4 (8 N–K2 N×B 9 Q×N P–B3)
8 ... N×B 9 Q×N 0–0 10 P–B4 P–B3 11 B–Q2 N–R3=.

If **5 B×N** P×B 6 N×P B–Q3 7 Q–K2 B×N= (Capablanca–Redding, New York,
1905!).

LINE 1 (*Continue from Diagram 20*)

5 ...   **B–Q3**

This move and 5 ... B–K2 (Line 2) are Black's soundest replies. Whilst 5 ... B–Q3 is the
more enterprising, 5 ... B–K2 is reputed to be the more solid.

6 0–0

If White tries to force the attack, **6 P–QB4,** Black could simply castle, after which White
can hardly do better than to transpose to the text play. If 6 ... B–N5 ch 7 K–B1! and White
threatens to win material. (7 ... 0–0 2. Q–32.)

6 N–QB3 N×N (not 6 ... N–KB3 7 0–0 0–0 8 R–K1 N–B3 9 B–KN5 B–K3 10 N–N5
B–K2 11 B–KB4 N×N 12 P×N, Gligorich–Alexander, Dublin, 1957, nor 6 ... B–QN5
7 0–0! N×N 8 P×N B×P 9 B–R3±, or if 7 ... B×N 8 P×B N×QBP 9 Q–R5±) 7 P×N
N–Q2 (7 ... Q–R5 8 0–0 0–0 9 R–K1 N–Q2 10 P–N3 Q–R6 11 B–B1 Q–B4 12 B–Q3 Q–R6=,
Smyslov–Lilienthal, Moscow, 1941, or 7 ... 0–0 8 Q–R5 P–KN3 9 Q–R6 P–KB3 10 N–B3
Q–K2 ch= according to Levenfish, or 7 ... 0–0 8 0–0 N–Q2 9 P–KB4 P–QB4 10 Q–B3 P–B5
11 B–K2 Q–R4=, Tal–Benko, Hastings, 1973–4) 8 0–0 (8 Q–R5 P–KN3, or more safely
8 ... B×N 9 P×B N–B4) 8 ... 0–0 9 P–KB4 P–QB4= (Kupreichik–Dvoretsky, U.S.S.R.
Championship, 1974). Black has considerable counter-play in view of the possibility of
attacking the doubled pawn by Q–R4.

6 Q–K2 B×N 7 P×B N–B4=.

6 N–Q2 B×N 7 P×B N–B4=.

6 ...   **0–0**

6 ... **N–QB3** is sometimes played here. Black thereby offers a pawn: 7 N×N P×N and
now 8 Q–K2 0–0 (8 ... Q–K2 9 R–K1) 9 B×N P×B 10 Q×P R–K1, or 8 R–K1 0–0 9 B×N
P×B 10 R×P P–QB4. In either case Black gains the bishop pair, and a good attack.
White usually declines the offer, playing 7 N×N P×N 8 N–B3 transposing back to the
next note.

6 ... **B×N** 7 P×B N–B4 8 N–B3 with some advantage to White (Fred–Hadziotis, Tel-
Aviv, 1964); but 7 ... 0–0 is better here.

7 P–QB4

See Diagram 21.

21

Instead White can attack the centre with his pieces by **7 N–QB3**. Black must not underrate this attack. **7 ... N×N** (not the passive 7 ... N–KB3 transposing to Gligorich–Alexander, see note to White's 6th move) **8 P×N N–Q2** (8 ... Q–R5 9 P–KB4 N–B3 10 R–N1 N–K2 11 P–B5±, Aronin–Kamyshov, Moscow, 1949, but not 8 ... P–QB4 9 Q–R5! when White's last move has more effect than before when both sides were uncastled, 9 ... P–B4 10 R–K1 P–B5 11 B–N5! Q–K1 12 B–K2! Q×Q 13 B×Q N–R3 14 B–B3 N–B2 15 QR–N1 +, Ribli–S. Garcia, Arrecife, 1973) **9 R–K1** (9 P–KB4 P–QB4) **9 ... Q–R5** as in Smyslov–Lilienthal in the note to White's 6th move.

A good fighting line after **7 N–QB3** is 7 ... B×N 8 P×B P–KB4 9 Q–R5 B–K3 10 R–Q1 Q–K1 11 Q–R4 (Réti–Spielmann, Stockholm, 1919) 11 ... N–QB3 with chances for both sides.

7 P–KB3 B×N 8 P×B N–B4 9 N–B3 N×B= (Mukhin–Noakh, Leningrad, 1966).

7 N–Q2 N–QB3 (not 7 ... N–KB3 8 QN–B3 N–B3 9 P–B3, Penrose–Milner-Barry, Sunderland, 1966) 8 N×QN P×N 9 B×N P×B 10 N×P B×P ch 11 K×B Q–R5 ch 12 K–N1 Q×N 13 R–K1 Q–N3 with good equalizing chances in view of the opposite coloured bishops. Black can also seek white square counter-play by 7 ... B×N 8 P×B N–B4 9 N–N3 N×B 10 Q×N N–B3 11 P–KB4 (Ljubojevich–Razuvayev, Amsterdam, 1975) when 11 ... N–N5 seems best. 11 ... P–KB3 is possible.

7 R–K1 B×N (or 7 ... N–QB3) 8 P×B N–QB3 9 B–KB4 and now 9 ... P–B4 10 P–B4 B–K3 11 P×P Q×P 12 B×N Q×Q= (Alvarez–Ayerra, Montevideo, 1960) or 9 ... N–B4 10 N–B3 N–N5 11 B–B1 P–Q5 12 N–K4 N×N= (Klovan–Kuzminikh, Riga, 1966).

LINE 1 (A) (*Continue from Diagram 21*)

7 ...   N–QB3

This move (from a game Torquay–Paris, 1913) used to be considered best here. Black develops fast and attacks the centre.

8 N×N

8 P×P gives White no advantage, **8 ... N×QP 9 B×N** (9 B–KB4 Q–B3 10 R–K1 Q×B 11 R×N Q–B3 12 Q–R5 P–KN3 13 N–N4 B×N 14 Q×B N–B6 ch +, A. R. B. Thomas–Hallmark, York, 1959; or if 9 N–B4 then 9 ... Q–R5 10 N×B N×N 11 N–B3 B–B4=,

Euwe, or 9 ... N–KB3 10 B×P ch K×B 11 Q×N N×P=, Szabó–Michell, Mar del Plata, 1948, e.g. 12 P–QN3 B–K2! 13 B–N2 B–B3 14 N–K5 R–K1) **9 ... B×N 10 P–B4** (10 N–B3, B–B4 11 B–K3 B×B 12 B×N and now not 12 ... B–B7 which only gives White a tempo later on, e.g. 13 Q–Q2 B×B 14 Q×KB R–K1 15 QR–QB1 B–N3 16 Q–QN4, or in this 14 ... Q–Q2 15 KR–K1 P–QR3 16 R–K2±, Tal–Osnos, Kiev, 1965, but simply 12 ... B×B 13 Q×B B–N3 14 QR–B1 P–QR3 15 Q–QN4 Q–Q3=, Matulovich–Hecht, Belgrade, 1969) **10 ... B–B3** and now;

(1) 11 N–B3 B–B4 12 Q–Q3 B×B (Alekhine–Alexander, Hastings, 1933–4) 13 Q×B=,

(2) 11 Q–Q3 R–K1 (or 11 ... P–KN3 12 N–B3 B–B4 13 B×B N×B 14 P–KN4 N–Q3=, Yanofsky–Schulman, Winnipeg, 1958) 12 N–B3 (12 B×P ch K–R1 13 B–K4 R×B+) 12 ... P–KN3 13 B–Q2 (13 B–K3 N–B4) 13 ... B–N2 14 QR–K1 B–B4= (Henley–Wheeler Bristol, 1960).

(3) 11 P–KN4 R–K1 12 N–B3 N–N4∓.

8 P–B4 and now 8 ... B×N 9 QP×B P–B4=, or 9 BP×B N×QP= (Keres) or 8 ... N×P 9 B×N B×N 10 B×P ch K×B 11 P×B (Steiner–Rejfir, Maribor, 1934) 11 ... P×P with good play for Black.

8 ...	**P×N**
9 P–B5	**B–K2**

See Diagram 22.

22

10 N–B3

10 P–B3 N–N4 11 N–B3 P–B4 transposes to the text.

10 Q–B2 B–B3 11 B–K3 R–K1 and if 12 N–B3 or 12 N–Q2, then 12 ... B–B4. Here 10 ... P–B4 is also playable.

10 N–Q2 and now (1) 10 ... B–B3 hitting White's QP as recommended by Keres, perhaps giving up a pawn, but getting counter-play; (2) 10 ... B–B4 11 N–B3 B–N5! 12 B–K2 B×N 13 B×B P–B4 with an excellent game for Black, who has given up his bad bishop for the enemy knight (Aitken–Hooper, Felixstowe, 1949); (3) 10 ... P–B4? 11 N–B3! B–B3 12 B–KB4 P–N4 13 B–K5 P–N5 14 B×B R×B 15 N–K5±, if 15 ... R–R3 16 Q–B1!; (4) 10 ... N×N 11 B×N B–B3 12 B–B3 P–QR4 13 B–B2! Q–Q2 14 P–KR3± (Geller–Naranja, Palma, 1970).

10 ...	**P–B4**

Having a weak Q-side Black naturally seeks space on the other side of the board. This move leaves a hole at his K4, but it would take White a long time to occupy it.

10 . . . N–B3 is passive, 11 Q–R4 B–Q2 12 R–K1 N–K1 13 R–K2± (German–Maragliano, Brazilian Championship, 1951).

10 . . . N×N Black voluntarily surrenders the spearhead of his position as in (4) above, 11 P×N P–B4 12 B–KB4 B–B3 13 Q–R4 Q–Q2 14 Q–R5 R–B2 15 KR–K1 P–N4 16 B–K5± (German–Sallamini, Brazilian Championship, 1951).

11 P–B3   **N–N4**

See Diagram 23.

23

This position offers chances for both sides as the following lines show. Black must be careful not to exchange minor pieces in such a way that he is left only with his QB which becomes a bad bishop. White, in turn, has to defend a weak QP.

12 B–K3 N–K3 13 B–QB2 (13 P–QN4 P–B5 14 B–KB2 B–R5 15 P–N5 B–Q2 16 Q–B2 B×B ch=, Matulovich–Zuidema, Hamburg, 1965) 13 . . . P–B5 14 B–B2 B–R5 15 B–R4 B–N2 16 Q–Q2 R–B4 17 KR–K1 B×B ch 18 Q×B Q–B3 19 QR–Q1 R–KB1= (Parma–Trifunovich, Belgrade, 1964).

12 Q–R4 Q–Q2 13 N–K2 N–K3 14 N–B4 N–Q1! 15 R–K1 B–B3 (Schmid–Krebs, correspondence, 1951–2).

LINE 1 (B) (*Continue from Diagram 21*)

7 . . .   **B×N**

This defence dating from about 1905 has been revived by Trifunovich with success, and has had a great deal of attention devoted to it. Its reputation has now been confirmed as a good drawing line for a player to adopt when he is satisfied with a draw. This was presumably the reason for Karpov's adoption of it against Tal at Milan in 1975. Black gives up a bishop for a knight so that he can get ahead as fast as possible with his development.

8 P×B   **N–QB3**

8 . . . B–K3 is less precise, 9 P×P (9 B–K3 N–QB3 10 P–B3 P–Q5 11 B×N P×B 12 Q–B2 N×P∓, Duckstein–Trifunovich, Vienna, 1962) 9 . . . Q×P 10 R–K1 (Euwe gives 10 Q–B2 as superior, 10 . . . P–KB4 11 P×P e.p. N×P(3) 12 N–B3 Q–K4 13 N–K4 N–N5 14 N–N3±, Liberzon–Hennings, Debrecen, 1968. 12 . . . Q–B3 may be an improvement) 10 . . . R–Q1 11 B–K2 Q×Q= (Parma–Trifunovich, Vrnjačka Banja, 1962). In this position Stein–Korchnoy, U.S.S.R. Championship, 1967 was agreed drawn.

See Diagram 24.

24

9 P×P

The modern main line. Other possibilities:

(1) **9 P–B4 B–B4!** (Hammond–Wallwork, Southport, 1905) **10 P×P** (10 P–KN4? P×P+; Ivkov suggests 10 Q–K1, overlooking 10 . . . P×P! 11 B×N Q–Q5 ch; if 10 N–B3 then simply 10 . . . N×N 11 P×N B×B 12 Q×B P×P 13 Q×BP Q–Q2 14 R–N1 P–QN3∓, Jansa–Makarychev, Amsterdam, 1975, but not 10 . . . N–N5 11 B–N1 Q–K2 12 P×P Q–B4 ch 13 K–R1 N×N 14 P×N Q×BP 15 B–N2 Q×B 16 B×B with excellent prospects, Janoshevich–Tóth, Madonna di Campiglio, 1973) **10 . . . Q×P 11 B×N Q×B∓** (Kostro–Dvoretsky, Polanica, 1973), or **10 B–K3** and now **10 . . . P–Q5** with excellent prospects, rather than the complicated 10 . . . N–N5 11 B×N B×B 12 N–B3 B–Q6 13 B–B5 B×R 14 Q×B? (14 K×B or 14 P×P is unclear) 14 . . . P–Q5 15 R–Q1 P×N! (Nichevsky–Dvoretsky, Polanica, 1973); after 9 P–B4 N–N5? 10 P×P Q×P 11 B×N Q×B **12 N–B3** Q–N3 13 B–K3 B–K3 14 Q–B3 N–B7 White has a slight advantage (Damjanovich–Trifunovich, Vrnjačka Banja, 1963).

(2) **9 B–B4 B–K3 10 N–R3 N–B4** (or 10 . . . B–B4 11 B–N1 B–N3! Euwe) 11 P×P Q×P 12 B–QN5 KR–Q1, ½–½ (Haygarth–Clarke, Brighton, 1972). 9 . . . N–N5 is also feasible, 10 N–R3 N–B4 (10 . . . B–B4 intending . . . Q–Q2 and . . . KR–Q1 seems better) 11 B–N1 P–Q5 12 N–B2 N(N5)–Q6 13 Q–Q2 B–B4 14 B–N3! N×NP 15 N×P B×B 16 QR×B N(N7)–R5 17 Q–K3 with a slight initiative (Schmid–Medina, Gstaad, 1973).

(3) **9 R–K1,** as suggested by Euwe, who gives 9 . . . N×KP 10 P×P N×B 11 Q×N N–Q3 12 N–B3 with a slightly freer game for White in view of 12 . . . B–B4 13 Q–Q4, or 12 . . . Q–B3 13 Q–KN3 with play on the black squares. Black can improve by maintaining the knight at its central post for as long as possible, 11 . . . B–B4! 12 B–B4 (12 R×N? B×R 13 Q×B R–K1 14 Q–QN4 Q×P intending . . . QR–Q1 or . . . R–K7; or 12 P–KN4 Q–R5 13 R×N B×R 14 Q×B QR–K1 15 Q–N4 P–KB4 with excellent attacking chances; or 12 N–B3 N×N winning the QP) 12 . . . R–K1=.

9 . . .	**Q×P**
10 Q–B2	

10 Q–B3 B–B4 11 Q×B Q×B 12 N–B3 N–B4= (Klovan–Zaidel, Riga, 1966), but not 10 . . . P– B4 11 P×P e.p. N×P(3) 12 Q×Q ch N×Q 13 B–QB4 B–K3 14 R–Q1± (Gufeld–Mikenas, U.S.S.R. Championship, 1965).

10 . . .	**N–N5**

10 . . . N–B4? 11 B×P ch K–R1 12 B–K3 N–K3 13 P–B4 P–KN3 14 N–B3 Q–B5 15 B×P P×B 16 Q×P with a strong attack. If Black wants to complicate matters and avoid the exchange of queens he can try the risky **10 . . . B–B4** 11 N–B3 N×N 12 B×B N–Q5 13 B×P ch K–R1 14 Q–Q3 N(6)–K7 ch 15 K–R1 Q×P 16 Q–KR3 N–B5 17 B×N Q×B (Knaak–Kostro, E. Germany–Poland, 1973) when White retains pressure by 18 QR–Q1 KR–Q1 19 B–K4 ch Q–R3 20 Q–N4 according to Kostro.

11 B×N	**N×Q**
12 B×Q	**B–B4**

If **12 . . .** N×R 13 B–K4, or even stronger, 13 P–K6 B×P 14 B×B P×B 15 N–R3 P–QN4 16 B–Q2 KR–Q1 17 B–R5 +, as given by Bellin and Harding.

13 P–KN4	**B×P**

13 . . . B–Q6 14 R–Q1 P–B3 15 B–N3 N×R 16 R×B, or **13 . . . B–N3** 14 P–B4 P–B3 15 B–N3 N×R 16 P–B5, or in this 14 . . . QR–Q1 15 P–B5 R×B 16 N–B3 R×P 17 R–N1, and in every case White wins material. *13... BN3 14 PB4 BQ6 15 RQ1 BR3 ∞*
BROWNE–ACERS MATCH 1970

14 B–K4

14 P–K6 P×P 15 B–K4 B–B4, or **14 N–R3** N×R 15 B–K3 QR–Q1.

14 . . .	**N×R**
15 N–B3	

The only move tried so far. **15 B–K3** and **15 N–R3** also come into consideration, e.g. **15 B–K3** P–KB4! (this move is the key to Black's counter-play in every variation) 16 B–Q5 ch K–R1 17 N–R3 P–B5! 18 B–B5 R–B4 19 R–K1 R–K1 20 R×N QR×P, or in this 19 R×N R×P 20 B×NP R–QN1 21 B–Q4 R–KN4 22 P–R4 R–N3 23 B–R1 B–K7 ch 24 K–R2 R–KN5 with good counter-chances; or **15 N–R3** P–KB4 16 P×P e.p. R×P 17 B–K3 R–K1 18 B–Q5 ch B–K3 19 B×B ch QR×B 20 R×N R–QR3 with a drawish ending.

15 . . .	**B–R6**
16 R–K1	**P–KB4**

Black has adequate counter-chances. There can follow 17 P×P e.p. QR–K1 18 B–Q2 (18 B–K3 R×B 19 N×R N–B7 20 R–QB1 N×B 21 P×N R–B1 22 P–B7 ch K–B1 23 N–N5 B–B4 24 R–B1 P–KR3 25 R×B P×N, ½–½, Butnoryus–Makarychev, Chelyabinsk,

1975) 18 ... R×B 19 N×R N–B7 20 R–QB1 N–Q5 21 R×P R–B2 (or 21 ... N–B6 ch 22 K–R1 N×B 23 R×P ch K–R1 24 N–N5, Klovan–Levchenkov, Riga, 1971, and now 24 ... R×P 25 R×RP ch K–N1 26 R×B R×P with a likely draw) 22 R×R N–B6 ch 23 K–R1 K×R 24 P×P K×P 25 B–K3 P–N3 26 N–Q2, the only way to free his king, but it leaves a drawn ending, 26 ... N×N 27 B×N P–QR4 and agreed drawn three moves later (Tal–Karpov, Milan, 1975).

LINE 1(C) (*Continue from Diagram 21*)

7 ...	N–KB3

Playable, but rather passive.

8 B–N5

Better than 8 N–B3 QN–Q2 9 P–B4 P×P 10 B×P N–N3.

8 ...	P×P
9 N×QBP	

9 B×P is somewhat better, as 9 ... B×N 10 P×B Q×Q 11 R×Q N–N5 does not solve all Black's problems.

9 ...	N–B3
10 N–B3	

So far, Chigorin–Halprin, Vienna, 1898. After 10 ... B–K2 White has only a slight advantage.

LINE 1(D) (*Continue from Diagram 21*)

7 ...	P–QB3

A defensive move which is more often than not a bad move in Petroff's Defence. Here is no exception.

7 ... **P–KB3** is not good, 8 P×P P×N 9 B×N Q–R5 10 P×P (better than 10 Q–Q3 P×P 11 P–KN3 Q–R4 12 Q×P B–KR6 13 B–N2 N–Q2, and Black has some attack for the pawn) 10 ... B×P 11 P–B4 B×BP 12 B×B R×B 13 R×R Q×R 14 N–B3 N–Q2 15 Q–Q4± (Stoltz–Andersen, Copenhagen, 1931).

8 N–QB3

The natural move, considered best by theory.

8 Q–B2 is the main alternative, and now:

(1) 8 ... R–K1 9 P–B3 (9 P×P P×P 10 B×N P×B 11 Q×P P–B3 12 Q–Q5 ch R–K3 13 P–B4 B–B2!∓) 9 ... N–B3 10 P–B4 P×P 11 B×P B–K3 12 B×B R×B 13 N–QB3 N–R3 = (Euwe–Olland, Club game, 1922).

(2) 8...N–Q2 (a promising counter-gambit) 9 P×P (9 N×N B×N 10 B×N P×B 11 Q×P N–B3 12 Q–Q3 B–KN5 13 B–K3 Q–R5 14 P–KN3 Q–R4∓) 9 ... P×P 10 B×N P×B 11 Q×P RK1 12 Q–R4 R–K1 13 B–B4 (13 B–N5 P–KR3 14 B×N Q×B, Black's bishops compensate for the pawn; Black could also avoid the endgame by 13...B–K2 followed by 14 ... P–KR3) 13 ... B–K2=. A correspondence game, Weenink–Olland, 1932, continued 14 B–K3 N–N5 15 Q–N3 B–Q3 16 B–B4 P–KN4.

(3) 8 ... N–B3 9 P×P (9 B–N5 P–KR3 10 B–R4 QN–Q2 11 P–B4 P×P 12 B×P N–N3 13 B–QN3 B–K2 14 N–B3 KN–Q4=, Konstantinopolsky–Shamayev, Kiev,1938) 9 ... P×P 10 B–KN5 with some advantage to White according to Keres.

8 P×P P×P 9 Q–B2 N–Q2! transposes to the gambit line of (2) above.

8 ...	**N×N**

This gives White the better game. Black prepared to defend his centre by his 7th move, so it seems illogical that he should now give it up. For better or worse he should try **8 ... B–KB4,** a move ignored by theory. After 9 Q–B2 B×N 10 P×B N–R3 (Pillsbury–Chapman and Brooke, Canterbury, 1903) Black was able to defend his game.

8 ... N–Q2 9 KN×N (9 QN×N P×N 10 B×P Q–R5 11 P–B4 B×N=) 9 ... B×N (9 ... N×N 10 B×P ch +, or 9 ... Q×N 10 N×N+) 10 P×P (10 N×N P×N 11 B×P B×P ch=) 10 ... N×N 11 P×N P×P 12 Q–R5 P–B4 13 Q–B3 B–K3 14 R–K1 Q–Q2 15 R–N1 K–R1 16 B–QN5 Q–B1 and now 17 B–KB4±, but not 17 B–R4 P–B5 with a good game for Black (Shamayev–Baranov, correspondence, 1935–6).

8 ... P–B3 9 P×P N×N 10 Q–R5 P–KB4 11 P×N±.

9 P×N

See Diagram 25.

25

In this position **9 ... N–Q2** is relatively best, 10 P–B4 (10 N×N Q×N! so that after 11 P×P P×P 12 Q–R5 Black's QP is guarded) 10 ... N–B3 and now 11 Q–B2 P×P 12 N×P(B4) B–K3 13 N×B Q×N 14 P–B5, White has the advantage, but Black won (Chigorin–Pillsbury, Paris, 1900), or 11 P–KB5 P–B4 12 B–N5 R–K1 13 R–K1±(Jansa–Kupka, Czech Championship, 1962).

9 ... **B–K3** is weak, 10 Q–R5 P–KN3 11 Q–R6 N–Q2 12 P–B4± (Schmid–Reitstein, Wilderness, 1964).

By playing 9 ... **B×N 10 P×B P×P 11 B×P** Black abandons the centre, cedes the bishop-pair, and remains behind in development. In 1889 Steinitz condemned this line; the superiority of White's position was demonstrated by a number of master games at the turn of the century; Black gets a positionally lost game, yet this line continues to harvest a crop of victories for White. As Alekhine once wrote it is a failing of even strong players that they exchange queens at the wrong time.

Play has continued:

(1) 11 ... Q×Q 12 R×Q R–K1 (12 ... B–B4 13 P–KR3, slow, P–QN4 13 B–N3 N–R3 15 B–R3 KR–K1 16 B–Q6±, Kostich–Andersen, 1931) 13 B–R3 B–B4 14 P–KB4 N–Q2 15 P–K6 + (Maróczy–Marshall, Paris, 1900).

(2) 11 ... B–K3 12 B×B P×B 13 Q–N3 Q–B1 14 B–R3 P–B4 15 QR–Q1 P–QN3 16 R–Q6 R–K1 17 Q–R4 Q–R3?? 18 Q×R mate. 1 : 0 (Maróczy–Showalter, Paris, 1900, Game 8).

(3) 11 ... Q–K2 12 P–QR4 R–Q1 13 Q–R5 R–K1 14 B–R3 + (Chigorin–Lebedev, Moscow, 1901).

(4) 11 ... Q–K2 12 P–QR4 B–K3 13 B–R3 P–QB4 14 B–Q3 N–B3 15 P–KB4 + (Pogáts–Androvitsky, Hungarian Championship, 1962).

(5) 11 ... B–B4 12 Q–B3 B–N3 13 Q–N3 Q–R4 14 B–K3 R–K1 15 P–B4 B–B4 16 QR–Q1 N–R3 17 B–Q4 P–B4 18 P–K6 + (Schorr–de Loughry, Tel-Aviv, 1964).

LINE 2 (*Continue from Diagram 20*)

       5 ...   **B–K2**

A positional line. On the one hand, if Black withdraws his KN then the bishop is better placed on K2; on the other hand, because his KB masks the open file, Black may delay castling and attack White's central position at once, see next note.

       6 0–0

After **6 N–Q2** Black can equalize by 6 ... N–Q3! 7 P–QB3 P–QB3 8 0–0 B–KB4 9 B×B N×B 10 R–K1 0–0= (Geller–Bronstein, U.S.S.R., 1969). Keres suggests 7 Q–R5 which is met by 7 ... N–Q2 and 8 ... N–B3.

See Diagram 26.

26

      6 ...   **0–0**

This is the usual move, but Napier's **6...N–Q2** is possible, **7 P–QB4** (Euwe suggests 7 B–KB4 N×N 8 QB×N, and Keres 7 N×N B×N 8 B×N P×B 9 R–K1) **7 ... N×N 8 P×N** and now:

(1) 8 ... B–K3! 9 P×P B×P (9 ... Q×P? 10 Q–R4 ch) 10 Q–R4 ch (10 Q–B2 is White's best chance of keeping the initiative, 10 ... N–B4 11 R–Q1 N×B 12 R×N P–QB3 13 N–B3, Ciocaltea–Rogoff, Malaga, 1971) 10 ... Q–Q2 11 Q×Q ch K×Q 12 R–Q1 K–K3! 13 B×N B×B 14 N–B3 KR–Q1∓ (Fox–Napier, Cambridge Springs, 1904).

(2) 8 ... P–QB3 9 P×P Q×P (9 ... P×P 10 N–B3 N×N 11 P×N 0–0 12 B–K3 with positional advantage to White, Gligorich–Olafsson, Hastings, 1956–7) 10 Q–K2 (10 Q–B3 P–KB4) 10 ... N–B4 11 B–B2 B–K3 12 N–B3 Q–B5! 13 Q–K3 0–0–0 and White has nothing much to speak of, e.g. 14 P–QN3 Q–R3! 15 Q–N3? N–Q6 16 B–N5 B×B= (Nunn–Jones, England–Wales, Birmingham, 1975). Black could even boldly play 15 ... N×P! 16 B×N (16 P×N Q×R 17 B–N5 Q–R6) 16 ... B×B 17 B–N5 R–Q6 18 P×B R×Q 19 R×Q R×B 20 R×RP K–B2 with at least an equal ending.

6 ... N–QB3 is also playable, 7 N×N P×N 8 P–QB4 0–0 9 P–B3 N–N4 10 P–B5= (Niephaus–Schuster, Essen, 1949). See also Game 12.

7 P–QB4

7 N–Q2 P–KB3 8 KN–B3 P–KB4 with chances for both sides (Matanovich–Udovchich, Yugoslav Championship, 1952). White's attack against Black's stonewall formation is less effective with his knight at Q2.

7 R–K1 N–QB3 8 N×N P×N 9 B×N (9 N–B3 P–KB4 10 N–K2 P–B4 11 P–QB3 P×P 12 P×P P–B4 13 P–B3 P–QB5 14 B–B2 N–N4 15 N–B4 B–B3 16 N–R5 P–N3 17 N×B ch Q×N 18 B×N Q×B= Matanovich–Trifunovich, Palma, 1966) 9 ... P×B 10 R×P P–QB4 (Schmid–Bhend, Venice, 1953). Black's attack and his bishop-pair compensate for the pawn. This is often the case when White has to give up his bishop to gain control of his K4 square. See Game 12.

7 ...   N–KB3

This simple move is best, although it represents a loss of time. White has as it were gained two moves: the advance of the QBP, which is not of much account now, and the advance of his KN to K5; but Black has no weaknesses, and can hope to gain time by attacking White's KB as happens in the text.

7 ... P–QB3 is weaker, 8 N–QB3 (in 1920 Bunger suggested 8 P×P P×P 9 B×N P×B 10 N–QB3 winning a pawn, but after 10...B–KB4 11 R–K1 N–Q2 12 N×N Q×N 13 N×P KR–Q1 Black has practical chances according to Mikenas) 8 ... N×N (8 ... N–B3 is better) 9 P×N N–Q2 10 P–B4 (10 P×P P×P 11 N×N Q×N with about level chances, Stein–Udovchich, Berlin, 1962) 10 ... P×P 11 B×P±.

7 ... B–K3 is also weak, 8 N–QB3 (8 Q–B2 is stronger) 8 ... N–KB3? (8 ... N×N 9 P×N P×P 10 N×QBP N–Q2 gives Black a playable game) 9 P–B5 KN–Q2 10 Q–R5 P–B4 11 R–K1 N–KB3 12 Q–K2 B–B1 13 B–KB4 R–K1 14 Q–B2 P–KN3 15 P–KN4 K–N2 16 P×P N–R4 17 B–R6 ch 1 : 0 (Alekhine–Levitsky, St. Petersburg, 1914, Game 9).

8 N–QB3   QN–Q2

8 ... P×P 9 B×P QN–Q2 (9 ... N–B3 10 B–K3 B–Q3 11 P–B4±) 10 Q–N3 N×N 11 P×N N–N5 12 B–B4 P–B3 13 P–KR3± (Lasker–Mason, Paris, 1900).

8 ... P–B3 9 Q–N3 (Mikenas recommends 9 R–K1 "with the better prospects for White") 9 ... QN–Q2 (if 9 ... Q–N3 10 P–B5) 10 P×P P×P 11 B–KB4 (Andrich–Udovchich, Yugoslav Championship, 1952) White has a small advantage.

9 B–N5

9 P–B5 P–B3 10 Q–B2 N×N! 11 P×N N–Q2 12 B×P ch K–R1 13 B–B5 N×KP 14 R–K1 B–B3 15 B–B4 R–K1 16 R–K3 B×B 17 Q×B N–N3 18 R–R3 ch K–N1 19 Q–R5 N–R5! and Black's break-up of the centre is shown to be more important than the slight weakness of his K side. Black has good counter-play (Tseitlin–Karasev, Leningrad, 1970).

9 ...	P×P
10 B×P	N–N3
11 B–N3	

See Diagram 27.

27

Black can now consider **11 ... P–B3,** but the only two moves tried in this position are:

11 ... B–K3, the safer move, 12 QB×N! KB×B 13 B×B P×B 14 Q–N4 (This speedy play against the KP is the point of his surprising 12th move) 14 ... Q–K2 15 QR–K1 QR–Q1 16 N–B3 KR–K1 17 R–K2, White will double on the K file and tie Black down, but his own QP will need protection too (Matulovich–Malich, Lugano, 1968).

11 ... KN–Q4, sacrificing a pawn for active counter-play, 12 B×B N×B 13 Q–B3 B–K3 14 B×B P×B 15 Q×P Q×P 16 Q×BP N(2)–Q4 17 Q–Q6 R–B3 18 QR–Q1 Q–KR5 19 N×N P×N 20 Q–K7 Q–R4 21 N–Q3 QR–KB1 22 Q–K5 Q–N5, Black has free play for his pawn, but White has no weaknesses and the long-term prospects (Gligorich–Gudmundsson, Amsterdam, 1950).

LINE 3 (*Continue from Diagram 20*)

5 ...	B–K3

Played by Blackburne (1888) and reintroduced by Malich in the 1960s. Black blocks the K-file, so that if now 6 0–0 he can attack White's centre at once by 6 ... N–Q2! when 7

P–KB4 P–KB4 8 N–Q2 QN×N gives about level chances.

6 Q–K2	**N–Q3**
7 0–0	**B–K2**
8 R–K1	

8 N–Q2 0–0 9 R–K1 B–B4 (10 N×P was a threat) 10 N–N3 B×B 11 Q×B N–Q2 12 N–B5± (Minich–Rogoff, Zagreb, 1971).

8 ...	**N–Q2**

See Diagram 28.

28

If **8 ... 0–0?** 9 N×P+, or if **8 ... Q–B1** 9 N–QB3 0–0 10 Q–R5 P–KB4 11 N–K2± (Steinitz).

There is not enough experience yet to state confidently whether Black's game is satisfactory. The line has been played very little, almost certainly because of its rather passive approach. There can follow:

9 N–QB3 P–QB3 10 B–KB4 N×N 11 B×N 0–0 12 Q–R5 P–KN3= (Unzicker–Malich, Sochi, 1965).

9 B–KB4 N×N 10 B×N 0–0 11 N–Q2 and now 11 ... R–K1= is better than 11 ... B–B3 12 Q–R5 P–KN3 13 Q–R6 B×B 14 P×B N–B4 15 B×N B×B 16 N–B3 P–KB3 17 N–Q4 P×P 18 R×P± (Fuchs–Malich, Leipzig, 1965).

9 N–Q2 N×N 10 P×N N–B4 11 N–B3 0–0 12 B–KB4 with about level chances (Lein–Malich, Sochi, 1965).

LINE 4 (*Continue from Diagram 20*)

5 ...	**N–QB3**

A counter-gambit known since about 1892, and introduced into master practice by Schlechter (1900). It is doubtful whether it is sound, but practical results have been good for Black.

6 N×N

6 N–QB3 B–QN5 7 N×N N×N= (Gligorich–Trifunovich, Kragujevac, 1959).

6 ...	P×N
7 Q–K2	

7 B×N P×B 8 0–0 P–N3 9 R–K1 P–KB4 10 P–KB3 B–KN2 11 P–B3 0–0 12 P×P P×P, with good attacking chances for Black, since if 13 R×P B–QR3 14 N–Q2 P–B4.

7 ...	Q–K2

7 ... P–KB4 8 P–KB3 B–Q3 9 0–0 Q–K2 (9 ... 0–0 is better, but after 10 P×N BP×P 11 R×R ch Q×R 12 B×KP P×B 13 Q–B4 ch White has the advantage according to Keres) 10 P×N BP×P 11 Q–R5 ch P–N3 12 Q–R6 P×B 13 B–N5 Q–K5 14 B–B6× (Ilyin-Zhenevsky–Rokhlin, Leningrad, 1930). The gambit 7 ... B–K2 8 B×N P×B 9 Q×P 0–0 (Pillsbury–Teichmann, Monte Carlo, 1903) is inadequate.

8 0–0	P–N3

8 ... N–Q3 is more discreet, a game Showalter–Marshall, Paris, 1900, continuing 9 R–K1 Q×Q 10 R×Q ch K–Q1 11 N–Q2 B–KB4 12 N–N3 B×B 13 P×B with the better endgame for White.

9 B×N	

Spielmann recommended **9 R–K1** so as to keep a pin on the K-file after 9 ... B–N2 10 P–QB3.

9 ...	Q×B

9 ... P×B 10 R–K1 P–KB4 11 P–KB3±.

10 Q–Q2	

With advantage to White (Keres). If instead 10 Q×Q ch P×Q 11 R–K1 P–KB4 12 P–KB3 B–KN2 13 P–B3 0–0 14 B–B4 P–B4 15 QP×P R–N1 16 R–K2 B–QR3∓ (Pillsbury–Schlechter, Munich, 1900).

LINE 5 (*Continue from Diagram 20*)

5 ...	N–Q2?

This line is no longer considered sound for Black.

6 Q–K2

6 N×N B×N 7 Q–K2 (7 0–0 Q–R5 8 P–QB4 0–0–0 9 N–B3 B–Q3 10 P–KN3, Tringov–Radulov, Bulgarian Championship, 1962, 10 ... N×NP; or in this 9 P–B5 P–KN3 10 N–B3 B–N2 11 N–K2 P–KN4 12 P–KB3 N–B3 13 B–K3 P–N5 14 P–KN3±, Kotkov–Khachaturov, U.S.S.R., 1971, but 9 ... P–KN4 may be an improvement) 7 ... Q–K2 8 0–0 0–0–0 and now: 9 P–QB4 N–Q3 10 P×P Q×Q 11 B×Q N–B4 12 R–Q1 B–K2 13 B–KB4 P–KN4 14 B–K5 P–KB3= (Sakharov–Gindin, Kiev, 1959–60); or 9 B–KB4 P–KN4! (Euwe); or 9 P–KB3 N–Q3= (Damjanovich–Malich, Bad Liebenstein, 1963).

6 0–0 N×N 7 P×N N–B4= (Suetin–Malich, Minsk, 1964).

6 N×P? K×N (6 ... Q–K2 7 N×R N–B6 ch 8 K–Q2 N×Q 9 R–K1 N×BP 10 B×P N–K5 ch, the safest, 11 R×N P×R 12 B–N6 ch K–Q1 13 N–B7 ch draws, I. Zaitsev–Karpov, Leningrad, 1966) 7 Q–R5 ch K–K3 and the attack peters out, e.g. 8 Q–N4 ch K–K2 and 9 ... QN–B3 follows, but 8 Q–K2 is a better chance.

6 ...	**Q–K2**

6 ... N×N 7 B×N P×B 8 Q×P+.
8... B-K3 9. Q×N Q-Q2 10. O-O O-O-O 11. B-K3 B-N5 12 N·B3 B×N ∞ (KARPOV-LARSON)

7 B×N

Best. 7 N×N B×N 8 0–0 0–0–0 9 R–K1 wins a pawn but gives Black some play, while **7 B–KB4** N×N 8 QB×N P–KB3 9 B–KB4 N–Q3= is tame (Matanovich–Udovchich, Skopje, 1962).

7 ...	**P×B**
8 B–B4	

Black's KP is fatally weak, 8 ... N×N 9 B×N P–KB3 10 B–N3 P–KB4 11 N–B3 P–B3 12 0–0–0 Q–N4 ch 13 K–N1 B–N5 14 N–N5! P–B5 15 N–B7 ch K–B1 16 Q×P. 1 : 0 (Dely–Malich, Pécs, 1964, Game 10).

The Symmetrical Variation is no less satisfactory for Black than the 3 ... P×P variations, and leads to much more varied lines of play. On the rare occasions Karpov has chosen the Petroff this has been his preference.

Summarizing the conclusions that Black should draw, Line 1(A) is probably his best chance of a good scrap with plenty of practical chances. Line 1(B) may be recommended as laying stress on development. White gets the bishop-pair, so Black must make the most of his faster development and sound pawn formation. The line also has the slight drawback nowadays that it is no longer virgin territory, since it has been extensively analysed in the last few years.

In Line 2 Napier's 6 ... N–Q2 is perhaps the soundest form of the Symmetrical, and has still been tried only rarely. The main variation of Line 2 leads to a long defensive game along positional lines unless Black is prepared to try Gudmundsson's pawn sacrifice with its practical chances—and long-term probable loss in the endgame. The untrodden ground of Line 3 may appeal to those who want to avoid long book variations, though it is rather passive.

Finally, we mention the transposition to Philidor's Defence by 3 ... P–Q3. This is a sound if cramped way of meeting 3 P–Q4 and because of the absence of early exchanges, such as are common in the Petroff, it leads to a close positional game. See Chapter 12.

Game 11 Sokolsky–Lilienthal, U.S.S.R. Championship Finals, 1937. 1 P–K4 P–K4 2 N–KB3 N–KB3 3 P–Q4 N×P 4 P×P P–Q4 5 QN–Q2 N–B4 6 N–N3 N×N 7 RP×N B–K2 8 B–Q3 N–B3 9 B–KB4 B–KN5 10 P–R3 B–R4 11 Q–K2 N–Q5 12 Q–K3 N–K3 13 P–B3 B–B4 14 Q–Q2 Q–K2 15 B–N3 P–KR3 16 N–R4 0–0–0 17 P–N4 B–QN4 18 N–B5 Q–Q2 19 0–0 P–N4 20 Q–B2 K–N1 21 KR–B1 N–B5 22 N–Q4 Q–K2 23 N–N5 P–QB3 24 N–R3 Q×KP 25 P–B4 P×P 26 N×P Q–Q5 27 B–B1 B–B2 28 Q–N3 KR–K1 29 P–N5 P×P 30 Q×P N×P ch 31 K–R2 B×B ch. 0 : 1 It is interesting to see how White's advanced KP finally fell.

Game 12 Schmid–Bhend, Venice, 1953. 1 P–K4 P–K4 2 N–KB3 N–KB3 3 P–Q4 N×P 4 B–Q3 P–Q4 5 N×P B–K2 6 0–0 N–QB3 7 N×N P×N 8 R–K1 0–0 (speculative) 9 B×N P×B 10 R×P R–N1 11 N–Q2 (or 11 P–QN3!) 11 ... P–KB4 12 R–K1 P–B5 13 P–QB3 K–R1 14 P–QN4 R–N4 15 N–B3 R(N4)–KB4 16 P–QR3 P–QR4 17 R–K5 (17 R–R2!) 17 ... R×R 18 N×R B–Q3 19 N×P? (better 19 N–B3 although Black still has some attack for his pawn) 19 ... Q–K1 20 P–N5 P–B6 21 P–N3 Q–R4 22 P–B4 (overlooking a brilliant forced winning combination, 22 N–K5 is best, when Black's attack is probably not decisive) 22 ...B×NP! 23 RP×B B–R6 24 B–N5 B–N7 25 B–R4 Q–N5 26 N–K5 Q–R6. 0 : 1.

Chapter 2

The Classical Attack

1 P–K4	P–K4
2 N–KB3	N–KB3
3 N×P	

This move has been analysed a great deal, and at present is rather less popular than 3 P–Q4.

3 ...	P–Q3

Petroff rediscovered this reply in the 1830s, hence the name of the opening. However, in the few games he played which have been preserved for posterity there is no evidence that he played the defence. Black's third move had previously been mentioned only by Cozio, and then only with the continuation 4 N–KB3 N×P 5 Q–K2.

4 N–KB3	N×P
5 P–Q4	

The Classical Attack, first analysed by Petroff and Jaenisch, and the strongest move here.

5 ...	P–Q4

Black has gained a tempo, represented by his advanced knight. He must try to maintain this outpost, exchanging or withdrawing the knight only for some compensating gain.

White should attack the knight, undermine its position, or force its exchange or retreat, or force Black awkwardly to defend it. In short, White tries to prove that the knight is prematurely advanced, that Black's tempo-gain is incorrect.

6 B–Q3	B–K2

6 ... **B–KN5** is premature, 7 0–0 (7 Q–K2 Q–K2 8 0–0 and if 8 ... N–QB3 9 B–QN5, Lilienthal–Alatortsev, U.S.S.R. Championship, 1944; if 7...P–KB4 then as Keres points

out 8 P–KR3 B–R4 9 P–KN4! P×P 10 N–K5±) 7 ... P–KB4 8 P–B4 N–QB3 9 N–B3 B×N 10 P×B N×QP 11 P×N QP×KP 12 B×P! P×B 13 Q–R5 ch + (Sir George Thomas–A. R. B. Thomas, Hastings, 1937–8).

7 0–0

After **7 Q–K2** White's queen is not particularly well placed on the open file, 7 ... B–KB4 (7 ... 0–0 and 7 ... N–Q3 are also sound) 8 0–0 (8 QN–Q2 N–Q3 9 B×B N×B=, since 10 Q–N5 ch N–B3 11 P–B3 P–QR3! favours Black somewhat) 8 ... 0–0 9 P–B4 R–K1=.

7 QN–Q2 N–Q3 (or 7 ... B–KB4) 8 Q–K2 0–0 (8 ... B–B4= is simpler) 9 0–0 N–B3 10 P–B3 R–K1 11 N–K5 B–B1 12 B–KB4 P–B3 13 Q–R5 P–KN3 14 N×P P×N 15 B×P and White has a strong attack, 15 ... R–K2 16 Q×P ch B–K3 17 Q–KR5 R–N2 18 P–B5 B–B2 19 N–B3 N–K2 20 N–R4 (Cohen–Kashdan, New York, 1934) 20 ... Q–K1! and Black can probably hold the position, but his game is not easy.

7 N–B3 N×N 8 P×N, and now 8 ... N–B3 (see note to move 8 by White in the Chigorin Variation), or 8 ... B–KN5.

7 ...   N–QB3

Black's last two moves, advocated by Jaenisch (1842), are still considered best. The bishop masks the open file, the QN is poised for counter-attack.

See Diagram 29.

29

THE JAENISCH VARIATION

8 P–B4   N–B3

This leads to an equal game. White's loosened pawns compensate Black for his loss of time in retreating the knight.

8 ... N–N5 was long considered sound, **9 P×P** (9 B–K2 P×P 10 B×P 0–0=) **9 ... N×B 10 Q×N Q×P 11 R–K1 B–KB4 12 N–B3** (12 N–K5 B–R5? 13 P–KN3 N×NP 14 Q–B3 +, Zuidema–Barendregt, Amsterdam, 1966. Black should play 12 ... P–KB3 or 12 ... N–Q3) **12 ... N×N 13 Q×N P–QB3?** (13 ... B–K3 14 Q×P B–Q3 15 Q–B3 0–0 with some white square play to compensate for the pawn is Black's best chance) **14 B–R6!** (This is a move which escaped the attention of analysts and players for decades. Previous tries were 14 B–Q2, Yates–Kashdan, Hastings, 1931–2, when 14 ... B–K3 is good enough, 14 B–N5 P–B3 15

Q–K3 Q–Q2 16 B–B4 K–B2 17 R–K2 KR–K1=, Williams–Clarke, Brighton, 1972, and Fine's 14 R–K5 Q–Q2 15 P–Q5 0–0=, though 15 ... P×P 16 R×B ch Q×R 17 Q×P K–Q2 18 N–K5 ch K–K3 is unclear) 14 ... R–KN1 (14 ... P×B 15 R–K5 Q–Q2 16 QR–K1 B–K3 17 P–Q5 P×P 18 R×B P×R 19 Q×R ch B–B1 20 Q–B6 R–B1 21 R×P ch B–K2 22 P–KN3+, or 14...B–K5 15 B×P R–KN1 16 B–B6 B×N 17 R×B ch K–B1 18 P–KN3 B–R8 19 P–B3 B×P 20 Q–R3+, or in this 16...B×B 17 R×B ch Q×R 18 R–K1) 15 R–K5 Q–Q2 16 QR–K1 B–K3 17 N–N5 + (Browne–Bisguier, Chicago, 1974).

8 ... B–KN5 is recommended by Euwe (and Jaenisch in his day!) **9 P×P** (9 N–B3 N×N 10 P×N N–B3 11 R–K1 P×P 12 B×BP N–R4 13 B–Q3 P–QB4=, Ermenkov–Radulov, Vraca, 1975, or 9 R–K1 N–B3 transposing to Chigorin's Variation) **9 ... Q×P 10 N–B3 N×N 11 P×N B×N** (Black could consider 11 ... 0–0 12 R–N1! R–N1 13 R–K1 B×N 14 Q×B Q×Q 15 P×Q B–Q3, but after 16 P–KB4 the bishops and possession of open lines gives White the advantage, Purdy–Kerfil, correspondence, 1948) **12 Q×B Q×Q 13 P×Q 0–0–0 14 R–K1 B–Q3** (Tarrasch–Marshall, Ostend, 1905). Black is at some disadvantage, but he drew the game.

8 ... 0–0 (Blackburne) **9 P×P** (9 N–B3 N×N 10 P×N P×P 11 B×P B–KN5=, if 12 B–B4 B–Q3, or if 12 R–N1 N–R4 13 B–Q3 P–QB4) **9 ... Q×P 10 R–K1** (10 B×N Q×B 11 R–K1 Q–N3 12 P–Q5 B–KR6!) **10...N–B3 11 N–B3 Q–Q1** with about level chances.

8 ... B–K3, a developing move not so bad as its reputation, **9 R–K1** (9 P×P B×P 10 N–B3 N×N 11 P×N 0–0=) **9 ... N–B3** (9 ... P–B4? 10 N–B3 N×N 11 P×N P×P 12 R×B P×B 13 Q–N3+, Steinitz) **10 P–B5 0–0 11 N–B3 B–N5 12 B–K3 P–QN3,** and Black has a playable game.

9 N–B3

9 P–B5 0–0 10 B–QN5 N–N1 11 N–K5 P–B3 12 B–Q3 P–QN3 13 P×P RP×P= (Chekhover–Kamyshov, Leningrad, 1938).

9 ...   0–0

If Black fears the further advance of White's QBP he may safely play **9 ... P×P 10 B×BP,** and now 10 ... 0–0 11 P–Q5 N–QR4 12 B–Q3 P–B3=, or 10 ... B–KN5 11 P–Q5 N–K4 12 B–N5 ch N(K4)–Q2 with about level chances.

9 ... B–KN5 is sound, if less precise, 10 P×P KN×P 11 B–K4 and now 11 ... B–K3, or 11 ... N–B3, but not 11...N×N 12 P×N±.

10 P×P

10 P–B5 B–N5 11 B–K3 Q–B1? (11 ... P–QN3=) 12 R–K1 R–K1 13 P–KR3 B–K3 14 P–R3 N–N1 15 Q–B2± (Kashdan–Kupchik, New York, 1940).
10 P–KR3, or **10 B–K3,** then 10 ... N–QN5=, or **10 N–K5** N×QP∓.

10 ...   KN×P

10 ... N–QN5 is not so good, (1) 11 R–K1 QN×QP, 12 B–KN5 B–K3 13 N–K5 (Veitch–

Hooper, London, 1954), or (2) 11 B–QB4 QN×QP 12 R–K1 P–B3 13 B–KN5 B–K3 14 Q–N3 N×N 15 B×B (Unzicker–Rabar, Munich, 1954), and in both cases White has somewhat better chances, although he won neither of the games.

11 R–K1

11 Q–N3 B–K3 12 Q×P? N(Q4)–N5∓.

11 ...   **B–K3**

See Diagram 30.

30

The chances are even.

12 N–K4 N–B3 (not good, says Capablanca, 12...P–KR3 being indicated) 13 N(B3)–N5 B–KB4 14 N×N ch B×N 15 B×B B×N 16 P–Q5 N–N5 17 R–K4 P–QR4 with about level chances (Capablanca–Kostich, New York, 1918).

This variation offers Black satisfactory chances. He does best to saddle White with an isolated pawn as in the text. Kashdan's 8...N–QN5 now seems inferior.

Game 13 Browne–Bisguier, U.S.A. Championship, Chicago, 1974. 1 P–K4 P–K4 2 N–KB3 N–KB3 3 N×P P–Q3 4 N–KB3 N×P 5 P–Q4 P–Q4 6 B–Q3 B–K2 7 0–0 N–QB3 8 P–B4 N–N5 9 P×P N×B 10 Q×N Q×P 11 R–K1 B–KB4 12 N–B3 N×N 13 Q×N P–QB3 14 B–R6! R–KN1 15 R–K5 Q–Q2 16 QR–K1 B–K3 17 N–N5 0–0–0 (17 ... B×N 18 B×B P–KR3 19 B–R4 P–KN4 20 B–N3 K–B1 21 R×B P×R 22 P–Q5 and 23 Q–B6 ch, or 20 ... 0–0–0 21 P–Q5! B×P 22 R–K7 Q–N5 23 Q–K5; or 17 ... P×B 18 N×B P×N 19 R×P R–N2 20 P–Q5 K–B1 21 Q×R ch!) 18 N×BP (18 P–Q5 is also good) 18 ... B×N 19 R×B Q×P 20 R×B Q×Q (20 ... P×B 21 Q–QN3) 21 P×Q P×B 22 R–N1 R–N4 23 P–KR4 R–N4 24 R×R P×R 25 R×RP R–Q8 ch 26 K–R2 R–Q7 27 R×RP R×RP 28 P–R5 R×P 29 R–R8 ch K–B2 30 P–R6 K–N3 31 K–R3 P–R4 32 P–N4 P–N5 33 P×P P×P 34 R–K8 R–B8 35 K–N2 R–B5 36 P–N5 R–B4 37 P–R7 R×P ch 38 K–B3 R–KR4 39 P–R8(Q) R×Q 40 R×R 1 : 0.

THE CHIGORIN VARIATION

(*Continue from Diagram 29*)

8 R–K1

Without in any way compromising his pawns White forces Black to make a decision about his advanced knight.

8 P–KR3 0–0 9 R–K1 P–B4 10 P–B4 B–K3= (Teichmann–Hodges, Cambridge Springs, 1904).

8 P–B3, a passive move giving Black a free hand, (1) 8 . . . 0–0 9 QN–Q2 B–KB4 10 Q–B2 N×N=, or (2) 8 . . . B–KB4, and if 9 Q–N3 N–B4 +, or 9 QN–Q2 N×KBP +, or finally, (3) 8 . . . B–KN5 9 QN–Q2 N×N 10 B×N 0–0 11 P–KR3 B–R4 12 R–K1 B–Q3=.

8 N–B3 N×N (8 . . . B–KB4 is also good) 9 P×N 0–0 (9 . . . B–KN5 is also sound, 10 R–N1 R–N1 11 R–K1 0–0 12 B–KB4 Q–Q2 13 R–K3! with slight pressure, Browne–Murray, Vancouver, 1971) 10 P–KR3 B–K3 11 R–K1 Q–Q2 12 B–KB4 (Aronin–Zhilin, R.S.F.S.R., 1959) 12 . . . B–B3=.

8 P–QR3 B–KN5 9 B–K3 0–0 10 P–B4 P–B4 11 P×P Q×P 12 Q–B1 K–R1 13 B–QB4 Q–Q3 14 N–K5 N×N 15 P×N Q×KP 16 P–B3 P–B5 17 P×N P×B 18 N–B3 B–Q3 19 P–KN3 P–K7 0:1 (O. Penrose–Hooper, Buxton, 1950, Game 14).

8 . . .   B–KN5

Black indirectly protects his KN.

8 . . . N–B3 is weak, because Black has little compensation for this loss of time, 9 P–B3 0–0 (for 9 . . . B–N5 see Berger's Variation, note to Black's 9th move) 10 B–KB4 (or 10 QN–Q2 B–Q3 11 N–K5±) 10 . . . B–Q3 11 N–K5± (German–Azevedo, St. Paulo, 1960).

8 . . . N–Q3 9 N–B3 (9 B–KB4 0–0 10 P–B3 B–K3 11 QN–Q2 Q–Q2 12 N–B1 P–KB4 13 Q–K2±, R. Byrne–Reshevsky, New York, 1972) 9 . . . B–K3 10 N–K2± (Steinitz), but after 10 . . . B–KB4 Black has little to fear.

8 . . . P–B4? 9 P–B4±.

9 P–B4

9 B×N P×B 10 R×P B×N 11 Q×B N×P 12 Q–Q3 N–K3=, or 11 P×B P–KB4 12 R–B4 0–0∓; while for other moves see the Berger and Krause Variations.

9 . . .   N–B3

Black now "justifies" this retreat on the grounds that White has slightly compromised his pawns to force it. It is in fact the only sound move here.

9 . . . B×N 10 Q×B N×QP 11 Q–K3, White will regain his pawn and then he has the advantage of he two bishops and the freer game, 11 . . . N–KB4 (11 . . . P–QB4 12 P×P N–KB3 13 N–B3±) 12 Q–B4 (or 12 Q–KR3 QN–Q3 13 P×P N–B3 14 B–N5 Q–Q2 15 Q–R4 0–0–0 16 N–B3± as in the stem-game for 9 P–B4, Chigorin–Schiffers, St. Petersburg,

1879) 12 ... N(B4)–Q3 13 P×P N–QB4 14 B–B2 0–0 15 Q–K3 N–B1 16 N–B3 B–Q3 17 Q–R3 P–KN3 18 B–R6 R–K1 19 Q–R4 B–K2 20 Q–Q4 P–KB3 21 P–Q6 1 : 0 (Wolf–Bardeleben, Munich, 1900, Game 15).

9 ... P–B4 is incorrect because Black cannot maintain his centre, so this advance merely weakens his game, 10 P×P Q×P 11 N–B3 N×N 12 P×N B×P (12 ... 0–0 13 Q–R4) 13 Q×B Q×Q 14 P×Q±.

10 P×P

10 N–B3 0–0 (10 ... P×P is also sound) 11 P×P and now 11 ... KN×P transposing to the text, but not 11 ... B×N? 12 Q×B QN×P 13 Q–B4, and if now 13 ... B–B4 14 Q–R4 P–KR3 15 R–K5±.

10 ...   KN×P

Pillsbury's **10 ... Q×P** has been played very little, but is quite good, 11 N–B3 B×N (11 ... Q–KR4? 12 B–QN5 B×N 13 P×B N–Q4 14 Q–R4 N×N 15 P×N! K–B1 16 B×N Q–N3 ch 17 K–B1 P×B, exchanging queens is no better, 18 B–B4 Q–Q6 ch 19 K–N2 Q–N4 20 Q×Q+, Vitolins–Heida, Riga, 1972) 12 N×Q B×Q 13 N×B (13 N×N ch! P×N 14 P–Q5 B–R5 15 P×N B×P 16 B–KB4 looks a slight improvement) 13 ... N×N 14 R×B 0–0–0 15 B–QB4 KN–Q4. Black's knights can maintain an effective blockade on his Q4 square.

11 N–B3   0–0
12 B–K4

See Diagram 31.

31

12 N×N Q×N 13 B–K4 Q–Q3 14 B×N P×B. Black's bishop-pair and his strengthened command of his Q4 square compensate for his weakness on the QB file.

12 P–QR3 B–K3 13 N–K4 P–KR3 14 B–B2 (14 N–N3 N–B3 15 B–B2 Q–Q4 16 B–B4 B–Q3 17 B×B Q×B with easy play, Barnsley–Wason, correspondence, 1939–40) 14 ... B–KB4 15 N–N3 B×B= (Wolf–Teichmann, Monte-Carlo, 1902). Black won, exploiting the isolated pawn.

12 P–KR3 drives the bishop where it wants to go, 12 ... B–K3=. But not 12 ... B–R4? 13 B×P ch + (Grenholm–Wennberg, Stockholm, 1900; Olafsson–Persitz, Hastings, 1955–6; and others).

Continuing from Diagram 31 Black has two sound lines:

12 ... B–K3, a solid and logical move blocking the isolated pawn. Black loses time by this retreat, yet still remains ahead in development. A few masters feel that White's freedom of action is worth just a little more than his pawn weakness; but most agree that the chances are about even. If 13 Q–Q3 P–KR3 14 P–QR3 (14 Q–N5 QN–N5 15 Q×P R–N1 16 Q×RP R–R1, draw by repetition) 14...B–B3 15 B–Q2 P–R3 16 QR–B1 QN–K2 17 N–K5 (Meyer–Liegl, correspondence, 1952–3) 17 ... N×N=. Or 13 Q–B2 P–B4 (13 ... P–KR3 may still be best) 14 B–Q3 KN–N5 15 Q–K2 N×B 16 Q×B ch K–R1 17 R–Q1 N×B 18 QR×N Q–Q3 19 Q–N3 P–QR3 20 N–QR4 N–Q1 21 N–B5 P–QN3 22 N–Q3 (Tseshkovsky–Dvoretsky, Vilnius, 1975). White still has some pressure. Or 13 P–QR3 B–B3 14 N–QR4 R–N1 15 Q–Q3± (Sax–Bednarski, Vraca, 1975). Haag suaggests 13 ... P–KR3 intending R–K1 and B–KB1 followed by Q–Q2 or Q–B3 and QR–Q1.

12 ... N–B3 allows White to push forward in the centre, but Black eases his game by exchanges, 13 P–Q5 (Keres suggests 13 B×N P×B 14 P–KR3±) 13 ... N–N5 14 P–QR3 N×B 15 R×N B×N 16 Q×B N–R3 (16 ... N–B7? 17 R–N1 P–QB4 18 P×P e.p. N–Q5 19 R×N +, Teschner–Schuster, Berlin, 1953) and now: 17 B–K3 when White has nothing substantial according to Keres; or 17 P–QN4 B–B3 18 B–B4 Q–Q2 19 QR–K1 QR–K1= (Levenfish, 1940).

Not, however, **12 ... N×N 13 P×N B–Q2 14 R–N1±,** nor **12 ... B–N5?** 13 N×N B×R 14 Q×B P–B4 15 B–N5! Q–Q3 (15 ... Q–Q2 16 B–B2 B×N 17 P×B N×P 18 Q–Q1! +) 16 N–K7 ch + (Chigorin and Schiffers–Alapin and Petrovsky, St. Petersburg, 1879).

In theory, 8 R–K1 should be stronger than 8 P–B4 (better to retain options if no clear advantage can be forced), yet, as these variations show Black can level up the chances. Usually a typical isolated-pawn situation arises: White gets more freedom of action with some prospect of attack; Black gets positional and long-term chances because of White's isolated pawn.

THE KRAUSE VARIATION

(*Continue from Diagram 29*)

8 R–K1	**B–KN5**
9 P–B3	

Now White threatens to win a pawn safely by 10 B×N.

9 ...	**P–B4**

Black supports his knight, but slightly loosens his pawns. The move is feasible because he has first developed his QB outside the pawn chain. He gets good attacking chances, but his centre comes under some pressure.

10 P–B4

By this two-stage advance (Krause, 1895) White first induces a pawn-weakness and then attacks it. Black must know the following variations which show that he can defend his game satisfactorily, if not actually gaining the advantage.

See Diagram 32.

32

10 ...   **B–R5**

Maróczy's move (1902) and the only good one. All other continuations favour White:

10 ... 0–0 11 P×P Q×P 12 N–B3 N×N 13 P×N B×N 14 Q×B Q×Q 15 P×Q B–Q3 16 R–N1 QR–N1 17 R–N5± (Maróczy–Pillsbury, Monte-Carlo, 1902).

10 ... Q–Q3 11 N–B3 (11 P×P B×N 12 Q×B! N×QP 13 Q–K3 is also good) 11 ... N×N 12 P×N 0–0 13 R–N1 QR–N1 14 P–KR3± (Berger, 1903).

10 ... B×N 11 P×B N–B3 12 P×P Q×P 13 N–B3 Q–Q2 14 B–QN5 P–QR3 15 B×N Q×B 16 B–N5±.

10 ... P×P 11 B×P B×N 12 P×B Q×P (12 ... N–B3 13 P–Q5+) 13 Q×Q N×Q 14 P×N N–B7 15 R–K2 N×R 16 P×P 0–0–0 (16 ... R–Q1 17 N–B3+) 17 R×B R–Q8 ch 18 K–N2 R×B 19 N–B3 (Schlechter, 1916).

See Diagram 33.

33

The following analyses are so convincing for Black that White has long since abandoned the Krause Attack.

11 P–KN3 and now: (1) 11 ... B×N 12 Q×B N×P 13 Q–K3 (13 Q–Q1 seems to be better) 13 ... B–B3 14 P×P (14 P–B3 0–0) 14 ... 0–0 15 B×N R–K1+ (4th Edition, *Modern Chess Openings* (2) 11 ... B–B3 12 P×P N×P 13 Q–R4 ch (13 B×N 0–0) 13 ... Q–Q2 14 Q×Q ch K×Q 15 N×N B×N 16 B×N QR–K1∓ (Hooper). (3) 11 ... N×P (given in most books) 12 B×N QP×B 13 Q×N B×N 14 Q–K5 ch (14 Q×NP B–B3 15 Q–R6 Q–K2 16 N–B3 P–B3∓) 14 ... B–K2? (14 ... Q–K2 15 Q×KBP P–KN3 16 Q–R3 B–N4 17 B×B Q×B 18 Q–K6 ch K–B1=) 15 B–N5 R–KB1 16 N–Q2 R–B2 17 N×B P–KR3

18 QR–Q1 Q–B1 19 B×B R×B 20 Q–Q5. 1 : 0 (Black–Schroeder, match, New York, 1918, Game 16).

11 B–K3 0–0 12 P×P (12 P–KN3 P–B5 13 P×BP N×BP 14 B×N B×B ch 15 K×B R×P 16 N–Q2 Q–R5 ch 17 K–N1 B×N 18 N×B Q–N5 ch 19 K–B2 QR–KB1 20 R–K3 N×P 21 B–K2 Q–R5 ch +, Vignoli, 1911) 12 ... N–N5 13 P–Q6 (13 N–B3 B×N 14 P×B N–N4 +) 13 ... N×B 14 Q×N B×N 15 P×B and now 15 ... P–B5 (Vignoli) or 15 ... N×QP∓ (Keres).

11 R–B1 P×P 12 B×P Q–B3, and now (1) 13 Q–K1 0–0–0 14 N×B Q×N 15 P–B3 Q×Q 16 R×Q N×P 17 P×B N–B7 18 R–B1 N×R 19 N–R3 N–Q7∓ (Krause, 1903). (2) 13 B–K2 0–0–0 14 B–K3 P–B5 15 N×B B×B 16 Q×B Q×N 17 P–KN3 Q–R6 18 B×P KR–K1 +. (3) 13 N–B3 0–0–0 14 N–Q5 B×N 15 N×Q B×Q 16 N×N N×P+ (Vignoli, 1911).

11 P×P? B×P ch 12 K–B1 B×R 13 P×N B×N and now, (1) 14 P×B Q×P 15 Q–K2 0–0–0 16 P×P ch K–N1 17 K×B KR–K1 18 P×N R×P 19 B×R Q–N8 ch 20 Q–B1 R–Q8 ch + (Maróczy and Teichmann, 1903). (2) 14 Q×QB Q×P 15 P×P R–Q1 16 B–N5 P–B3 17 B×P ch K–K2 18 B×N P×B 19 B–N5 ch K–K1 20 Q–K3 R–B1 ch + (Krause, 1903).

11 B×N QP×B 12 P–Q5 N–K4 13 Q–R4 ch P–N4 14 Q×P ch P–B3 15 P×P N×N ch 16 P×N·B×P ch 17 K×B Q–R5 ch 18 K–B1 0–0 +.

11 R–K2? N×P 12 N×N B×P ch +.

THE BERGER VARIATION

(Continue from Diagram 29)

	8 R–K1	B–KN5
	9 P–B3	P–B4

See Diagram 34.

34

This leads up to a pawn sacrifice, for which Black gets a strong attack. At this point there is no better move for Black, so if he does not want to play 9 ... P–KB4 he should not play 8 ... B–KN5.

9 ... N–B3 loses time without compensation, and now: (1) 10 QN–Q2 0–0 11 N–B1 Q–Q2 12 N–N3 N–KR4, and White wins the bishop-pair. (2) 10 B–KN5 Q–Q2 (10 ... 0–0 11 QN–Q2 R–K1 12 Q–N3!) 11 QN–Q2 0–0–0 12 Q–R4 P–KR3 13 B–R4 P–KN4 14 B–N3

B×N 15 N×B P–N5 (Keres–Alexander, Hastings, 1954–5) 16 B–N5 +. (3) 10 P–KR3 B–R4 with about level chances.

9 ... N–Q3 10 B–KB4 0–0 11 Q–B2! but not 10 QN–Q2 B–B4= (Kindij–Germek, Sarajevo, 1951).

10 QN–Q2

This position was first analysed by Berger (1880).

10 Q–N3 0–0 and now:

(1) 11 QN–Q2 (best) transposing to the text variation.

(2) 11 Q×P B×N (or 11 ... R–B3 12 Q–N3 R–N1 13 Q–B2 R–KN3 14 B–K2 B–Q3 and Black is a move ahead as compared with the text, as he has not had to spend a move on K–R1) 12 P×B B–R5 13 B×N BP×B 14 Q×N R–B3 15 Q–N5 (Zuidema–Hort, World Junior Championship, 1961) 15...R×P 16 B–K3 B×P ch 17 B×B Q–N4 ch with a winning attack (Averbakh).

(3) 11 KN–Q2 N×KBP 12 K×N B–R5 ch 13 P–N3 P–B5 14 K–N2 P×P 15 P×P (15 B–K4 B–R6 ch 16 K–N1 P×P ch 17 K×P Q–Q3 ch 18 K–R1 B×R +, Ljubojevich–Makarychev, Amsterdam, 1975; if 16 K×B Q–Q2 ch 17 K–N2 R–B7 ch. Clearly the modern grandmasters are not always familiar with the legacy of the past!) 15...Q–Q3 16 P×B R–B7 ch 17 K×R Q–R7 ch 18 K–K3 Q–N6 ch 19 N–B3 R–K1 ch 20 K–Q2 R×R + (Schlechter, 1902).

(4) 11 B–KB4? B×N 12 P×B N–N4 13 K–N2 Q–Q2∓ Lasker–Pillsbury, St. Petersburg, 1895–6).

10 Q–B2 0–0 11 KN–Q2? N×KBP 12 R×B B–Q8!! 0 : 1. A bolt from the blue—by correspondence, Kugaevsky–Khmielevsky, 1897, Game 17.

10 ...	**0–0**
11 Q–N3	

Other moves leave Black with the initiative:

11 N–B1 B–R5 (11 ... B–Q3 is also good, if then 12 N–K3? B×P ch +, Janowski–Schlechter, match, Karlsbad, 1902) 12 P–KN3 B–K2 13 N–K3 B–R4 14 N–N2 B–Q3 (Mason–Napier, London, 1904).

11 B–K2 B–Q3 12 P–KR3 B×N 13 N×B N–K2 14 N–K5 P–B3 (Mason–Napier, Monte-Carlo, 1902).

11 Q–B2 B–Q3 (11 ... K–R1 is also sound) 12 Q–N3 K–R1 13 Q×NP Q–B3, and not 13 ... R–B3? 14 N×N BP×N 15 B–KN5 +.

11 ...	**K–R1**

Black offers a pawn for counter-attack. He can save the pawn by **11 ... N–R4 12 Q–R4 P–B4** (Flohr), or less effectively by **11 ... P–QN3** 12 N×N (12 N–K5? N×KN 13 P×N N×KBP +) 12 ... N–QR4 13 N–B6 ch B×N 14 Q–Q1.

12 Q×NP

12 B–N5 B–Q3 13 P–KR3 B–R4 14 B×N P×B 15 P–B4 Q–B3∓ (Penrose–Alexander, Hastings, 1956–7).

12 N–B1 and now (1) 12 ... B×N 13 P×B N×KBP, or (2) 12 ... B–Q3 13 KN–Q2? Q–R5 14 P–N3 Q–R6 15 Q×QP N–K2 16 Q–N3 N×KBP 0 : 1 (Duhrssen–Batik, correspondence, 1927, Game 18), or 12 ... Q–Q2 (weak) 13 KN–Q2 N×N 14 B×N± (Capablanca–Kostich, Havana, 1919).

12 B–K2 R–QN1 with attacking chances.

12 P–KR3! A significant innovation. After 12 ... B–R4 13 Q×NP R–B3 14 Q–N3 R–N3? 15 B–K2 B–R5 White's K side position proved to be too strongly defended (Karpov–Korchnoy, Moscow, 1974). Black can improve on his play by 12 ... B×N 13 N×B R–N1, or by 12 ... B–R4 13 Q×NP N–R4 14 Q–N5 P–B4 with an unclear position in both cases.

12 ...	**R–B3**

Black now threatens 13 ... R–N1 14 Q–R6 N–N5.

13 Q–N3	**R–N3**

13 ... R–N1 14 Q–Q1! R–KN3 15 N–B1 N–N4? 16 N×N!+ (Ribli–Bonner, Skopje, 1972).

See Diagram 35.

35

Some examples of play from Diagram 35:

14 B–K2 R–N1 (14 ... Q–Q3 is also good, 15 N–B1 P–B5 16 KN–Q2 N×KBP 17 B×B R×B 18 R×B N–R6 ch? 19 K–R1 N–B7 ch. Draw, Tukmakov–Dvoretsky, Odessa, 1974. If 18 K×N? B–R5 ch 19 K–B3 B×R 20 K×R Q–N3 ch 21 K–B3 Q–R4 ch +, while Black could have improved on the game continuation by 18 ... N×R 19 K×N Q–KN3 20 P–N3 P×P ch 21 P×P R–KB1 ch 22 N–B3 Q–R4 23 B–B4 N–N3 with a fine attack) 15 Q–B2 B–Q3 (the usual place for this piece) 16 P–QN3 with transposition to Game 19.

14 K–B1 R–N1 15 Q–B2 B–Q3 16 P–KR3 B–R4 17 P–R3 Q–B3 18 N–K5 (Showalter–Pillsbury, Cambridge Springs, 1904) 18 ... B×N 19 P×B Q–N4 +.

14 B–B1 Q–Q3 (14 ... B–R5 may be better) 15 Q–B2 R–KB1 16 P–N4 N×N (not usually a good move) 17 N×N P–B5 18 P–N5 N–Q1 19 P–QR4 N–K3 20 B–R3 and White eventually won (Unzicker–Alexander, Biel, 1960).

In Berger's Variation the consensus of opinion is that Black's attack is worth as much as, if not more than, the sacrificed pawn. This was the opinion of Lasker, Pillsbury, and

Tarrasch; and in modern times of Euwe, Keres, and Panov. The Tukmakov–Dvoretsky game quoted above was played after the Karpov–Korchnoy one, so opinion in the U.S.S.R. does not seem convinced that 12 P–KR3 is a decisive strengthening of White's play. On the other hand, the great masters of defence, Steinitz and Capablanca, took the view that White could defend his game, a view not altogether supported by the evidence of practical results which are in Black's favour. Black can, of course, avoid the sacrifice of a pawn, if he so chooses by 11...N–R4 as noted in the text.

From all this we may conclude that 9 P–B3 is no more effective for White than 9 P–B4.

Game 19 Gunsberg–Weiss, New York, 1889 (stem-game for Berger's Variation). 1 P–K4 P–K4 2 N–KB3 N–KB3 3 N×P P–Q3 4 N–KB3 N×P 5 P–Q4 P–Q4 6 B–Q3 N–QB3 7 0–0 B–K2 8 R–K1 B–KN5 9 P–B3 P–B4 10 QN–Q2 0–0 11 Q–N3 R–K1 12 Q×NP R–B3 13 Q–N3 R–N1 14 Q–B2 R–KN3 15 P–QN3 B–Q3 16 B–K2 B–KR6 17 B–B1 Q–B3 18 P–N3 B×B 19 K×B R–KB1 20 N×N BP×N 21 N–R4 R×P 22 P×R B×P 23 K–N2 (23 B–K3 B×N 24 K–K2 B×P) 23 ... B×N 24 B–K3 Q–B6 ch 25 K–R2 B–K2 26 K–N1 R–B3 27 K–B1 Q–N5 28 Q–Q1 R–B6 29 R–B1 Q–R6 ch 0 : 1 (30 K–K2 R×B ch mates or wins the queen).

Game 20 Karpov–Korchnoy, Candidates Final Match, Moscow, 1974 (first 11 moves as in Game 19) 12 P–KR3 B–R4 13 Q×NP R–B3 14 Q–N3 R–N3 (in the changed circumstances 14 ... P–N4 is the correct continuation according to Botvinnik) 15 B–K2! B–R5 (15 ... B–Q3 was the last attacking chance) 16 R–B1 B×N 17 N×B B×P ch (Despair, but Black had less than 10 minutes for his last 24 moves) 18 R×B N×R 19 K×N Q–Q3 20 N–N5 R–KB1 21 Q–R3 Q–Q1 22 B–KB4 P–KR3 23 N–B3 R–K1 24 B–Q3 R–K5 25 P–KN3 R–B3 26 Q–B5 P–N4 27 N×P P×N 28 B×NP R(5)–K3 29 R–K1 Q–KN1 30 P–KR4 R–N3 31 R×R. Black lost on time.

THE MASON VARIATION

1 P–K4	P–K4
2 N–KB3	N–KB3
3 N×P	P–Q3
4 N–KB3	N×P
5 P–Q4	P–Q4
6 B–Q3	B–K2
7 0–0	0–0

See Diagram 36.

36

This variation, first regularly played by the Irish Grandmaster James Mason, is again being tried. It avoids the complex lines which often follow 7 . . . N–QB3.

7 . . . B–KB4 is, however, the simplest way of equalizing, 8 R–K1 N–Q3 (8 . . . N–Q2 9 QN–Q2 N–Q3 10 B×B N×B 11 Q–K2±) 9 N–B3 P–QB3 10 B×B N×B 11 Q–Q3 P–KN3 12 B–N5 0–0 13 B×B N×B= (Teschner–Trifunovich, Vienna, 1957).

7 . . . B–KN5 most likely transposes to other lines after 8 R–K1 or 8 P–B4. The stonewall formation is not good here, e.g. 8 R–K1 P–KB4? 9 P–B4 P–B3 10 N–B3 0–0 11 Q–N3±.

7 . . . QN–Q2 is probably less good for Black. White could try (1) 8 R–K1 N–Q3 9 Q–K2; or (2) 8 P–B4 KN–B3 (8 . . . P–QB3 9 N–B3) 9 P×P N×P 10 N–B3 QN–B3 11 R–K1 0–0 12 B–KN5 with a slight advantage.

8 R–K1

8 P–B4 is also good, (1) 8 . . . N–KB3 9 N–B3 P×P 10 B×P B–KN5 11 R–K1! QN–Q2 12 P–KR3± (Ree–Langeweg, Amsterdam, 1968). (2) 8 . . . B–KN5 9 P×P N–KB3 10 N–B3 N×P 11 B–K4 B–K3 12 R–K1. (3) 8 . . . P–QB3 9 N–B3 B–KN5 (9 . . . N×N 10 P×N also favours White) 10 N×N P×N 11 B×P P–KB4 12 B–B2 B×N 13 Q×B Q×P 14 R–Q1 Q–K4 15 B–B4+ (Hartmann–Burzlaff, East German Championship, 1958).

8 . . .	N–Q3

8 . . . B–KB4 9 P–B4 P–QB3 10 N–B3 (10 Q–B2 is also good, as well as 10 Q–N3 P×P 11 B×P N–Q3 12 B–Q3 B×B 13 Q×B QN–Q2 14 N–B3 N–N3 15 B–B4 R–K1, Timman–Stumpers, Rotterdam, 1969 and now 16 N–K5±) 10 . . . N×N 11 P×N B×B 12 Q×B P×P 13 Q×P N–Q2 14 Q–N3 with pressure (Kavalek–Pfleger, Montilla, 1973).

8 . . . N–KB3 loses time, but is not too bad, as Black can attack the centre with his QBP, 9 N–K5 P–B4 10 P×P B×P 11 QN–B3 N–B3 12 B–KN5 B–K2 13 Q–B3 B–K3 14 B×N B×B 15 Q–R5 P–KR3 16 N–N4 QB×N 17 Q×B B×N 18 P×B Q–B3 19 R–K3± (Eisenberg–Pillsbury, Hanover, 1902).

8 . . . P–KB4? 9 P–B4 P–B3 10 N–B3±

9 B–KB4

To prevent Black playing . . . B–KB4.

9 . . .	B–N5
10 QN–Q2	

For **10 N–B3** see Game 21.

10 . . .	N–Q2
11 P–B3	

11 N–B1 N–B3 12 N–N3 R–K1 13 P–KR3 with about level chances (Bogdanovich–Krizhnik, 8th Yugoslav Championship, 1952). Here 12 . . . N–R4 is good.

11 . . .	N–B3

11...B–R4 12 Q–N3 N–N3 13 N–K5 R–K1 with reasonable prospects (R. Byrne–Reshevsky, Oberlin, 1975).

12 Q–B2	P–KN3
13 Q–N3	R–N1
14 R–K2	R–K1
15 QR–K1	B–KB1

With about level chances (Unzicker–Porreca, Opatija, 1953).

This is a quieter variation, suitable for those who want to avoid the sharper and more analysed lines of play. Black maintains his "mass of manoeuvre", that is he keeps most of his pieces on the board—but he must be careful not to get them too bunched.

Game 21   Pilnik–Olafsson, Reykjavik, 1955. 1 P–K4 P–K4 2 N–KB3 N–KB3 3 N×P P–Q3 4 N–KB3 N×P 5 P–Q4 P–Q4 6 B–Q3 B–K2 7 0–0 0–0 8 R–K1 N–Q3 9 N–B3 P–QB3 10 B–KB4 B–N5 11 P–KR3 B–R4 12 B–R2 P–KB4 13 N–K2 P–KN4! 14 N–N3 B–N3 15 N–K5 N–Q2 16 N×B RP×N 17 Q–K2 R–B2 18 N–B1 N–K5 19 P–KB3 N–Q3 20 P–B3 N–KB1 21 Q–QB2 N–K1 22 R–K2 B–Q3 23 P–KN3? N–N2 24 QR–K1 Q–B3 25 K–N2 N(N2)–K3 26 B–N1 R–Q1 27 R–Q1 R–R2 28 P–QB4 P–N5! 29 BP×NP B×P! 30 N×B R×P! 31 NP×P? N–B5 ch 32 K–B3 Q–R5 33 B–B2 N–R2 34 R–KN1 N–N4 ch 35 K–K3 R–K1 ch 36 K–Q2 N–B6 ch 37 K–B3 N×R ch 38 N×N Q×B 39 R×P ch K–R1 40 Q–B1 R–K6 41 N–B4 R–K8. 0 : 1 Black's twelfth move was bold, leaving a slight weakness on the K-file; 12 ... N–Q2 would have been safer. By permitting the exchange of bishops on his 23rd move White would have had a minimal advantage, because of his hold on the king's file. Later, instead of 31 NP×P he should have played 31 N–R5! according to Euwe. A brilliant win by Olafsson.

THE MARSHALL VARIATION

1 P–K4	P–K4
2 N–KB3	N–KB3
3 N×P	P–Q3
4 N–KB3	N×P
5 P–Q4	P–Q4
6 B–Q3	

See Diagram 37.

37

6 ...	B–Q3

Marshall's favourite variation, which, however, theorists consider less correct than 6 . . . B–K2 or 6 . . . N–QB3.

6 . . . N–QB3, and White's best answer is 7 0–0 (7 Q–K2 B–KB4 8 QN–Q2 Q–K2 9 0–0 and now 9...N–Q3=, or 9...N×N=) 7 . . . B–KN5 (this move is not bad, but 7 . . . B–K2 is best transposing to better known lines), and now (1) 8 R–K1 B–K2! but not 8 . . . P–B4? 9 P–B4 B–Q3 10 P×P B×N 11 Q×B N×QP 12 Q–K3 Q–B3 13 B×N P×B 14 Q×P ch K–B2 15 B–N5 ch + (Capablanca–Marshall, New York, 1910). (2) 8 P–B4 N–B3! but not 8 . . . P–B4? 9 R–K1 transposing to the above-quoted game, or 9 N–B3 with advantage to White. *✗9. Ne3*

6 . . . B–N5 is somewhat premature, **7 Q–K2** (7 0–0 B–K2 is likely to lead to normal lines) **7 . . . Q–K2** (7 . . . P–KB4? 8 P–KR3 B–R4 9 P–KN4 and now 9 . . . P ×P 10 N–K5±, or 9 . . . B–N3 10 P–B4±) 8 0–0 N–QB3 (8 . . . N–Q3 9 Q–Q2) 9 B–QN5 (9 P–B3 0–0–0 10 R–K1 P–KB4 11 B–QN5 Q–B3 12 Q–Q3 B×N=) 9 . . . P–QR3 10 B×N ch P×B 11 Q–Q3 (11 R–K1 gives White some advantage) 11 . . . B×N 12 Q×B Q–B3 13 R–K1 B–K2 14 Q×Q= (Lilienthal–Alatortsev, U.S.S.R. Championship, 1944).

7 0–0

7 P–B4 was popular at a time when it was thought advisable for White to avoid the Tarrasch Variation, 7 . . . B–N5 ch (or 7 . . . 0–0 8 0–0, but not 8 P×P B–N5 ch∓) 8 QN–Q2 (8 K–B1 0–0 9 P×P Q×P∓, e.g. 10 Q–B2 R–K1 11 N–B3? Q×N! Janowski–Marshall, match, Biarritz, 1912) 8 . . . 0–0 (8 . . . N×N 9 B×N Q–K2 ch 10 Q–K2 Q×Q ch? 11 K×Q B×B 12 K×B, Alekhine–Marshall, St. Petersburg, 1914. Here 10 . . . B×B ch gives approximate equality) 9 0–0 B×N (9 . . . R–K1 10 P×P N–KB3 11 N–K5 QN–Q2 12 QN–B3 N×P 13 N×P! K×N 14 N–N5 ch +. 1 : 0 Capablanca–Black, New York, 1913) 10 B×B B–N5 11 B–B4 N–QB3 12 R–K1 N×QP 13 B×N P×B 14 Q×N P×N= (Tarrasch–Marshall, St. Petersburg, 1914).

7 . . .	**0–0**

7 . . . B–KN5 is not good. (1) 8 P–B4 P–QB3 (for 8...0–0 see the Tarrasch Variation) 9 R–K1 0–0 10 B×N P×B 11 R×P P–KB4 12 R–K1 N–Q2 13 P–B5 +. (2) 8 R–K1 P–KB4 9 P–B4 P–B3 (for 9 . . . N–B3 10 P×P see note to Black's 6th move, above; 9 . . . 0–0 10 N–B3? B×P ch is Leonhardt–Marshall, Hamburg, 1911, for which see note to White's 9th move in the Tarrasch Variation. 10 N–B3 0–0 11 P×P P×P (Black can improve by the standard combination 11...B×P ch 12 K×B N×P 13 Q–K2 N×B 14 Q×N B×N 15 B–N5 Q×B 16 Q×N Q–R5 ch 17 Q–R3, Capablanca–Wolbrecht, St. Louis, 1909, and now 17 . . . Q×Q∓. Hence 8 P–B4 seems superior to 8 R–K1) 12 Q–N3 B×N 13 P×B N×N (13 . . . Q–R5 14 P×N +) 14 P×N N–B3 15 Q×P ch K–R1 16 P–KB4 +. (3) 8 Q–K2 is ineffective, 8...P–KB4 9 P–B4? N–B3 10 P×P N×P 11 Q–K3 N×N ch 12 P×N Q–R5 +, a game won by Marshall.

8 P–B4

See Diagram 38.

38

For **8 R–K1** R–K1 (or 8 ... B–KB4, but not 8 ... N–KB3 9 N–K5) 9 P–B4 P–QB3 see note to White's 9th move in the text.

8 N–B3 N×N 9 P×N B–KN5 10 R–N1 P–QN3 (10 ... N–Q2 is also playable) 11 P–B4 P–QB3 12 R–K1 N–Q2 13 P×P P P×P 14 P–KR3 B–R4= (Yates–Marshall, London, 1927).

8 QN–Q2 B–KB4 9 R–K1 R–K1 10 N–B1 (10 P–B4? N×KBP +) 10 ... B–N3 11 P–B3 N–Q2= (Rossetto–Pilnik, match, 1946).

(*Continue from Diagram 38*)

8 ...	P–QB3

For other moves see the Tarrasch Variation.

9 Q–B2

9 R–K1 is the best alternative when Black equalizes by 9 ... B–KB4 10 Q–N3 N–R3 11 P×P QN–B4 12 P×N N×QBP 13 B×B N×Q 14 P×N P×P. The alternatives 9 ... R–K1, as played by Marshall, and 9 ... N–B3 do not seem as good.

9 N–B3 appears to lead to no advantage, 9 ... N×N 10 P×N B–KN5 (10 ... P×P 11 B×P B–KN5 12 Q–Q3 N–Q2 13 R–K1±, or 10 ... N–Q2 11 P×P P×P 12 B–KN5 P–B3 13 B–R4 R–K1 14 Q–N3 N–N3 15 Q–B2±, Puc–Kindij, Sarajevo, 1951) 11 P–KR3 B–R4 12 P×P (12 R–N1 P×P 13 B×P N–Q2!) 12 ... P×P 13 Q–N3 (if 13 R–N1 then 13 ... P–QN3, or 13 ... N–Q2 14 R×P N–N3 with counter-play for the pawn, but not 13 ... Q–B2? 14 B×P ch +) 13 ... B×N 14 Q×NP N–Q2 15 P×B N–N3 16 R–N1 Q–B3 17 K–N2 QR–B1 18 Q×RP (if 18 R–N3 R–B2) 18 ... R×P 19 R×N R×B= (Capablanca–Marshall, New York, 1909).

9 Q–N3 B–KN5 (Krause, 1921) **10 B×N** (10 Q×P B×N) **10 ... P×B 11 N–N5** and now: (1) 11 ... B–K2 12 N×KP Q×P 13 Q×P Q×N 14 Q×R B–Q3 with chances for both sides (Duhrssen–Batik, correspondence, 1928). (2) 11 ... B–B2 12 N–QB3 (12 Q×P Q–Q2 13 K–R1 B–K7 14 R–K1 B×BP 15 Q×R B–N3 16 N×KP N–R3=, or 12 B–K3 P–QN3 13 QN–B3 Q–Q3 14 P–N3 Q–N3 15 KN×KP P–KB4∓, or 12 N×KP Q×P 13 Q×P Q×N 14 Q×R Q×P∓) 12 ... Q×P 13 Q×P Q–Q2 14 K–R1 B–QR4 15 Q×Q N×Q 16 KN×KP N–K4=.

9 ...	N–R3

With this move (Krause, 1921) Black gives up a pawn for counter-attack. He is under some pressure, and must take this calculated risk, or accept retreat. His chances are not unpromising and would suit those who seek tactical play: those who do not should avoid the 6 . . . B–Q3 variations.

9 . . . P–KB4 also involves risk, but may be less disadvantageous than usual, since White must lose a tempo to bring his queen on to the weakened diagonal, 10 Q–N3 K–R1 (10 . . . B–K3 11 N–B3 N×N 12 P×N P×P 13 B×BP±) 11 N–B3 and now 11 . . . N–R3 looks as good as anything, so that if 12 P×P P×P 13 N×P B–K3 14 B–QB4 R–B1 +; if instead 11 . . . N×N 12 P×N P–KR3 13 R–K1±. In view of this White would do well to consider 10 N–B3 or 10 P×P P×P 11 N–K5 intending 12 P–B3, and in either case he stands slightly better.

9 . . . N–B3, if played at all this retreat should come at move 8, 10 B–N5 P–KR3 (Steinitz advocated 10 . . . P×P so that if 11 B×P ch Black has chances with his queen-side pawn majority) 11 B–R4 P×P 12 B×P QN–Q2 13 N–B3± (Ilyin-Zhenevsky–Polyak, Leningrad, 1938).

9 . . . B–KN5? 10 N–K5 B×N 11 P×B B–KB4 12 P–B3 Q–N3 ch 13 P–B5 N×P 14 B×B N–N6 ch 15 R–B2 N×R 16 B×P ch + (Sanguinetti–Puiggros, Argentine Championship, 1957).

9 . . . B–KB4 10 N–B3 R–K1 11 R–K1±.

10 B×N

It is best for White logically to carry out his threat.

10 P–QR3 P–KB4! this is Black's idea, should White decline the pawn-offer, and now (1) 11 P–B5 B–K2! 12 P–QN4 N–B2 13 N–K5 N–K3 (Panov). (2) 11 P×P P×P 12 B×QN P×B 13 Q–B6 Q–N3! (3) 11 Q–N3 N–B2 and Black can defend his centre with a satisfactory stonewall position.

10 ...		P×B	
11 Q×P		R–K1	
12 Q–Q3			

12 Q–R4 Q×Q 13 N×Q N–N5 14 N–R3 R–K5 15 N–B3 B–N5 16 B–K3 B×N 17 P×B R–R5=.

12 ...		B–KN5	

Or **12 . . . N–N5** 13 Q–N3 B–KB4 14 B–KN5±.

See Diagram 39.

39

For his pawn Black has two bishops and the better development. Experience is lacking as to whether this compensation is sufficient. Suggested continuations: (1) 13 N–N5 P–KN3. (2) 13 QN–Q2 N–B4 14 Q–B2 N–K3. (3) 13 B–N5 P–B3 14 B–R4 N–B4 (or 14 ... B×N).

The defence 6 ... B–Q3, if not so correct, perhaps, as 6 ... B–K2 (or 6 ... N–QB3), is nevertheless quite playable, and gives fair practical results. Note in particular the number of occasions on which Black is able to meet a premature R–K1 by the combination B×KRP ch, then N×KBP, N×KB, QB×N and Q–R5 ch winning the unguarded rook at K1. In those cases when counter-attack is called for Black must not flinch from making sacrifices. In some cases he must accept that he cannot force a counter-attack, and then he must complete his development quickly and proceed along positional lines.

Game 22   Janowski–Marshall, Biarritz, 1912. 1 P–K4 P–K4 2 N–KB3 N–KB3 3 N×P P–Q3 4 N–KB3 N×P 5 P–Q4 P–Q4 6 B–Q3 B–Q3 7 P–QB4 0–0 8 P×P B–N5 ch 9 K–B1 Q×P 10 Q–B2 R–K1 ! N–QB3? (11 B×N R×B 12 N–QB3 B×N 13 P×B is a lesser evil) 11 ... N×N 12 P×N Q×N! 13 P×B N–B3 14 B–N2 (14 B–K3 B–R6 15 R–KN1 R×B 16 B×P ch K–R1 17 P×B N×QP) 14 ... N×NP 15 B×P ch K–R1 16 P×Q B–R6 ch 17 K–N1 N×Q 18 B×N R–K7 19 R–QB1 QR–K1 20 B–B3 (20 B–Q3 R–K8 ch 21 B–B1 R×R 22 B×R R–K8) 20 ... QR–K6! 21 B–N4 (21 P×R R–N7 ch 22 K–B1 R×B ch) 21 ... R×P(6) 22 B–Q1 R–B3 0 : 1.

Game 23   Desler–Andersen, Copenhagen, 1929. 1 P–K4 P–K4 2 N–KB3 N–KB3 3 N×P P–Q3 4 N–KB3 N×P 5 P–Q4 P–Q4 6 B–Q3 B–N5 7 Q–K2 Q–K2 8 0–0 N–QB3 9 P–B3 P–B4 10 P–KR3? B–R4 11 R–K1 0–0–0 12 B–KB4? R–N1 ! 13 B–QN5 P–N4 14 B×N B×N! 15 B×P ch K×B 16 Q–N5 ch K–B1 17 Q–R6 ch K–Q2 18 B×BP P–N5!! 19 B×R Q×B 20 Q–N7 ch K–K3 21 Q×KRP B–Q3 22 P–B4 P×RP 23 P×P ch K–B3 24 Q–R4 ch R–N4 25 P–KN3 K–N3 26 K–R2 R×P!! 27 Q×R ch N×Q 28 P×N Q–N4 29 R–K6 ch K–R4 30 R×B Q–K6. 0 : 1 If 15 Q×B P×QB 16 B–R4 N–N4! Later if 21 P×B Black mates in 4, and later still if 25 Q–R6 ch R–N3 26 Q–R4 ch K–N2! Black moves his king with remarkable coolness under fire, and wins brilliantly, without giving a single check himself.

THE TARRASCH VARIATION

(*Continue from Diagram 38*)

8 ...	**B–KN5**

A counter-attack invented by Tarrasch in 1906. Black wastes no time guarding his queen's pawn. Instead he brings the QN as quickly as possible to the king's side to assist the attack, and to regain or maintain control of the central light-coloured squares, his Q4 and K5 squares. The idea is now known to be unsound.

Pillsbury's **8 ... N–KB3** is worth consideration, (1) 9 N–B3 P×P 10 B×P N–B3 11 B–KN5 (11 P–KR3 P–KR3=) 11 ... P–KR3 12 B–R4 B–KN5. (2) 9 B–KN5 P×P 10 B×P QN–Q2 11 N–B3 N–N3 12 B–N3 B–KN5, and in either case Black has a playable game.

8 ... B–K3, a move which held the field for many years. (1) 9 R–K1 (Capablanca)

9 ... R–K1 10 Q–N3 P×P 11 B×P B×B 12 Q×B P–B3 13 N–B3 =. (2) 9 N–B3 N×N 10 P×N P×P 11 B–K4 Q–B1 12 R–N1 P–QB3 13 N–N5 B–KB4 (13 ... P–KR3 14 N×B Q×N 15 R–K1 and White has positional compensation for the pawn according to Krause, 1921) 14 B×B Q×B 15 R×P Q–B1 16 R–N1 N–Q2 and Black has an inferior but defensible game according to Keres. (3) 9 Q–K2 N–KB3 10 P–B5± (Panov), but 9 ... R–K1! is a better move for Black. (4) 9 Q–N3 P×P=. (5) **9** P×P B×P 10 N–B3 N×N 11 P×N N–Q2=. (6) 9 Q–B2 P–KB4 10 Q–N3 P×P (as in the stem-game for all 5 P–Q4 variations, Pest–Paris, correspondence, 1842) 11 B×P= and not 11 Q×NP N–QB3∓ (Steinitz).

9 P×P

9 P–B5 B–K2 10 P–KR3 B×N 11 P×B? N–N4 12 P–B4 N–K3 13 B–B5 N–B3∓ (John–Marshall, Hamburg, 1910).

9 N–B3 N×N 10 P×N P–QB3 as Marshall's Variation, note to White's 9th move. If 10 ... P×P 11 B×P N–Q2 12 Q–Q3! P–B4? (12 ... P–QB3 13 N–N5 N–B3 14 P–KR3±, Capablanca–Northrup, Manhattan C.C., 1909) 13 N–N5 N–B3 14 P–KR3 B–R4 15 P–B4 P–KR3 16 P–N4 P–N4 17 B–Q5 B–N3 18 Q×B± (Corzo–Marshall, Havana, 1913).

9 R–K1 P–KB4 10 N–B3? (10 P–KR3!) 10 ... B×P ch 11 K–B1 N–QB3 12 N×P B×N 13 Q×B Q–R5 (13 ... N×P is rather better) 14 B×N N×P 15 Q–KR3= (Leonhardt–Marshall, Hamburg, 1911).

9 ...	**P–KB4**
10 N–B3	

10 R–K1? B×P ch +.

10 ...	**N–Q2**
11 P–KR3	

11 N×N P×N 12 B×P N–B3, and now 13 B–N5 B×P ch +, or 13 Q–Q3 N×B 14 Q×N B×N 15 P×N K–R1 +.

11 R–K1 QN–B3 (11 ... B×P ch? 12 K×B N×P 13 B–KN5 +, one rare case of the typical bishop sacrifice not working!) 12 Q–B2 B×N 13 P×B N×N 14 P×N N–R4 15 B×P Q–R5 16 P–KR3 B–B5 + (the stem-game, Ruck–Tarrasch, Nuremberg, 1906).

11 B–K2 P–KR3 (to prevent 12 N–KN5) 12 B–K3 QN–B3 13 N×N P×N 14 N–Q2 B×B 15 Q×B N×P 16 Q–N4± (Janowski–Marshall, Biarritz, 1912).

11 ...	**B–R4**
12 N×N	**P×N**
13 B×P	**N–B3**

13 ... K–R1 is also inadequate, but leads to complex play, 14 Q–Q3 P–KR3 15 B–Q2 Q–B3 16 P–KN4 B–B2 17 P–N5 Q–Q1 18 P×P P×P 19 B×P + (Spielmann–Marshall, San Sebastian, 1912).

14 B–B5	**K–R1**

See Diagram 40.

40

15 P–KN4 (the best) **15 ... N×QP 16 B–K6** (16 Q–Q3 N–N5 17 Q–K4 B–B2 18 B–N5 Q–K1 19 N–K5 B–Q4 with about level chances) **16 ... B–B2 17 N–N5 B×B 18 N×B Q–R5** (18 ... Q–B3 19 N×R R×N 20 P–N5+) **16 Q–N3+** (Alexander–Mallison, Brighton, 1938).

Neither **15 Q–N3** N×P 16 B–N5 B–K2, nor **15 B–N5** P–KR3 16 B×N Q×B 17 B–N4 B×B 18 P×B Q–B5 19 Q–Q3 Q×NP leads to clear advantage for White.

15 B–K6 N–K5! 16 P–KN4 B–N3 17 K–N2 Q–B3 18 B–K3 QR–K1 19 P–KR4 R×B 20 P×R N–B6! 21 P×N B–K5 22 K–R3 and Black mates in 6 (Norman-Hansen–Andersen, Copenhagen, 1934, Game 24). A beautiful "ladder" mate. Note Black's use of his K5 square.

On the whole the Tarrasch Variation cannot be recommended for Black, except by way of surprise against an opponent who doesn't know it well—when he would be hard put to it to find the correct moves. The variations given in the note to Black's 8th move may be worth a try, especially 8 ... B–K3.

Game 25 Krause–Nielsen, Copenhagen, 1896. 1 P–K4 P–K4 2 N–KB3 N–KB3 3 N×P P–Q3 4 N–KB3 N×P 5 P–Q4 P–Q4 6 B–Q3 B–Q3 7 0–0 B–KN5 8 P–B4 P–QB3 9 P–KR3 B–R4 10 R–K1 0–0 11 B×N P×B 12 R×P N–Q2 13 N–B3 P–KB4 14 R–K1 N–B3 15 Q–Q3 N–K5 16 N×N P×N 17 Q×P B×N 18 P×B Q–B2 19 Q–K6 ch? K–R1 20 P–B5 R–B3! 21 Q–K4 R–N3 ch 22 K–R1 Q–Q2 23 Q–R4 Q–B4 24 R–K3 B–K2 25 Q–N4 R×Q 26 BP×Q Q–Q4 ch. 0 : 1 Perhaps this might be called the stem-game.

THE CLOSE VARIATION

1 P–K4	**P–K4**
2 N–KB3	**N–KB3**
3 N×P	**P–Q3**
4 N–KB3	**N×P**
5 P–Q4	**N–KB3**

A quieter plan than advancing the QP. Black's loss of time is not serious here, for he is not behind in development. White gets a nominal advantage in space, but there are no weaknesses in Black's position.

If, however, Black now advances his QP, he may give White a useful outpost on the open file (Black's K4 square). Black should therefore play ... P–Q4 only in certain circumstances: if White cannot profitably occupy the outpost; or if White plays slow or inexact moves—in this case advancing the QP may gain space for Black; or if White plays P–QB4 trying to gain space by moving up his pawns. In this last instance Black may regard the advance of his QP as an attacking move against White's pawns, with the probable consequence that White will be left with an isolated queen's pawn.

There has been considerable interest shown in the variation since the 1971 match between Fischer and Petrosian in Buenos Aires, though the idea is far from new since it was played in Lowenthal–Barnes, London, 1862. The move order preferred by Petrosian was 5 ... N–KB3 6 B–Q3 B–K2, but there have been a number of games which have gone 5 ... B–K2 6 B–Q3 N–KB3. It remains an open question whether against either fifth move White should play 6 P–Q5 emphasizing his space advantage.

6 B–Q3

If **6 P–KR3 B–B4=**.

6...   **B–K2**

6...B–N5 is sound enough if Black wants to make sure of getting this piece out early·

7 P–KR3

The modern preference, recommended by Tarrasch. After **7 0–0 B–N5** Black has fewer difficulties—8 P–KR3 B–R4 9 R–K1 0–0 10 QN–Q2 QN–Q2 11 N–B1 B–N3 12 N–N3 R–K1 13 B–KN5 N–Q4= (Kupper–Smyslov, Munich, 1958) since exchanges relieve Black's game, or 8 B–KN5 0–0 9 QN–Q2 N–B3 10 P–B3 P–KR3 11 B–R4 N–R4 12 B×B N×B= (Keres–Bronstein, U.S.S.R. Championship, 1961).

8 P–QN3 may be White's best chance, followed by QN–Q2, B–N2 and P–QB4. White builds a pawn attack which can be effective if Black gets his pieces too bunched together. However, he has a good square for his knight at KB5 and can try the same space gaining plan as in the main line—P–QB3, P–QR3, P–QN4, etc.

7...   **0–0**
8 0–0   **P–B3**

Perhaps the possibility of this move was suggested to Petrosian by the success of the same move in defending against the Cozio Attack (next chapter) in his 1969 match against Spassky.

8 ... R–K1 9 P–B3 N–B3 10 R–K1 B–Q2 11 QN–Q2 B–KB1 12 N–K4 P–Q4 13 N–N3 B–Q3= (Bronstein–Smyslov, U.S.S.R. Championship, 1971) is an example of steady playing for a draw by exchanges, but White can improve by 9 P–B4 N–B3 10 N–B3 P–KR3 11 R–K1 B–B1 12 R×R Q×R 13 B–B4 B–Q2 14 Q–Q2 Q–B1 15 P–Q5 when Black is badly cramped (Fischer–Gheorghiu, Buenos Aires, 1970).

8 ... P–B4 is too optimistic. 9 N–B3 N–B3 10 R–K1 P–QR3 (10 ... N–QN5 11 B–KB4 N×B 12 Q×N and 13 QR–Q1 when it is hard for Black to develop satisfactorily) 11 P–Q5

N–R2 12 P–QR4 B–Q2 13 P–R5 R–K1 14 B–KB1 P–KR3 15 B–KB4 B–KB1 16 R×R Q×R 17 B–R2 Q–Q1 18 N–Q2 and Black is under pressure (Karpov–Smyslov, Moscow, 1972).

9 R–K1	**QN–Q2**
10 B–KB4	**R–K1**
11 P–B4	**N–B1**
12 N–B3	**P–QR3**

Black's counter-play is based upon P–QN4.

13 Q–N3

13 P–QN4 N–K3 14 B–R2 B–B1 is no improvement. After 15 Q–N3 P–QN4 16 P–Q5 P×QP 17 P×QP N–B2 (Polgár–Tóth, Hungary, 1972) Black stands no worse. White could consider 13 P–QR4 (met by 13 . . . P–QR4 and ultimately N–QN5) or 13 P–Q5 P×P 14 P×P P–QN4 15 P–QN4.

13 . . .	**N–K3**
14 B–R2	

14 B–K3 looks no better in view of 14 . . . P–QN4 15 P–QR4 P×BP 16 B×BP P–Q4 17 B–Q3 B–Q3 with prospects on the Q3/KR7 diagonal.

14 . . .	**B–B1**
15 R–K2	**P–QN4**
16 Q–B2	**B–N2**
17 QR–K1	

17 P–Q5 P×QP 18 P×NP P–Q5 19 N–K4 N×N∓

17 . . .	**P–KN3=**

41

There are chances for both sides. Fischer–Petrosian, match, Buenos Aires, 1971 continued 18 P–QN4 P×P (18 . . . P–B4 is also good) 19 B×BP N–B2 20 B–QN3? (20 R×R or 20 Q–N3 is better) 20 . . . R×R 21 R×R QN–Q4 and Black has a firm centre and can put pressure on the QNP.

This is a suitable variation for those who like solid positional play, avoiding sharp tactics early in the game.

Game 26   Schlechter–Mason, London, 1899. 1 P–K4 P–K4 2 N–KB3 N–KB3 3 N×P P–Q3 4 N–KB3 N×P 5 P–Q4 N–KB3 6 B–Q3 B–K2 7 0–0 0–0 8 R–K1 B–N5 9 QN–Q2 QN–Q2 10 N–B1 R–K1 11 N–N3 N–B1? 12 P–KR3 B×N 13 Q×B P–B3 14 N–B5 N–N3 15 B–KN5 N–Q4 16 N×B ch N(Q4)×N 17 R–K2 P–B3 18 B–Q2 Q–Q2 19 B–B4 ch! P–Q4 20 B–Q3 N–KB1 21 QR–K1 N(K2)–N3 22 B–B5! Q–KB2 23 P–KN3 R×R 24 Q×R P–QR4 25 P–KR4! P–QN3 26 P–R5 N–R1 27 P–R6 N(R1)–N3 28 P×P K×P 29 K–N2 R–R2 30 Q–K8 Q×Q 31 R×Q K–B2 32 R–N8 P–N4 33 B–R6 R–B2 34 R–R8 P–R5 35 B–N4 N–K3 36 P–KB4 N–N2 37 P–B5 N–K2 38 B–R5 ch N×B 39 R–B8 mate. One of Schlechter's best games. If 36 ... N×QP 37 P–B5 N–K4 38 B–R5 ch K–K2 and White mates in 2.

In the Classical Attack, in those variations where Black also plays ... P–Q4, he has the problem of what to do about his knight on K5. If when threatened he retreats it, then he loses time. This is not always serious. On the other hand, the defence of this piece by "stonewall" methods (... P–KB4, ... P–QB3) is not as a rule successful, for the stonewall crumbles if White plays correctly; the knight is exchanged or withdrawn, and Black's defensive pawn moves will merely have weakened his game.

White's strategy is in the nature of things an attack on the centre so as to undermine the enemy knight. Whilst his central pressure grows his development may lag. Black should cross White's strategy, not by defence of his centre directly, but by rapid development.

Black then solves his problems in one of several ways: simplifying exchanges may release the central tension, and if his development is well ahead he should have few problems left. Or he may simply retreat his knight if and when White plays P–QB4, often arriving at the familiar "isolated QP" situation, in which White's greater freedom is counterbalanced by the weakness of his QP. Or Black may have available to him, because of his lead in development, sharp counter-strokes of a tactical kind. Examples of these are Kashdan's 8 ... N–QN5 in the Jaenisch Variation, or Maróczy's 10 ... B–KR5 in the Krause Variation.

At various times the Petroff has been regarded as a weapon of counter-attack. Specifically, most of these counter-attacks have been refuted. Instead you should regard this defence as you would regard any other defence. You may be called upon to play any kind of game, from defensive to offensive, partly depending upon White's actions.

A word of warning: in any kind of open game even the best defences tend to leave White a very slight and sometimes persistent initiative. This is not in any way decisive, but you should remember that some positions are less equal than others. You should not strike out aggressively until you are sure that this tiny advantage is finally eliminated. Not infrequently in such positions White tries too hard to make too much out of too little; and many games are won by Black because White overplays his hand.

Finally, of course, we may mention the Close Variation, where Black retreats his knight more or less at once. His slight disadvantage in space is not serious. The exchange of one or two pieces may ease his problems. This defence is not to everyone's taste. It is better to play the kind of game you like than to worry about theoretical niceties as to which kind of game is "best".

Chapter 3

The Cozio Attack

1 P–K4	P–K4
2 N–KB3	N–B3
3 N×P	P–Q3K
4 N–KB3	N×P
5 Q–K2	

A positional line first noted by Cozio (1766), first played by Morphy (1850), and reintroduced into master chess by Marco at Hastings, 1895.

White seeks small advantages. The queens are often exchanged and the tempo of the game slows down. Black must not take things too lightly, but masters are agreed that there are several ways by which he can secure equal chances; "Leads rapidly to equality" (Tarrasch, 1912). This seemed to be the view of Schlechter too in view of his comments in the last edition of the Handbuch (1916) and the fact that 5 Q–K2 had only three columns allotted to it, compared to ninety-four columns for 5 P–Q4!

More recently this opinion has been restated thus by Gligorich (1951): "It is not enough to retain an advantage for White." This view was confirmed when Spassky failed to make anything of it in the 1969 world title match with Petrosian in face of the innovation 9 ... P–B3.

5 ...	Q–K2
6 P–Q3	N–KB3
7 B–N5	

See Diagram 42.

42

7 N–B3 is just as good, but is rarely played; it would in all probability transpose, 7 ... Q×Q ch 8 B×Q P–KN3 9 B–N5 B–N2 10 0–0–0 0–0=, while Haag prefers 7 ... QN–Q2 8 N–QN5 N–K4! or 8 B–K3 N–N3=.

LINE 1 (*Continue from Diagram 42*)

 7 ...   Q×Q ch

Thus White gains a tempo, which is of less value to him than having the queens on the board. Therefore Black should exchange them now or later.

 8 B×Q   **B–K2**

8 ... N–B3 is playable, if not so precise. If White now takes on KB6 Black's bishops are considered adequate compensation for the doubled pawn. 9 N–B3 B–K3 10 0–0–0 B–K2 11 P–Q4 P–Q4 and now 12 B–KB4 0–0–0 13 N–KN5 B–Q3 14 N×B P×N 15 B×B P×B= (Marco–Schlechter, Hastings, 1895) or 12 N–K5 (Pachman–Heidenfeld Marianske-Lazne, 1951) 12 ... N–Q2=.

The attempt to avoid the doubled pawn by 8 ... N–Q4 is not good, 9 P–B4 N–N5 10 K–Q2 P–KR3 11 B–K3 B–K2 12 B–Q4! 0–0 13 P–N4 B–K3 14 R–N1 QN–B3 15 B–B3± (Mukhin–Voronov, Uzbekistan, 1975).

9 N–B3

After **9 QN–Q2** N–Q4 (Ciocaltea–Karpov, Caracas, 1970) Black has no difficulties at all.

 9 ...   P–B3

This move must now be considered the main line. Credit for the idea must go to Schlechter who in the 1916 edition of the Handbuch gave 9 ... B–Q2, and then the laconic note, "to prevent 10 N–N5, yet 9 ... P–B3 is better". The move was recommended by Marshall in his autobiography (1942), first played by Bolbochan (1949) and finally confirmed by Petrosian in his 1969 match with Spassky.

9...B–Q2 is also good. At this point Tarrasch claimed that White's QB was better placed than Black's QB. A modern master might well take the opposite view; it can be argued that White's QB is committed, perhaps misplaced, and may have to lose time moving again, whereas Black's QB is safely ensconced behind his pawns ready for action on either wing. Play might continue 10 0–0–0 (10 0–0 N–B3 11 KR–K1 0–0? 12 P–Q4 KR–K1 13 B–N5 P–QR3 14 B–QR4 with slight advantage, Capablanca–Kostich, Havana, 1919. Black should have castled on the Q side) 10 ... N–B3 11 KR–K1 (11 P–KR3 0–0–0=) 11 ... 0–0–0 (not 11 ... 0–0 12 P–Q4 N–KN5? 13 B×B N×B 14 B–N5+, Lasker–Teichmann, Cambridge Springs, 1904) 12 P–Q4 (12 B×N B×B 13 N–Q5 B–Q5 14 N–K7 ch N×N 15 N×B=, Lein–Spassky, Sochi, 1967) 12 ... QR–K1=.

9 ... N–B3 10 N–N5 K–Q1 11 0–0 (better 11 0–0–0) 11 ... P–QR3 12 QN–Q4 (Kashdan–Mikenas, Folkestone, 1933) 12 ... N×N 13 N×N N–Q4=.

9 ... P–KR3. The former main line. Black does best to develop quickly in such a way that he can soon castle on the Q side. **10 B–R4** (10 B–B4 N–B3 11 0–0–0 B–B4 12 P–KR3 0–0–0 13 KR–K1 P–Q4 14 P–Q4 B–QN5=, Grechkin–Lilienthal, U.S.S.R., 1938, or in this 11 P–KR3 B–B4 12 0–0–0 0–0–0 13 KR–K1 KR–K1 14 B–B1 B–B1, Draw, Ivkov–Smyslov, Wijk aan Zee, 1972; or 10 B–K3 N–B3 11 0–0—if 11 0–0–0 N–KN5—11 ... B–Q2 12 P–QR3 0–0 13 P–Q4 P–R3=, Gligorich–Rossetto, Amsterdam, 1964) **10 ... B–Q2** (10 ... P–B3 is still feasible) **11 0–0–0 N–B3 12 P–Q4 0–0–0 13 B–B4** (13 KR–K1 QR–K1 14 B–B4 N–Q1=) **13 ... KR–B1 14 KR–K1 QR–K1** (14 ... B–N5 is also good, 15 R–K3 P–Q4=, Fine—Alexander, Hastings, 1935–6). See Diagram 43.

43

15 P–Q5 N–QN1 16 B–QN5 (16 N–QN5 P–R3 17 QN–Q4 B–Q1=) 16 ... P–R3 17 B×B ch QN×B 18 P–KR3 B–Q1= (Tan–Fred, Leipzig, 1960).

10 0–0–0

10 N–Q4 N–R3 11 0–0 B–Q2 12 KR–K1 P–KR3 13 B–R4 P–KN4 14 B–N3 K–Q1= (Rossolimo–Bolbochan, Trenčianske Teplice, 1949).

10 ...	**N–R3**
11 N–K4	

11 KR–K1 N–B2 12 B–B1 (12 N–K4 N×N 13 P×N B×B 14 N×B, Hazai–Tóth, Budapest, 1972 and now 14 ... K–K2! 15 P–KB4 P–B3=) 12 ... N–K3 13 B–Q2 (13 B–R4 N–R4!) 13 ... B–Q2 14 P–Q4 P–KR3 15 B–Q3 P–Q4 16 P–KR3 R–Q1= (Spassky–Petrosian, Moscow, 1969).

11 ...	**N×N**
12 P×N	**N–B4**
13 KR–K1	**B×B ch**

13 ... N×P 14 B×B K×B 15 B–Q3 P–Q4 16 B×N P×B 17 R×P ch B–K3 18 N–Q4±, but Black could equalize easily by 13 ... P–B3 14 B–KB4 N×P 15 B–Q3 P–KB4 16 B×N P×B 17 R×P B–B4.

14 N×B	**K–K2**
15 N–B3	**R–Q1**
16 N–Q4	**P–KN3=**

6*

Spassky–Petrosian, Moscow, 1969. Black follows up with K–B1 and N–K3, and the position is too tame for either side to achieve much. The actual game was drawn 9 moves later.

LINE 2 (*Continue from Diagram 42*)

7 ...   **B–K3**

The refusal to exchange queens favours White, according to Keres. This may be true, but White gets very little advantage. If you are a tactical player this is the defence to choose as the risks are not very great.

8 N–B3

See Diagram 44.

44

If **8 P–Q4** QN–Q2, and not 8 ... P–Q4 9 N–B3 P–B3 10 N–K5± (Duras–Marshall, San Sebastian, 1912).

8 ...   **P–KR3**

Though considered the main line this may well be suspect and Black should consider rather **8 ... QN–Q2** preparing to recapture with knight at KB3. Then 9 0–0–0 P–KR3 10 B–R4 transposes to the text, while avoiding the unpleasantness of the lines arising from 9 B×N in the next main note.

8 ... N–B3 is not wholly satisfactory, 9 0–0–0 (9 N–K4 0–0–0 10 N×N P×N 11 B–K3 also favours White; however, in a correspondence game Shukov–Schiffman, 1953, Black was able to defend himself after 11 ... P–Q4 12 P–Q4 B–N5 13 Q–Q2 Q–K3 14 B–K2 K–N1 15 P–QR3 N–K2 16 0–0–0 N–B4 17 B–KB4 N–Q3) 9 ... 0–0–0 (9 ... P–KR3 10 B×N P×B, and it is generally held that Black's bishop-pair does not compensate for the doubled pawn. Black has, of course, lost a tempo in provoking this exchange, and the pawn at KR3 is weaker than if it were still unmoved. Yet in a game Hirsch–Herrman, correspondence, 1929, Black obtained sufficient counter-play after 11 P–Q4 P–Q4 12 Q–N5 0–0–0 13 Q–R4 Q–N5 14 B–N5 N–R4 15 KR–K1 P–R3 16 B–B1 P–KR4) 10 P–Q4 P–Q4 11 N–K5 Q–K1 12 Q–K3 (12 P–B3 B–K2 13 B–K3 B–Q3=, Pogrebyssky–Yudovich, match, 1937; or 12 Q–B3 N×N 13 P×N B–KN5 14 Q–B4 B×R 15 P×N B–R4 16 B–N5 Q–K3∓.)

12 ... B–K2 13 B–N5 B–Q2 14 N×B Q×N 15 B×N (QB6) ± (Kieninger–Schuster, Essen, 1948).

9 B–R4

9 B×N seems White's best chance of gaining an advantage, **9 ...ʹQ×B 10 P–Q4,** and now (1) 10 ... B–K2, the most enterprising, 11 Q–N5 ch (11 0–0–0 0–0 12 Q–K4 P–B3 13 B–Q3 P–KN3, Malevinsky–Gusev, U.S.S.R., 1970, and now not 14 P–Q5 as played, but 14 Q–K3 with slight advantage) 11 ... N–Q2 12 B–Q3 (12 N–Q5 B×N 13 Q×B P–B3 14 Q–N3 Q–K3 ch=, Rossolimo–Tartakover, match, 1948) 12 ... P–KN4 13 Q×QNP! (13 P–KR3 0–0 14 Q×QNP QR–N1 15 Q–K4 Q–N2 with a good attacking position for the pawn, since if 16 P–QN3, Capablanca–Marshall, St. Petersburg, 1914, 16 ... N–B4 17 Q–K3 B–B3 18 0–0 KR–K1 19 Q–Q2 P–N5 +, Tarrasch) 13 ... R–QN1 14 Q–K4 R×P 15 0–0 Q–N2 (15 ... N–B4 16 B–N5 ch! R×B 17 Q–B6 ch B–Q2 18 Q–R8 ch B–Q1 19 N–Q5 +) 16 B–N5 preventing castling, Warburton–Hunter, correspondence, 1962–3. White has a marked advantage.

(2) 10 ... P–B3 11 P–Q5 (the less energetic 11 0–0–0 P–Q4 12 N–K5 is also good, and is the stem-game for the Cozio, Morphy–Loewenthal, New Orleans, 1850) 11 ... P×P 12 0–0–0 with strong pressure.

(3) 10 ... Q–K2, rather slow, 11 0–0–0 P–Q4 12 N–K5 P–QB3 13 P–B4 N–Q2 (Steiner–Kashdan, match, 1930) 14 P–KN4± (Levenfish).

9 ...   QN–Q2

9 ... N–B3 now seems to be playable, 10 0–0–0 0–0–0 11 P–Q4 P–Q4 12 N–K5 N×N! 13 P×N Q–N5 with about level chances (Israel–Fazekas, Felixstowe, 1949).

9 ... P–KN4 10 B–N3 B–N2 (better 10 ... QN–Q2; if 10 ... N–B3 11 0–0–0 preparing 12 P–Q4) 11 P–Q4 N–B3 12 0–0–0 N–Q4 (Kupchik–Marshall, New York, 1915). Black has avoided P–Q4 so as to have this square available for his pieces, writes Marshall, who does not explain how he would have met 13 Q–N5!

10 0–0–0   0–0–0

10 ... P–KN4 11 B–N3 N–R4? 12 P–Q4 N×B 13 RP×N± (Lasker–Marshall, St. Petersburg, 1914) 13 ... N–N3 is now best

11 P–Q4

11 Q–K3 N–N3 12 P–Q4 P–N4 13 B–N3 N–R4 14 P–Q5 B–Q2 15 Q–Q4 B–N2∓ (G. F. Harris–Hooper, Hastings, 1953).

11 ...   P–KN4
12 B–N3

See Diagram 45.

45

12 ... N-Q4! or **12 ... N-N3** 13 Q-N5 P-R3 14 Q-R5 B-B5 15 N-Q2 B×B 16 KR×B N-R4 17 KR-K1 Q-Q2 18 N-Q5 (von Holzhausen–Richter, correspondence, 1929) and now 18 ... N×N with hardly any advantage to White, but not 18 ... P-KB4 19 Q×N+.

LINE 3 (*Continue from Diagram 42*)

7 ...   QN-Q2

Milner-Barry's defence. Black develops his KB very effectively on the long diagonal, and hopes to show that White's QB is misplaced. The line has been popular in the Soviet Union in recent years, and rightly so.

8 N-B3

8 QN-Q2 is tame, 8 ... P-KR3 (or 8 ... Q×Q ch 9 B×Q B-K2, Rabar–Udovchich, Opatija, 1953) 9 B-R4 Q×Q ch 10 B×Q P-KN3 11 0-0 B-N2 12 KR-K1 0-0 13 B-B1 N-N3= (Johansson–Trifunovich, Halle, 1963).

8 ...   Q×Q ch

This is better than **8 ... P-KR3** 9 B-K3 N-N3 10 0-0-0 B-K3 (Keres gives 10 ... B-Q2 or 10 ... N-Q4 as improvements) 11 N-Q4 0-0-0 12 N×B Q×N 13 P-KN3 QN-Q4 14 B-Q2 N×N 15 Q×Q ch P×Q 16 B×N P-K4 17 B-R3 ch± (Gufeld–Lein, Tbilisi, 1966).

9 B×Q   P-KR3

Once again this is a good move, putting the question to White's QB.

See Diagram 46.

46

10 B-R4

Consistent. The bishop does not do much on the K side, but it is doubtful whether other moves are any better.

10 B×N N×B 11 N–N5 K–Q1 ∓ in view of the two bishops.

10 B–Q2 P–KN3 (Gutman prefers 10 ... N–B4 11 0–0–0 B–Q2 12 QR–K1 0–0–0=, e.g. 13 B–Q1 P–KN3 14 P–Q4 N–R5! Rytov–Vistanetskis, Riga, 1971) 11 0–0–0? 11 N–QN5 K–Q1 12 P–B4 B–N2 13 0–0 R–K1 14 KR–K1 retains some pressure, Gutman) 11 ... B–N2= (Redolfi–Trifunovich, Munich, 1958). The fianchetto is the main idea for Black in this variation, and the bishop becomes very strong on the long diagonal.

10 B–B4 P–KN3 11 0–0–0 (so that White's king defends the Q-side pawns. If 11 N–Q4 N–N3) 11 ... B–N2 12 P–KR3 (time-consuming) 12 ... N–N3 13 N–Q2 QN–Q4 14 N×N N×N 15 B–R2 0–0∓. Black's KB, commanding the long diagonal, may be contrasted with White's QB, impotent on the K side. Now 16 B–B3 N–N5 17 P–R3 N–B3 18 P–B3 (18 QR–K1 is better) 18 ... P–QR4 19 KR–K1 B–Q2 20 P–Q4 P–QN4 21 P–Q5 N–R2 22 N–N3 P–N5 23 RP×P P×P 24 P×P KR–N1 25 R–K4 B–R5 26 R–Q3 P–KB4 27 R–K7 R×P 28 B–Q1 R–B5 ch 29 K–N1 N–B1 30 R–K6 K–B2 31 P–KN4 N–K2 32 P×P N×P 33 R–KB3 R–QN1 34 B–B2? (White is lost in any event) 34 ... R×B. 0 : 1 (Trifunovich–Bronstein, Leningrad, 1957, Game 27).

10.N–N5 N–Q4 11. P–QB4 P–QR3

10 ...   **P–KN4**

The slower but less compromising **10 ... P–KN3** has not been well tested, 11 0–0–0 B–N2 12 KR–K1 (12 N–QN5 K–Q1 13 KR–K1 R–K1 14 KN–Q4 N–B1=, Kholmov–Bronstein U.S.S.R., 1959) 12 ... P–R3 13 B–B1 ch K–Q1 14 P–KR3 (Naroditsky–Khachaturov, Moscow, 1964) 14 ... N–B1=.

10...P–B3 to prevent N–QN5 is feasible, 11 N–K4 B–K2 12 0–0–0 P–Q4 13 N×N ch B×N 14 B×B N×B 15 KR–K1 0–0= (Gufeld–Savon, Moscow, 1970).

11 B–N3   **B–N2**

Better than **11 ... N–R4** 12 N–Q5 K–Q1 13 P–Q4! (Minich–Trifunovich, Yugoslav Championship, 1961).

11 ... N–N3 is also good, 12 0–0–0 B–Q2 13 P–KR4 P–N5 14 N–Q2 B–N2 15 P–B3 0–0–0 and White has nothing (Arulaid–Vistanetskis, Tallinn, 1964).

12 N–Q4

12 P–KR4 P–N5 13 N–Q2 0–0 14 0–0–0 N–N3 15 P–R5 (weak) 15...B–Q2± (Kramer–Milner-Barry, London, 1948).

12 ...   **N–N3**
13 KN–N5   **QN–Q4**

A game Alexander–Milner-Barry, Margate, 1938, continued 14 N×N N×N 15 B–B3 P–R3 16 N×QP ch P×N 17 B×N B×NP 18 R–QN1 B–B6 ch 19 K–K2 0–0=.

LINE 4 (*Continue from Diagram 42*)

7 ...   B–N5

If **7 ... N–B3** 8 N–B3, then (1) 8 ... Q×Q ch (best) 9 B×Q B–K3, a variation considered in the note to Black's 8th move in Line 1. (2) 8 ... B–N5 9 B×N P×B 10 N–Q5 B×N 11 Q×Q ch B×Q 12 P×B with some advantage to White.

8 N–B3

White should probably prefer 8 B×N P×B, proceeding with his threat to break up the K-side pawns. Note that Black cannot maintain symmetry by 8 ... B×N in view of 9 Q×Q ch! B×Q 10 B×P R–N1 (10 ... B×P 11 B×B R–N1 12 B×P+) 11 B–B3 winning a pawn (11 ... B×P? 12 R–N1+). After 8 ... P×B 9 Q×Q ch B×Q 10 QN–Q2 N–B3 11 0–0–0 0–0–0 12 P–KN3 (Sokolsky–Raizman, U.S.S.R., 1963) the bishops may not be sufficient compensation.

8 ...   Q×Q ch

As in Lines 1 and 3, the queen exchange is correct.

8 ... QN–Q2 9 0–0–0 0–0–0 10 Q–Q2 N–N3 11 R–K1 Q–Q2 12 N–Q4 B–K2 13 P–KR3± (Chistyakov–Shamayev, Kiev, 1938).

<table>
<tr><td>9 B×Q</td><td style="text-align:right">B–K2</td></tr>
<tr><td>10 0–0–0</td><td></td></tr>
</table>

10 N–Q4 B×B 11 QN×B (11 K×B P–KN3 12 QR–K1 K–Q2) 11 ... N–Q4 12 B×B N×B= (Geller–Solmanis, 17th U.S.S.R. Championship Preliminaries).

<table>
<tr><td>10...</td><td style="text-align:right">P–KR3</td></tr>
<tr><td>11 B–R4</td><td></td></tr>
</table>

See Diagram 47.

47

11 ... QN–Q2 12 P–KR3 B–R4 13 P–KN4 B–N3 14 N–Q4 0–0–0 15 P–B4 QR–K1=. A game Rabinovich–Kan, Moscow, 1935, continued 16 B–B3 B–Q1 17 B–N3 P–R3 18 N–N3

B–R2 19 N–R5 P–B3 20 N–B4 B–B2 21 P–N5 P–Q4 22 P×N P×N 23 P×NP KR–N1 ∓.
Black won, his king's side attack outweighing the sacrificed pawn.

11 ... N–B3 12 P–KR3 B–R4 13 P–KN4 B–N3 14 B–N3 0–0–0 15 P–Q4 N–K5! 16 N×N
B×N 17 KR–K1 B–B3 18 P–QB3 (Chistyakov–Yudovich, Moscow, 1935) 18 ... QR–K1=.

The various defences against 5 Q–K2 have been so strengthened in recent years that Black
gets a wide and satisfactory choice of alternatives.

Line 1 was once thought to be the only "correct" defence; but it tends to be drawish,
and indeed most examples from play are drawn. This is the line to choose if you wish to
avoid risks at all cost.

Lines 2 and 3 give good practical results for Black. In both lines the fianchettoed position
for Black's KB can be very strong. The queens may be exchanged but there are plenty of
pieces left on the board, with reasonable chances of complications if you are seeking a
win.

Line 4 is less explored and would suit players who want to strike out on their own. It is,
of course, not certain that the development of Black's QB to KN5 is altogether correct.
White is tempted to advance his king's side pawns, which may become weakened thereby.
The queen exchange draws White's KB to K2, whereas after the advance of the pawns on
this wing he really wants the bishop at KN2.

Chapter 4

The Nimzowitsch Attack

1 P–K4	P–K4
2 N–KB3	N–KB3
3 N×P	P–Q3
4 N–KB3	N×P
5 N–B3	

See Diagram 48.

48

This move was mentioned by Jaenisch in 1842. It became popular at the turn of the century, and was favoured by Nimzowitsch. White aims at rapid development, but achieves very little and the line has all but disappeared from modern play.

5 ...   **N×N**

Best, according to theory.

The quiet **5 ... N–KB3** is also sound and may be compared with the Close Variation of the Classical Attack. **6 P–Q4 B–K2** (Gutman suggests 6 ... B–B4, so that if 7 B–KN5 B–K2 8 Q–Q2 N–K5 9 N×N B×N 10 Q–K3? B×N 11 P×B N–B3∓) **7 B–Q3** (If 7 P–KR3, recommended by Tarrasch, 7 ... B–B4=. Pachman suggests 7 B–N5 followed by 0–0–0, which can once again be met by Gutman's 7 ... B–B4)`7 ... B–N5` (to prevent White regrouping his QN; however, 7 ... 0–0 8 N–K2 R–K1 9 0–0 QN–Q2 10 N–N3 N–B1 as also satisfactory for Black) **8 P–KR3 B–R4 9 0–0 N–B3** (after 9 ... 0–0 Tarrasch shows an interesting pawn offer, 10 P–KN4 B–N3 11 N–KR4 B×B 12 Q×B N×P 13 N–B5 N–KB3 14 K–R1) **10 B–K3 0–0=**.

5 . . . P–Q4, a gambit played in the stem-game (for 5 N–B3), Daniells–Walker, London, around 1844. It was reintroduced to master play by Schlechter and refuted sixteen years later by Alekhine in the games quoted below; **6 Q–K2 B–K2 7 N×N P×N 8 Q×P 0–0 9 B–B4** (other moves give Black at least equality, if not a good attack, 9 P–Q4 R–K1 10 N–K5 N–B3 11 B–QB4 N×N 12 P×N B–N5 ch 13 P–B3 B–Q3 14 P–B4 Q–R5 ch; 15 P–N3 Q–R4 16 B–K2 B–KN5, and if here 11 B–Q3 P–B4 12 B–B4 ch K–B1; or 9 B–K2 R–K1 10 0–0 B–Q3 11 Q–Q3 N–B3 12 P–B3 Q–B3∓; or 9 B–Q3 P–KN3 10 Q–Q4 B–Q3 11 Q–KR4 R–K1 ch 12 B–K2 Q×Q 13 N×Q N–B3 14 P–QB3 P–KN4 15 N–B3 P–N5 16 N–N1 N–K4∓, Gunsberg–Schlechter, Monte-Carlo, 1902) **9 . . . B–Q3 10 0–0** (10 P–Q4 R–K1 11 N–K5 B×N 12 P×B N–B3 13 B–B4 Q–R5=) **10 . . . R–K1 11 Q–Q3 N–B3 12 P–QN3 Q–B3 13 B–N2 +** (Alekhine–Rabinovich, Moscow, 1918), after 13 . . . Q×B 14 N–N5 White has a winning attack.

6 QP×N

White speeds up his development and gains space in the centre. The doubled pawn is not much of a weakness in view of the compact pawn structure on the Q side.

6 NP×N weakens the pawns without compensation, 6 . . . B–K2 7 P–Q4 0–0 8 B–Q3 B–N5 9 0–0 N–Q2 10 R–N1 P–QN3= (Bilguer).

6 . . .   **B–K2**

See Diagram 49. Black does not play . . . P–Q4, because White could play P–QB4 eliminating his only weakness.

49

In the play that follows White sometimes castles on the Q-side, Black on the K-side, and each player attacks the enemy king. In a general way this is easier for White who has rather more manoeuvring space. Also, his doubled pawn may help defend his king's position. One remedy for Black is to castle on the same side as White, and for this purpose he must not castle too soon.

Black should not, however, altogether forego the possibility of opposite wing castling. It offers more chances for both sides, and may in some circumstances favour Black. Often he may employ the time-honoured strategy of countering a wing attack by active play in the centre.

Line 1 (*Continue from Diagram 49*)

7 B–K3

On this square the bishop may deter Black from castling on the queen's side.

7 ...	N–B3

7 ... **0–0** is premature, 8 B–Q3 N–Q2 (8 ... R–K1 9 P–KR4 N–B3? 10 B×P ch +) 9 P–KR4! P–KB4 10 B–B4 ch K–R1 11 N–N5 Q–K1 12 Q–K2 N–K4 13 0–0–0 N×B 14 Q×N P–B3 15 B–B4 P–Q4 16 Q–Q3 P–QN4 17 QR–K1 + (Showalter–Halprin, Vienna, 1898).

8 Q–Q2

8 B–Q3 B–N5 (8 ... B–B3 9 Q–Q2 N–K4 is too slow, 10 N×N B×N 11 P–KB4 B–B3 12 0–0–0 0–0 13 P–KR3 P–B3 14 P–KN4 Q–R4 15 P–R3 P–Q4 16 Q–B2 KR–K1 17 P–N5±, Wolf–Pillsbury, Monte Carlo, 1903, White's attack is ahead) **9 B–K4 Q–Q2 10 Q–Q2 0–0–0 11 0–0–0,** and now 11 ... B–B3=, or 11 ... KR–K1 12 N–Q4 P–Q4 (12 ... B×R? 13 N×N+ but 12 ... N×N! 13 Q×N P–QB4 14 Q–Q3 P–B4 is better) 13 N×N Q×N 14 B×QP Q–QR3 15 Q–Q3 (Nimzowitsch–Marshall, St. Sebastian, 1911) and either 15 ... B×R 16 Q×Q P×Q, or 15 ... Q–R4 16 P–B3 P–QB3 17 Q–B4 R×B 18 R×R Q×R 19 Q×Q P×Q 20 P×B B–Q3 21 K–Q2 R–K5 (as played) 22 P–KR3, leaves Black a difficult endgame.

8 P–KR3 and now (1) 8 ... B–B4 9 B–Q3 Q–Q2 10 Q–Q2 0–0 11 0–0–0 N–K4 (Black plays in the centre) 12 N×N P×N 13 B×B Q×B 14 Q–Q5 P–QN3 15 P–KB4 B–Q3 16 KR–B1 QR–K1∓ (Michell–Scott, London, 1920) Black won with his king's side pawn majority. (2) 8 ... P–QR3 9 Q–Q2 B–K3 10 B–K2 (10 0–0–0 Q–Q2 with equal chances, but not 10 ... P–QN4? 11 P–KN4 P–QR4 12 N–N5 Q–Q2 13 N×B P×N 14 P–KB4 0–0 15 B–N2 +, Atkins–Sherrard, Southport, 1905) 10 ... Q–Q2 11 N–Q4 N–K4 12 N×B Q×N 13 P–QN3 B–B3 14 0–0 0–0=, if 15 P–KB4 N–B3 16 B–N4 Q–K2 17 QR–K1 P–Q4! 18 Q×P B×P∓ (Atkins–Scott, Hastings, 1920–1).

8 B–K2 B–B3 9 Q–Q2 B–B4 10 0–0–0 Q–Q2= (Flórián–Alexandrescu, Bucharest, 1951).

8 ...	B–N5

8 ... **B–K3** is probably sound, Black thus avoiding known lines.

8 ... **B–B4** is relatively untried, 9 0–0–0 0–0 (better 9 ... Q–Q2) 10 N–Q4 (too tame, 10 R–N1 is better) 10 ... N×N 11 B×N B–N4 12 P–KB4 B–B3= if 13 B–B2 Q–Q2 14 P–KR3 Q–R5 15 P–R3 P–QN4 16 P–KN4 B–K5 17 R–N1 P–B4 18 R–K1 P–Q4 19 B×BP KR–B1 20 B–N4 P–QR4! 21 P–N3 P×B + (D. E. Lloyd–Allen, London, 1961).

9 B–K2	Q–Q2
10 P–KR3	B×N
11 B×B	B–B3
12 0–0–0	0–0
13 KR–K1	QR–K1

The position is level. White dare not attack on the wing because Black is too strong in the centre. White's bishop - pair is not particularly effective in this compact position.

Nimzowitsch–Marshall, St. Petersburg, 1914, now continued 14 B–N4 (driving the queen back, otherwise Black himself might start a wing attack) 14 ... Q–Q1 15 P–KN3 (15 P–KB4 B–R5) 15 ... R–K2 16 P–KB4 KR–K1 17 B–B2 R×R 18 R×R R×R ch 19 Q×R P–KN3 20 B–B3 Q–Q2 21 B–N4 Q–Q1 ½ : ½, Game 28.

LINE 2 (*Continue from Diagram 49*)

7 B–KB4

White keeps the K-file open and puts another guard on his K5 square, the only one of the four centre squares contested by Black. A disadvantage of this line is that in the event of exchanges on White's Q4 square he cannot recapture there with a bishop.

7 **P–KR3** might transpose, or Black could reply 7 ... N–Q2 and perhaps later ... N–QB4.

7...	N–B3

7 ... 0–0 8 Q–Q2 N–Q2 9 0–0–0 N–B4 10 P–KR3 R–K1 11 P–KN4 N–K5 12 Q–K1 B–B3= (Tseshkovsky–I. Zaitsev, U.S.S.R., 1975).

8 Q–Q2

8 **B–Q3 B–N5** (or 8 ... B–K3 9 Q–Q2 Q–Q2 10 0–0–0=) 9 P–KR3 (9 B–K4 Q–Q2 10 Q–Q3 0–0–0 11 P–KR3 B–K3 12 N–Q4 P–Q4=) 9 ... **B–R4,** and now (1) 10 Q–K2 transposing to Romanovsky–Travin in Line 3, or (2) 10 P–KN4 B–N3 11 P–KR4 (a premature pawn advance) 11 ... Q–Q2 12 R–KN1 0–0–0∓ (Louma–Milner-Barry, London, 1947).

8 ...	B–N5

8 ... **B–K3** is playable; and also probably 8 ... **B–KB4** and if then 9 B–Q3 Q–Q2=.

9 B–K2	Q–Q2

9 ... **0–0** leads to opposite wing attacks, 10 0–0–0 R–N1! (these attacks must be played at top speed, so 10 ... P–QR3 would be too slow) 11 K–N1 (inaccurate; 11 P–KR3! should be played at once) 11 ... B–B3 12 P–KR3 B×N 13 B×B N–K4 14 B–K2 P–QN4! with about level chances (Michell–Tylor, Hastings, 1935–6).

10 P–KR3	B–R4
11 0–0–0	0–0–0
12 KR–K1	KR–K1

12 ... **P–QR3** leaves White a lead in development as well as in space, 13 Q–Q5 B–N3 14 N–Q4 N×N 15 Q×N K–N1 16 B–N4 P–KB4 17 B–B3 B–B3 18 Q–N4 Q–N4 19 Q×Q P×Q 20 R–Q5 + (Foltys–Szapiel, Sczawno-Zdroj, 1950).

13 P–KN4	B–N3

The chances are even. A game Schmid–Alexander, Dublin, 1957, continued: 14 B–QN5 P–QR3 15 B–R4 P–N4 16 B–QN3 N–R4 17 B–Q5 P–QB3 18 B–K4 N–B5 19 Q–Q3 B×B 20 R×B P–Q4 (now White's doubled pawn is held in restraint) 21 R–K2 B–Q3 22 B×B R×R 23 Q×R N×B 24 Q–K3 R–K1 25 Q–N6 Q–N2 26 Q×Q ch K×Q. ½ : ½, Game 29. Black might well have continued as he has the better endgame.

LINE 3 (*Continue from Diagram 49*)

7 B–Q3	B–N5

Black does well to defer castling, since if **8 ... 0–0** then 9 B–K3 followed by Q–K2, 0–0–0, P–KR4, etc., follows, with attacking chances for White.

7 ... **N–B3** is also good, 8 P–KR3 (8 B–K3 or 8 B–KB4 transposes into earlier lines) 8 ... B–K3 9 N–Q4 N×N 10 P×N P–Q4 11 B–KB4 B–Q3= (Puc–Kostich, Ljubljana, 1947).

8 Q–K2	N–B3
9 B–KB4	Q–Q2!
10 P–KR3	B–R4
11 P–KN4	B–N3
12 0–0–0	B×B
13 P×B	0–0–0

This is Romanovsky–Travin, Leningrad, 1923. The position is level since Black's king is safe on the Q-side.

In this variation Black must develop rapidly, but he should not castle too soon. In the best played lines he castles only when White's intentions in this respect are clear. Black then has no real difficulties. In a general way, if White castles on the queen's side and Black on the king's side, then with correct play White will have a slight edge in the opposite wing attacks which may follow—see notes to Wolf–Pillsbury and Michell–Tylor games.

The advance of pawns on the wings is incorrect if made before castling intentions are defined. In the Atkins–Sherrard game, because Black has prematurely advanced his queen's side pawns he later has to castle on the king's side, where in due course he succumbed to an attack. In the Louma–Milner-Barry game White advanced his king's side pawns, which merely became weak when Black castled on the other side.

Opposite wing castling (White 0–0–0, Black 0–0) may suit Black in certain circumstances: firstly, if White plays slow moves or himself fails to develop quickly; secondly, if one or two pieces are exchanged. This slows down White's attack. Black's attack on the queen's side, however, depends more on a pawn advance than a piece attack. First he induces White to play P–QR3, then he advances a pawn to his QN5 (White's QN4) breaking open one or more files—see the Lloyd–Allen game.

Finally, as we have pointed out in the text, Black must remember that central manoeuvring often forestalls or refutes a wing attack—see the Nimzowitsch–Marshall game in Line 2.

Chapter 5

The Kaufmann Attack

1 P–K4	P–K4
2 N–KB3	N–KB3
3 N×P	P–Q3
4 N–KB3	N×P
5 P–B4	

Attributed to the Viennese amateur Kaufmann, this move first appeared in master play in the game Marco–Tinsley, Hastings, 1895. See Diagram 50.

White hopes for strong central pressure if Black plays ... P–Q4. However, by not further advancing his QP Black gets a very satisfactory game. White will merely have made a useless and in some cases a weakening pawn-move.

50

5 ...	B–K2

5 ... **P–KN3** is also a good idea, 6 P–Q3 N–KB3 7 N–B3 B–N2 8 Q–K2 ch Q–K2 9 Q×Q ch K×Q 10 B–N5 R–K1 11 0–0–0 K–B1 12 P–KR3 P–QR3= (Keres–Rossetto, Buenos Aires, 1964).

5 ... **P–Q4,** Black unnecessarily sets up a target for White, 6 N–B3 and now (1) 6 ... N–KB3 (this and the relatively untried 6 ... B–K3 7 P–Q4 are Black's best chances here) 7 P–Q4 B–K2 8 P×P N×P 9 B–QB4 N×N 10 P×N 0–0 11 0–0 (not 11 N–K5 N–Q2 12 P–B4 P–B4 13 Q–N3 P×P 14 N×P Q–R4! Levenfisch) 11 ... N–Q2 12 R–K1 ± (Marco–Goncharov, Moscow, 1907). (2) 6 ... B–QB4? Black deliberately loses a tempo so that he will not be forced to retreat the knight from K5. The idea is not tested properly, but re-

sults have favoured White. 7 P–Q4 B–QN5 8 B–Q2 (or 8 Q–N3 Q–K2, see Game 30) 8 ...
N×B 9 Q×N 0–0 10 P×P N–Q2? (10 ... B–N5) 11 P–QR3 R–K1 ch 12 B–K2 B–B1
13 0–0± (Keres–Keller, Zurich, 1959). (3) 6 ... N×N 7 QP×N P–QB3 8 Q–Q4 B–K3
9 N–N5± (Keres–Ribeiro, Leipzig, 1960).

6 N–B3

Since Black has not played ... P–Q4 White's 5th move has lost its point. The text-move
attempts to steer clear of the regular variations; yet **6 P–Q4** is still the logical continuation,
and now 6 ... 0–0 (6 ... P–Q4 is playable in the changed circumstances!) 7 B–Q3 N–KB3
8 0–0 (8 P–KR3 P–Q4=, or 8 N–B3 B–N5 9 P–KR3 B–R4 10 0–0 P–Q4? 11 P×P N×P?
12 B×P ch K×B 13 N–KN5 ch K–N1 14 Q×B B×N 15 B×B +, Tseitlin–Karasev,
Leningrad, 1971. Black should have played 10 ... N–B3 or 10 ... QN–Q2, and next move
11 ... QN–Q2 was his last chance) 8 ... B–N5 9 P–KR3 B–R4 10 N–B3 N–B3 11 B–K3
Q–Q2 12 B–K2 QR–K1 and Black, ahead in development, has equalized. Or 6 P–Q4 B–N5!?
7 P–KR3 B–R4 8 Q–N3 N–Q2! 9 Q×P B×N 10 P×B N–N4 11 B×N B×B 12 Q–K4 ch
K–B1 13 N–B3 N–B3 and Black has adequate compensation for the pawn (Tal–Smyslov,
Moscow, 1974).

6 ...	N×N

6 ... B–B4! has not been played much, but seems best, 7 N×N B×N 8 P–Q4 P–Q4
9 Q–N3 N–B3 (Ludolf–Maslov, Baltic Championship, 1961). If 7 N–Q5 0–0 8 P–Q3 N–B3
9 N×B ch Q×N ch 10 B–K2 R–K1 11 P–KR3 P–Q4 12 P–R3 P–B4∓.

7 QP×N

7 NP×N 0–0 8 P–Q4 B–B4 9 B–Q3 Q–Q3 10 0–0 N–B3 with good play for Black in view
of White's weak pawns (Michell–Hooper, Club game, London, 1952).

7 ...	0–0

7 ... **N–B3** is less flexible, 8 B–Q3 (8 B–KB4 B–N5 9 B–K2 Q–Q2=) 8 ... B–N5 (8 ...
N–K4 9 N×N P×N 10 Q–B2±) 9 B–K4 0–0 10 0–0 and if 10 ... N–K4 (10 ... R–N1 is
better) 11 B×P R–N1 12 B–K4 K–R1 13 P–KR3 B×N 14 B×B N×P 15 B–Q5 N–N3
16 B–N3± (Keres–Mikenas, Parnu, 1960).

8 Q–B2

Euwe suggests **8 B–Q3** at once retaining QB2 for the bishop.

8 ...	N–Q2
9 B–Q3	P–KR3
10 B–K3	N–B4

This is a strong square for the knight, while if P–QN4 to drive it away the doubled pawn becomes weaker.

After 11 B×N P×B 12 0–0–0 B–Q3 13 B–R7 ch K–R1 14 B–B5 (Weenink–Kashdan, Prague, 1931) Black has at least equality.

Game 30   Evans–Bisguier, New York, 1958. 1 P–K4 P–K4 2 N–KB3 N–KB3 3 N×P P–Q3 4 N–KB3 N×P 5 P–B4 P–Q4 6 N–B3 B–QB4 7 P–Q4 B–QN5 8 Q–N3 P–QB4 9 B–Q3 Q–R4 (if 9 ... 0–0 10 P×QP±) 10 0–0 N×N 11 P×N B×P 12 B–N2 B×B 13 QR–K1 ch! (a neat (**Zwischenzug**) 13 ... K–B1 14 Q×B BP×P 15 P×P N–Q2 16 Q×QP N–B3 17 Q–K5 Q–B4 18 N–N5 B–Q2 19 N–K4 N×N 20 R×N R–K1 21 Q–B4 Q×P 22 KR–K1 R×R 23 B×R Q–K3 (pinning the rook, but not for long) 24 Q–N8 ch B–K1 25 Q×RP P–QN3 26 Q–R3 ch Q–K2 (moving the king loses the queen) 27 B–B6! 1 : 0.

Chapter 6

The French Attack

1 P–K4	P–K4
2 N–KB3	N–KB3
3 N×P	P–Q3
4 N–KB3	N×P
5 P–Q3	

An uncommon move, not altogether without sting, but too tame for most tastes nowadays. Black should know something about it, so that he is not taken by surprise.

5 ...	N–KB3

5 ... **B–K2** 6 P×N 1 : 0 (Tarrasch–Alapin, Breslau, 1889, Game 31) is a terrible warning against playing the openings by rote. As soon as White touched his QP Black assumed it was being moved two squares, and replied accordingly. As a curiosity it may be quoted as the shortest decisive tournament game between masters.

6 P–Q4	P–Q4

This position could arise from an old-fashioned variation of the French Defence, and most of the games quoted arose in this way. Black is in no real difficulty, but if he wants to avoid symmetry he may instead equalize by **6 ... B–K2** when he is a move ahead as compared with the Close Variation of the Classical Attack.

Or 6 ... **B–N5** 7 B–K2 B–K2 8 0–0 0–0 9 P–B4 P–Q4 10 P–B5 N–B3 11 P–KR3 B–R4 12 B–K3 N–K5!= (Pietzsch–Mikenas, Leningrad, 1960).

7 B–Q3	

7 P–B4 N–B3 8 N–B3 B–KN5 9 B–K3 B–K2 10 P–KR3 B–R4 11 P–B5 0–0 12 B–QN5 N–K5= (Alekhine–Bogolyubov, Salzburg, 1942).

7 ...	B–Q3

7 ... **B–K2** has not been at all successful in practice, 8 0–0 (8 N–K5 N–B3=, or 8 B–N5 QN–Q2 9 QN–Q2 N–K5=) 8 ... B–KN5 9 R–K1 0–0 10 P–B3, and now (1) 10 ... N–B3 11 B–KB4 Q–Q2 12 QN–Q2 N–KR4 13 B–N3 N×B 14 RP×N B–KB4 15 B–N5! (Yanofsky–Suesman, Ventnor City, 1942) or (2) 10 ... QN–Q2 11 B–KB4 R–K1 12 QN–Q2 N–B1 13 Q–N3, with advantage to White in either case.

8 0–0   **0–0**
9 N–B3

9 B–KN5 B–KN5 (or 9 ... P–B3; but not 9 ... N–B3 10 P–B3 when Black's KN is awk-wardly pinned) 10 QN–Q2 QN–Q2=, a well-known grandmaster draw variation. Instead Black can liven it up by 10 ... P–KR3 11 B–R4 B–B5 12 P–B3 (12 R–K1 P–KN4 13 B–N3 N–R4 14 N–B1 Q–B3 15 N–K3=, Puc–Nedeljkovich, Yugoslavia, 1952) 12 ... Q–Q3 13 Q–B2 QN–Q2 14 KR–K1 P–B4, and now if 15 B–B5? (15 P–KR3 is correct) 15 ... P×P 16 N×P B×P ch+ (Johner–Rotlewi, Carlsbad, 1911).

9 N–K5 P–B4! and White is defending a Petroff's Defence!

9 ...   **B–KN5**

9 ... **P–B3** allows White to regroup his QN, but this does not seem to give him any ad-vantage, 10 N–K2 B–KN5 (10 ... R–K1 11 N–N3 QN–Q2 12 N–B5 N–B1 13 N×B Q×N 14 N–K5 KN–Q2 15 B–Q2! P–B3 16 Q–R5 R×N±, Larsen–Petrosian, Havana, 1966. Black could have improved by 11 ... N–K5) 11 N–N3 Q–B2 12 P–KR3 B–K3 (12 ... QB×N 13 Q×B R–K1 14 N–B5±) 13 N–B5 (if 13 N–N5 Black must not reply 13 ... B×N? 14 P×B Q×P because of 15 R×N winning at once) 13 ... B×N 14 B×B QN–Q2=.

9 ... **R–K1** 10 B–KN5 P–B3 11 R–K1 R×R ch 12 Q×R QN–Q2= (Larsen–R. Byrne, Havana, 1966).

10 B–KN5

See Diagram 51.

51

10 ... **N–B3,** the most enterprising move, 11 K–R1 (Zukertort's move, also recommended by Maróczy. If 11 N×P B×P ch, or 11 B×N Q×B 12 N×P Q–R3 13 Q–B1=) 11 ... B–K2 (this is alleged to be a better position for White, but the proof is not clear) 12 Q–Q2 B×N 13 P×B N×P 14 B×P ch N×B 15 B×B (a classic game of the old days, Zukertort–Mason,

Vienna, 1882). A good struggle ensues, Black having a Q-side majority, and White some chances on the K-side.

10 ... P–B3, a solid move, 11 P–KR3 (11 N–K2 P–KR3 12 B–R4 B×N∓) 11 ... B×N (11 ... B–R4 12 P–KN4 B–N3 13 N–K5±) 12 Q×B QN–Q2=. If 13 N–Q1 (13 N–K2 is better) 13 ... Q–N3 14 P–B3 KR–K1 15 R–N1 (15 B–B5 is better) 15 ... N–K5∓ (Walbrodt–Maróczy, Budapest, 1896). As so often in this opening, Black may find opportunities of reoccupying his thematic square K5.

Game 32   Mackenzie–Mason, Vienna, 1882. 1 P–K4 P–K3 2 P–Q4 P–Q4 3 P×P P×P 4 N–QB3 N–KB3 5 N–B3 B–Q3 6 B–Q3 0–0 7 0–0 N–B3 8 B–KN5 N–K2? 9 B×N P×B 10 N–KR4 K–N2 11 Q–R5 R–R1 12 P–B4 P–B3 13 R–B3 N–N3 14 QR–KB1 Q–B2 15 N–K2 B–Q2 16 N–N3 QR–KN1. White mates in 6 starting 17 Q–R6 ch. Black should have played 8 ... B–KN5, transposing to the position after Black's 10th move in the Zukertort–Mason game quoted above.

Chapter 7

The Paulsen Attack

1 P–K4	P–K4
2 N–KB3	N–KB3
3 N×P	P–Q3
4 N–B4	

An attack first played by Louis Paulsen (1833–91). It was revived by Yugoslav players shortly after the Second World War. White's KN does not block the KBP which soon advances to form part of an attack on the K-side. The KN often plays later to K3. The idea has few supporters nowadays.

4 ...	N×P
5 N–B3	

5 P–Q4 has not been played enough for an accurate assessment to be made:

(1) 5 ... P–Q4 6 N–K3 B–K3 (6 ... N–QB3 7 B–QN5 P–QR3 8 B–R4 Q–R5 9 0–0? B–Q3 10 P–KN3 Q–R6 11 N–B3 P–KR4 12 KN×P P–R5! with a winning attack, Safonov–Gusev, Moscow, 1960. White has to try 9 P–KN3) 7 B–Q3 P–KB4 8 0–0 (L. Paulsen–Schallopp, Frankfurt, 1887, the stem-game) 8 ... B–Q3 with about level chances according to Levenfish.

(2) 5 ... P–Q4 6 Q–K2 N–B3 7 P–QB3 B–K2 8 B–B4 0–0 9 N–K3 N×QP! 10 P×N B–N5 ch 11 K–Q1 Q–B3 12 B–K5 N×P ch 13 K–B1 Q–B3 ch 14 N–B2 N×R 15 Q–B3 R–K1 16 B–Q3 B–N5 17 Q×B R×B 18 P×R Q–R3 ch. 0 : 1 (Gehl–Marshall, New Orleans, 1913, Game 33).

5 P–Q3 leads to sedate play, 5 ... N–KB3 6 P–Q4 B–K2 7 B–Q3 0–0 8 0–0 N–B3 9 P–QB3 R–K1 10 B–N5 P–Q4= (Padevsky–Kolarov, Sofia, 1955).

5 Q–K2 has little to recommend it, 5 ... Q–K2 6 N–K3 P–QB3 (also 6 ... N–KB3 7 P–KN3 B–Q2! 8 B–N2 B–B3 9 P–KB3 P–KN3 10 N–B3, Planinc–Jones, Nice, 1974, 10 ... QN–Q2 11 P–Q4 N–N3∓) 7 P–Q3 (7 P–QB4 is untried) 7 ... N–B3 8 N–Q2 QN–Q2= (Pilnik–Bogoljubov, Zurich, 1951).

5 ...	N×N

See Diagram 52.

52

LINE 1 (*Continue from Diagram 52*)

> **6 QP×N**

The position is similar to the Nimzowitsch Variation, with the difference that White's KN is at QB4 instead of KB3. If anything this difference favours Black.

| 6 ... | **B–K2** |
| **7 B–B4** | |

Not **7 B–K3** because this square is needed for the KN.

7 B–Q3 N–B3 8 Q–R5 B–K3 9 0–0 Q–Q2 10 N–K3 N–K4 11 P–KB4 N×B (Lehmann–Hooper, Bognor, 1955), the chances are about equal.

7 ...	**N–B3**
8 Q–Q2	**B–K3**
9 0–0–0	**0–0**
10 K–N1	**B–B3**
11 P–KR3	**R–K1**
12 N–K3	**B–K4**

Black has a very satisfactory position (Karaklajich–Bajec, Sarajevo, 1951). White's K-side attack foreshadowed by 11 P–KR3 does not get off the ground because of the lack of cohesion of his forces.

LINE 2 (*Continue from Diagram 52*)

> **6 NP×N**

Alexander points out that White can now try for an advance of his pawns on either side of the board. The idea is not very promising, however, as Alexander himself demonstrated. White runs grave risks of being left with weak pawns.

| 6 ... | **P–KN3** |

Black directs the bishop towards the broken pawns.

6 ... B–K2 is playable, 7 P–Q4 N–Q2 (better than 7 ... N–B3 8 B–Q3 B–B3 9 0–0 0–0 10 N–K3 P–KN3 11 P–KB4 N–K2 12 P–B5 with attacking chances for White, Gligorich–Vidmar, Ljubljana, 1951, or than 7 ... 0–0 8 B–Q3 R–K1 9 0–0 N–Q2 10 P–B4 N–B1 11 Q–B3 P–KB4 12 N–K3 P–KN3 13 P–N4 when the same comment applies, Matanovich–Paoli, Bad Pyrmont, 1951) 8 B–Q3 N–N3 9 N–K3 0–0 10 0–0 P–KB4 11 P–KB4 B–K3 12 R–K1 (Puc–Milner-Barry, London, 1951) 12...P–KN3∓.

Black should not try to block White's threatened pawn advances by playing both ... P–Q4 and ... P–KB4. Such a stonewall defence is not effective when Black lacks a supported knight on K5 (see illustrative game). Black may in time be forced to advance his KBP, but the QP is best held back at Q3.

6 ... P–Q4 is therefore inferior, 7 N–K3 B–K3 8 R–QN1 P–QN3 9 P–Q4 B–Q3 10 Q–B3 P–QB3 11 P–B4± (Rossolimo–Alexander, Birmingham, 1951).

7 P–Q4

This part of White's idea, but it would be better not to play it.

7 P–KR4 B–N2 8 P–R5 0–0, Black meets White's premature wing attack by play in the centre, 9 N–K3 N–Q2 10 B–B4 K–R1 11 P–Q4 N–N3 12 B–Q3 K–N1 13 Q–B3 P–QB4, and White's pawns are under fire (Bertok–Bajec, Sarajevo, 1951).

7 N–K3 B–N2 8 P–KR4 P–KR4 9 R–QN1 N–Q2 10 P–N3 N–B3 11 B–N2 P–B3= (Milich–Germek, Yugoslavia, 1952) is a sound method of play.

7 ...	**B–N2**
8 B–K2	

After the obvious **8 B–Q3** it is more difficult for White to advance his pawns. Black replies 8 ... N–Q2 9 0–0 0–0 (it is better to delay castling until White has done so to reduce the attacking potential behind P–KR4) 10 N–K3 N–N3.

8 P–KR4 0–0 9 B–N5 Q–K1 ch 10 N–K3 P–QB4 11 P–R5 N–B3∓ (Fuderer–Matanovich, Sarajevo, 1951).

8 ...	**N–Q2**
9 0–0	**0–0**
10 N–K3	**N–N3**

Black has at least an equal game.

11 P–QB4 B–K3 12 P–QB3 P–KB4 13 Q–N3 Q–K2 14 B–B3 (or 14 P–B4 P–B4±) 14 ... Q–B2 15 B×P? (15 N–Q5 is less disadvantageous) 15 ... QR–N1 16 B–R6 P–B5 17 P–Q5 B–Q2 18 N–Q1 N×QP 19 Q–R3 N–N5! 20 P×N B×R 21 N–B3 B–K3 22 B–Q2 B×N 23 Q×B R–N3 24 B–N5 P–QR3 25 B–R4 B×P 26 B–B1 P–Q4! (far safer than 26 ... B×R 27 B–N2) 27 B–N2 Q–B3 28 Q–Q2 (preferring to struggle on in the middle game, than have a bad ending a pawn down) 28 ... Q–K2 29 Q–B3 R(B1)–B3 30 B–N3 B×R 31 B×P ch K–N2 32 K×B R×P 33 B–N3 P–B4 34 P–N4 P×P e.p. 35 P×P R–Q5 36 Q–B2 Q–K5 37 Q×P Q–R8 ch 38 K–K2 Q–B6 ch 0 : 1 Mate next move (Matanovich–Alexander, London, 1951, Game 34).

Game 35   Fuderer–Kostich, 6th Yugoslav Championship, 1950. 1 P–K4 P–K4 2 N–KB3 N–KB3 3 N×P P–Q3 4 N–B4 N×P 5 N–B3 N×N 6 NP×N B–K2 7 P–Q4 N–Q2 8 B–Q3 N–N3 9 N–K3 P–Q4? 10 0–0 0–0 11 P–KB4 P–KB4 12 Q–R5 P–N3 13 Q–B3 P–B3 14 P–N4 N–B5 15 P×P N×N 16 P×P N–N5? 17 P–B5 N–B3 18 B–R6 R–K1 19 P×P ch K–R1 20 K–R1 B–B1 21 B–KN5 B–N2 22 R–KN1 Q–K2 23 R–N2 B–Q2 24 QR–KN1 R–KB1 25 B–R4 R–B2 26 R–N6 QR–KB1 27 Q–N2 1 : 0.

White was awarded the brilliancy prize for this game, but as he had a positional advantage at the time of the sacrifice on move 14 it is questionable whether he chose the right course. Had Black found 16 . . . N–B4, a thematic move not hard to see since it holds back White's KBP, it is difficult to see how White could have won. If then 17 Q–R5 P×P 18 Q×P ch K–R1 19 Q–R5 ch K–N2 20 R–B2 Q–K1 21 R–N2 ch K–B3 22 Q–N5 ch K–K3 23 R–K2 ch K–B2 24 Q–R5 ch K–B3, and White has nothing better than perpetual check.

Chapter 8

Cochrane's and Other Variations

THIS chapter contains some old variations, now discarded; but these include some interesting attacks and counter-attacks. It is advisable to know them, since the surprise element of the older lines can be considerable.

THE COCHRANE GAMBIT

1 P–K4	**P–K4**
2 N–KB3	**N–KB3**
3 N×P	**P–Q3**
4 N×P	

This gambit, dating from around 1848, is the invention of the British master Cochrane (given as Kohren in the *Yugoslav Encyclopedia!*). It is probably unsound despite Bronstein's recent advocacy of it.

4 ...	**K×N**

See Diagram 53.

53

From the diagram White has the choice of three lines of play. **5 N–B3** and now (1) 5 ... P–KN3 6 B–B4 ch K–N2 7 P–Q4 B–K2∓, Black threatens ... N×P. (2) 5 ... B–K3 6 P–Q4 B–K2 7 P–B4, and Black's QB becomes a target for White's pawns. If instead 7 P–Q5 B–Q2 8 B–QB4 (Ranken) (8 ... P–QB4∓, or if 7 P–B3 R–B1 8 B–K3 K–N1 9 P–KN4? P–Q4

P–QR4?

91

10 P–K5 N×P, a game played by correspondence, 1900. Black often has favourable ways of returning the piece. White, on the other hand, hopes to keep his pawn mass intact and gradually advance it. This was achieved in Rubenchik–Ofitserov, Minsk, 1971 after Black made several inaccurate moves: 5 N–B3 B–K3 6 P–Q4 B–K2 7 P–Q5 B–N5? 8 P–B3 B–QB1 9 B–QB4 QN–Q2 10 P–B4 N–N3 11 B–N3 P–QR4 12 P–QR4 R–K1 13 P–K5! B–KB1 14 P–K6 ch K–N1 15 P–B5 P–B3 16 0–0 QN×P 17 N×N P×N 18 P–N4 B–K2 19 P–N5 N–K5 20 B×P N×P 21 B×N Q–N3 ch 22 K–R1 B×B 23 Q–R5, etc. (3) 5 . . . B–K2 6 B–B4 ch B–K3 (not 6 . . . P–Q4 7 B×P ch N×B 8 N×N± for White's unbroken pawns form a compact mass worth more than a piece) 7 B×B ch K×B 8 P–Q4 P–B3 9 Q–K2 K–B2 10 B–K3 R–B1 11 0–0–0 K–N1 12 P–B4 Q–R4 13 P–KN4 QN–Q2 14 P–N5 with about level chances, as played by Staunton. (4) 5 . . . P–B3 6 B–B4 ch, and now 6 . . . P–Q4=, or 6 . . . B–K3 transposing to Staunton's line.

5 P–Q4 (Thorold, 1876) and now (1) 5 . . . B–K2 6 B–B4 ch (after 6 N–B3 Black could play 6 . . . P–KN3) 6 . . . P–Q4 (6 . . . B–K3 7 B×B ch K×B 8 0–0 K–B2 9 P–QB3±, Steinitz) 7 P×P B–Q3∓, White's mass of pawns has been split and his attack stopped. (2) 5 . . . P–KN3 6 N–B3 transposing, or (3) 5 . . . B–K3 6 N–B3 transposing. (4) 5 . . . P–B3 6 N–B3 and now 6 . . . P–KN3, or 6 . . . P–QN4, or 6 . . . B–K2 7 B–B4 ch P–Q4=. Finally not 5 . . . N×P? 6 Q–R5 ch K–K2 7 Q–K2+ (the only line quoted by Bronstein in support of his comment that the Cochrane is worth a try).

5 B–B4 ch, Cochrane's preference seeking direct attack, but it is probably the weakest of the three. 5 . . . P–Q4 (not 5 . . . B–K3 6 B×B ch K×B 7 P–Q4 K–B2 8 0–0 B–K2 9 Q–B3 N–B3 10 R–Q1 Q–B1 11 Q–QN3 ch K–N3 12 N–B3 P–KR3 13 P–B4 with good attacking prospects) 6 P×P (6 B–N3 B–KN5 7 P–KB3 B–K3 8 P–K5 N–R4∓, or 6 . . . N×P 7 Q–R5 ch K–K3±, both lines according to Steinitz) 6 . . . B–Q3 7 0–0 (7 P–Q3 R–K1 ch 8 B–K3 B–KN5 9 Q–Q2 QN–Q2 10 0–0 N–K4+, a game won by Minckwitz) 7 . . . R–B1 8 P–Q4 K–N1 +.

THE RUY LOPEZ VARIATION

1 P–K4	P–K4
2 N–KB3	N–KB3
3 N×P	Q–K2

This move was first given by Ruy Lopez (1561). It is probably not quite sufficient to equalize. **3 . . . N–B3?** 4 N×N QP×N 5 P–Q3+, or 5 P–K5 N–K5 6 P–Q4+, but not 6 P–Q3? B–Q B4+.

4 P–Q4

4 N–KB3, recently claimed as best by Gutman, and now (1) 4 . . . N×P (best) 5 B–K2 Q–Q1 6 0–0 B–K2 7 P–Q3 (7 P–Q4 P–Q4) 7 . . . N–KB3 8 P–Q4 0–0 with about level prospects—compare with the Close Variation of the Classical Attack; (2) 4 . . . Q×P ch 5 B–K2 B–B4 6 0–0 0–0 7 P–Q4 B–N3 (Anderssen–Kolisch, Paris, 1860) 8 P–B4± as played, or 8 N–B3 Q–K2 9 B–KN5 P–B3 10 Q–Q2±.

4 . . .	P–Q3
5 N–KB3	N×P

5 ... Q×P ch 6 B–K3 (6 B–K2 B–B4, and White has at best only a minimal advantage) 6 ... N–N5 7 Q–Q2 N×B 8 P×N P–Q4 (8 ... Q–K2 is more discreet, while Gutman thinks that 8 ... P–B3! 9 B–Q3 Q–K2 10 0–0 P–KN3 gives Black reasonable chances) 9 B–Q3 Q–K3 10 0–0 and Black's centre is overextended in view of 10 ... P–KB4 11 N–K5 P–KN3 12 P–B4 P–B3 13 P–KN4 P×NP 14 P×P P×P 15 P–K4+ (Levenfish, 1940).

6 B–K2

See Diagram 54.

54

6 ... Q–Q1 7 0–0 B–K2 8 B–Q3 N–KB3 (or 8 ... P–Q4) 9 R–K1, and White is a tempo ahead as compared with regular variations. He must therefore be considered to have a slight advantage.

6 ... P–Q4 7 0–0 B–K3 8 N–B3 N×N 9 P×N P–QB3 10 B–Q3 P–KR3 11 R–K1 Q–B3 12 R–N1 P–QN3 (Guerrero–Hadziotis, Tel-Aviv, 1964) 13 P–B4±.

THE DAMIANO VARIATION

1 P–K4	**P–K4**
2 N–KB3	**N–KB3**
3 N×P	**N×P**

The oldest defence of all, first analysed systematically by Damiano (1512). There is some new analysis here, and a recent flurry of interest demonstrates that the line may not be as hopelessly bad as once thought.

4 Q–K2	**Q–K2**
5 Q×N	**P–Q3**

See Diagram 55.

55

Line 1 (*Continue from Diagram 55*)

      6 P–Q4   **P×N**

All other moves are hopeless for Black:

    6 ... P–KB3 7 N–QB3 QP×N 8 N–Q5 Q–Q3 9 P×P P×P 10 B–KB4 P–B3 11 0–0–0 and White has a winning attack (Steinitz).

    6 ... N–Q2 7 N–QB3 P×N 8 N–Q5 N–B3 9 N×N ch P×N 10 B–N5 ch P–B3 11 B×P ch K–Q1 12 B–Q2 P–QR4 13 B–Q5 +.

    6 ... N–B3 7 P–KB4 (7 B–QN5 B–Q2 8 N–QB3 P×N 9 N–Q5? P–B4∓) 7 ... P×N 8 QP×P P–B3 9 N–B3 P×P 10 N–Q5 Q–Q1 (10 ... Q–Q3 11 P×P N×P 12 B–KB4 winning a piece) 11 **P×P +.**

                  7 P×P

This seems logical as White's queen is better placed than Black's. After **7 Q×KP Q×Q ch 8 P×Q** Black gets active play for his pawn, either by 8 ... N–B3 9 B–QN5 (9 P–KB4 B–KB4, or 9 B–KB4 B–KB4) 9 ... B–Q2, or even better according to Yaroslavyets (1974), 8 ... B–KB4. Now 9 B–Q3 B×B 10 P×B N–B3 11 B–B4 N–N5, or 9 P–QB3 N–Q2 10 P–KB4 B–B4 11 P–QN4 B–QN3 12 N–Q2 0–0–0 13 B–K2 (13 N–B4 P–KB3 14 N×B N×N) 13 ... P–B3! 14 P–N4 B–K3 15 P–B4 B–Q5 16 R–QN1 P×P∓ (Karmov–Yaroslavyets, Rostov, 1974), or 9 B–QN5 ch N–Q2 10 0–0 (10 B×N ch K×B=, or 10 B–R4 0–0–0=) 10 ... B×P 11 B–KB4 P–QB3 12 B–K2 B–QB4 13 N–B3 B–K2=.

          7 ...   **N–B3**

    7 ... P–KB3 8 P–KB4 (8 N–B3 is a good alternative, 8 ... Q×P 9 Q×Q N×Q 10 B–KN5 B–Q2, best, 11 0–0–0 P–KR3 12 B–R4 P–KN4 13 B–N3 N–B3± in view of Black's weak pawns, or 10 ... B–QN5 11 0–0–0 0–0 12 N–Q5 B–R4 13 B–QB4 K–R1 14 B–K7 R–K1 15 N–B6! N–B3 16 N×R N×B 17 R–Q8 +, Schindler–Chalupetsky, correspondence, 1904) 8 ... P×P (8 ... N–Q2 9 N–B3 P×P 10 B–B4! P–B3 11 0–0 Q–B4 ch 12 B–K3 Q×B ch 13 Q×Q B–B4 14 Q×B N×Q 15 QR–K1 +) 9 N–B3! (9 Q×KP Q×Q ch 10 P×Q N–B3 11 B–KB4 N–N5 with sufficient counter-play; or 9 P×P N–B3!—see Line 2) 9 ... P×P 10 B×P Q×Q ch 11 N×Q±, White has a nice lead in development and chances against the king on the open centre files.

                  8 B–QN5!

The strongest reply to the attempt by Yaroslavyets to rehabilitate the Damiano. White has two alternatives: (1) **8 P–KB4** B–Q2 9 N–B3 0–0–0 10 N–Q5 Q–K1 and now a correspondence game Yugai–Yaroslavyets continued 11 Q–K2 P–B3 12 P×P Q–B2 13 P–B4 B–N5 ch! 14 K–B2 (14 N×B? KR–K1) 14 ... KR–K1 15 B–K3 R×B 16 Q×R R–K1 17 Q–Q3 B–QB4 ch with a strong attack. If 16 N×R B–QB4. (2) **8 B–KB4** P–KN4 9 B–K3 (9 B–N3? P–B4 10 Q–K2 P–B5 11 Q–R5 ch Q–B2 12 Q×NP P×B 13 RP×B B–QB4 +, Nagaitsev–Yaroslavyets, Ivanovo, 1971) 9 ... B–N2 10 B–N5 B–Q2 11 N–B3 B×P 12 0–0–0

(12 N–Q5 P–B4 13 N×Q P×Q 14 N×N P×N, or 13 Q–QR4 Q–N2 with counter-play in both cases) 12 ... 0–0–0 13 KR–K1 (13 N–Q5? loses the queen) 13 ... B×N 14 Q×Q N×Q 15 B×B ch R×B 16 R×R K×R with a fairly level ending.

If White is satisfied with a slight positional plus he can avoid the complications by **8 N–B3** Q×P 9 Q×Q N×Q 10 B–KB4 B–Q3 11 B–N3! B–Q2 (Black cannot dispose his forces so as to prevent both N–N5 and N–K4) 12 0–0–0 0–0–0 13 N–K4 B–B3 14 N×B ch P×N 15 P–KB3 KR–K1 16 R–Q4 ± (Vasyukov–Chekhov, Kishinev, 1975).

8 ...	**B–Q2**
9 N–B3	

As already indicated White should play for development rather than compromise his position by trying to hang on to the pawn. Thus **9 P–KB4?** N×P. A sound alternative is **9 0–0** 0–0–0 10 N–B3 (10 B×N B×B 11 Q–K3 R–Q4 12 P–B4 Q–Q2 with counter-play, or 10 B–KB4 P–N4! 11 B–N3 P–KR4 12 P–KR3 P–R5 13 B–R2 B–N2) 10 ... N×P 11 B–K3! B×B (11 ... N–B3 12 Q–QB4±, Kholmov) 12 N×B N–B3 13 N×RP! N×N 14 Q–QR4 with winning chances (Kholmov–Belousov, Gorky, 1974).

9 ...	**0–0–0**

9 ... Q×P? 10 B×N+, or **9 ... N×P?** 10 N–Q5 Q–Q3 11 B×B ch K×B 12 B–KB4 R–K1 13 0–0–0+.

10 B–KB4	**P–QR3**

The standard counter-stroke of **10 ... P–KN4** is Black's best chance, 11 N–Q5 Q–B4, or 11 B×N B×B! 12 Q–B5 ch Q–Q2! 13 Q×Q ch (13 Q×NP B–K2) 13 ... R×Q 14 B×P R–N1 recovering a pawn and with play on the white squares.

11 B–QB4

Now **11 ... P–KN4** fails to 12 N–Q5. **11 ... B–K3?** 12 B×P K–N1 13 B–QN5 R–Q5 14 Q–K3 N–N5 15 B–R4 Q–B4 16 0–0 P–KN4 17 B×P N–Q4 18 N×N B×N 19 QR–Q1 1 : 0 (Sax–Hulak, Budapest, 1975, Game 36).

LINE 2 (*Continue from Diagram 55*)

6 P–KB4

As might be expected this is not as good as 6 P–Q4.

6 ...	**P×N**

6 ... P–KB3 7 P–Q4 N–Q2 (or 7 ... QP×N as in Line 1) 8 N–QB3 BP×N 9 N–Q5 N–B3 10 N×N ch P×N 11 B–N5 ch P–B3 12 B×P ch P×B 13 Q×P ch K–B2 14 Q–Q5 ch K–N2

15 Q×R B–N2 16 Q×P P×QP ch 17 K–B2 Q–K5 18 R–KN1, and Black's attack, obstructed by his pawn at Q3, is inadequate according to Steinitz.

6. . . N–B3 7 B–N5 B–Q2 also comes into consideration.

7 P×P

7 Q×P Q×Q ch 8 P×Q N–B3 9 B–N5 B–Q2 gives White no advantage.

7 . . .   **P–KB3**
8 P–Q4

White, as in previous lines, can surrender the pawn and remain content with some positional advantage, 8 N–B3 Q×P 9 Q×Q ch P×Q 10 P–Q4 B–QN5 (10 . . . P×P 11 N–N5 recovering the pawn at will and getting chances of attack on the K-file) 11 B–QB4 R–B1 12 B–K3 (12 P×P N–Q2 13 P–K6 N–B4) 12 . . . B–N5 13 P–KR3 B–KR4 14 P×P N–B3 15 P–KN4 (15 B–N5 is more ambitious) 15 . . . B×N ch 16 P×B N×P!= (Vitolins–Shmit, Riga, 1975).

8 . . .   **P×P**

8 . . . N–Q2 9 B–KB4 (better than 9 N–B3 P×P 10 N–Q5 N–B3 and now 11 N×Q N×Q 12 N×B P×P! or 11 N×N ch leading to a strong attack for Black, see Game 36) 9 . . . P×P 10 P×P P–KN4 11 B–N3 B–N2 12 N–B3 B×P 13 B×B Q×B 14 0–0–0 0–0 15 B–B4 ch K–R1 16 KR–B1 R–K1 17 QR–K1 +.

9 P×P   **N–B3**

After 10 B–KB4 P–KN4 11 B–N3 B–N2 12 N–B3 Black regains his pawn, 12 . . . B×P 13 B×B Q×B 14 0–0–0 0–0 15 Q×Q N×Q 16 R–K1 N–N3; White retaining some advantage, however.

Game 37 Ed. Lasker–Chalupetsky, correspondence, 1903. 1 P–K4 P–K4 2 N–KB3 N–KB3 3 N×P N×P 4 Q–K2 Q–K2 5 Q×N P–Q3 6 P–KB4 P×N 7 P×P N–Q2 8 P–Q4 P–KB3 9 N–B3 P×P 10 N–Q5 N–B3 11 N×N ch P×N 12 B–N5 ch P–B3 13 B×P ch P×B 14 Q×P ch K–B2 15 Q–Q5 ch K–N3 16 Q×R B–QN2 17 Q–N8 B–N2 18 Q×RP P×P ch 19 K–B2 R–K1 20 R–KN1 P–B4 21 Q–N6 ch B–B3 22 Q–N5 Q–K3 23 Q–Q3 B–R3 24 Q–Q1 (after 11 moves the queen goes home leaving Black nine tempi ahead) 24 . . . P–Q6 25 P×P Q–N3 ch. 0 : 1.

Chapter 9

The Three Knight's Game

1 P–K4	P–K4
2 N–KB3	N–KB3
3 N–B3	B–N5

See Diagram 56.

56

Black's third move is sound enough, but if he wishes he may play instead **3 ... N–B3,** making a Four Knights Opening. **3 ... P–Q3 4 P–Q4 QN–Q2** (Philidor's Defence) is also sound.

LINE 1 (*Continue from Diagram 56*)

      4 N×P

This move, recommended by the "Tarrasch School" which includes Dr. Euwe, gains for White the bishop-pair without his pawns being seriously weakened. As it gains very little else, Black having more than one way of getting a satisfactory game, there is much to be said from White's point of view for the more combative **4 B–B4,** see Line 2.

    4 ...   **0–0**

Best, Black reserving the option of moving his QP one or two squares.
However, after **4 ... P–Q3 5 N–B3 B×N 6 QP×B N×P 7 B–Q3 0–0 8 0–0 N–B4** (8 ...

N–KB3? 9 P–KR3 B–K3 10 B–KN5±, Tarrasch) 9 N–N5 P–KR3! White has no clear advantage.

4 ... Q–K2, and Black's queen is not well placed on the open file. (1) 5 N–B3 N×P 6 B–K2 B×N 7 QP×B P–Q3 8 0–0 B–K3 9 R–K1 N–Q2 10 N–Q4±. (2) 5 N–Q3 B×N 6 QP×B N×P (6 ... Q×P ch 7 B–K2 and now 7 ... 0–0 8 0–0 P–Q3 9 N–B4±, or 7 ... Q×P 8 B–B3 Q–R6 9 N–B4 with a good attack for the pawn) 7 B–K2 P–Q4 8 0–0 0–0 9 N–B4 P–QB3 10 P–B4 P×P 11 B×P B–B4 12 Q–K2 R–K1 13 R–K1 Q–Q2 14 B–K3 P–QN4 (Alapin–Alekhine, Carlsbad, 1911) 15 B–N3 N–R3 16 QR–Q1± (Alekhine).

5 B–K2

After **5 N–Q3** B×N 6 QP×B N×P 7 B–K2 P–Q4 (7 ... P–Q3 is also satisfactory) 8 0–0 B–B4 (8 ... N–QB3 9 P–B3 N–B3 10 B–N5±) 9 B–K3 N–Q2 10 N–B4 P–QB3 Alekhine recommends 11 P–B4 P×P 12 Q–Q4 Q–K2 13 P–KN4 B–N3 14 P–KR4, but Konkowski points out that Black gets the better game after 14 ... N–N3 threatening to trap White's queen. If 15 B–B3 KR–K1 16 P–R5 QR–Q1 +, or if 15 B–QB1 QR–Q1 16 Q–K3 Q×RP 17 N×B BP×N 18 Q×N QR–K1 +.

5 N–B3 B×N (or 5 ... R–K1 6 B–K2) 6 QP×B N×P 7 B–Q3 P–Q4 8 P–KR3 N–QB3=.

5 P–Q3 is weak, 5 ... P–Q4 6 P–QR3 B×N ch 7 P×B R–K1 8 P–KB4 P×P 9 P–Q4 N–Q4 10 P–B4 N–K2 11 B–K2 N–B4 + (Lupi–Alekhine, match, Lisbon, 1946).

5 ...	**R–K1**
6 N–Q3	

If **6 N–B3** either 6 ... B×N or 6 ... N×P is playable.

6 ...	**B×N**
7 QP×B	**N×P**
8 0–0	

See Diagram 57.

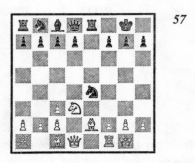

57

8 ...	**P–Q4**

In theory Black should advance this pawn one square only, so as not to provoke any opening up of the game which might favour White's bishops. In practice theory here subordinates itself to tactical necessity, for Black gains active play after the text-move, and there seems no way in which White can exploit the situation favourably to himself.

8 ... P–Q3 would suit a positional player—it is a matter of taste which move you choose. There might follow **9 N–B4** (9 B–K3 N–Q2 10 Q–B1 N–N3 11 P–B3? N×P+, Parkes–Hooper, club-game, London, 1955) **9 ... N–Q2 10 B–K3** (10 B–Q3 QN–B4 11 Q–B3 B–Q2 12 P–B4 N–N4 13 Q–R5 N×B 14 P×N R–K4∓, Spielmann–Rabinovich, Carlsbad, 1911), and now 10 ... QN–B4 or 10 ... N–N3 with about level chances; but not 10 ... N–K4, temporarily obstructing the open file, 11 P–B3 N–KB3 12 B–B2 P–KR3 13 P–QN3 B–B4 14 Q–Q2± (Tarrasch–Grunfeld, Vienna, 1922).

9 N–B4

9 B–B4 N–QB3 10 P–B3 N–B3 11 Q–Q2 B–B4=.
9 B–K3 N–Q2 10 N–B4 QN–B3 11 P–B4 P×P=.

9 ...	**P–QB3**
10 B–K3	**N–Q3**

Not **10 ... P–KB4** 11 P–B4 P–KN4 12 N–R5±.

11 B–Q3	**B–B4=**

Ed. Lasker–Marshall, Lake Hopatcong, 1926.

LINE 2 (*Continue from Diagram 56*)

4 B–B4

Other moves are somewhat less effective:
4 B–K2 P–Q3 5 P–Q3 N–B3 6 0–0 P–KR3 7 P–QR3 B×N 8 P×B P–Q4 9 P×P N×P 10 B–Q2 (Simagin–Kan, U.S.S.R. Championship, semi-finals, 1947), 10 ... Q–Q3=.
4 P–Q3 P–Q4 5 P×P N×P 6 B–Q2 0–0 7 B–K2 N–B3 8 0–0=.
4 P–QR3 B×N 5 QP×B N–B3 6 B–QB4 P–KR3 7 Q–Q3 0–0=, if 8 P–KN4? P–Q4∓ (Fahrni–Rabinovich, Carlsbad, 1911).

4 ...	**0–0**

See Diagram 58.

58

Black has two other satisfactory moves:

4 ... P-Q3 5 0-0 (5 N-Q5 N×N 6 B×N 0-0 7 P-B3 B-R4 8 P-Q3 P-B3 9 B-N5 Q-K1 10 B-N3 K-R1=, Becker-Euwe, Carlsbad, 1929; or 5 P-Q3 B-K3 6 B-N3 N-B3 7 0-0 P-KR3=) **5 ... N-B3 6 P-Q3** (6 P-Q4? B-KN5∓) **6 ... B×N** (6 ... B-N5 is enterprising, but insufficient, 7 N-Q5 N×N 8 P×N N-Q5 9 P-B3 N×N ch 10 P×N B-KR6 11 R-K1 Q-B3 12 K-R1 B-R4 13 P-B4±, Tartakover-Alexander, Hastings, 1935-6) **7 P×B** with level chances. Black may continue 7 ... B-K3, or 7 ... 0-0 8 B-KN5 N-QR4, or 7 ... P-KR3 8 P-KR 3 0-0= as in the stem-game for Line 2, Harrwitz-Loewenthal, match, London, 1853.

4 ... N-B3 5 N-Q5 (other moves transpose) 5 ... B-R4 (or 5 ... N×P 6 Q-K2 N-B3 7 N×KP 0-0=) 6 P-B3 or 6 0-0 P-Q3 7 P-Q3 N×N=) 6 ... 0-0=, see Game 39.

5 0-0

5 P-Q3 P-Q4 (5 ... P-B3 is also good) **6 P×P N×P,** and now:

(1) 7 B-Q2 N×N (simpler is 7 ... B×N as in the text, or 7 ... N-B5 8 0-0 B-N5 9 P-KR3 B-KR4=) 8 P×N B-Q3 9 Q-K2 (9 N-N5 P-KR3 10 N-K4 Q-K2 11 Q-R5 B-K3 12 B×P B×B 13 B×P K×B 14 Q-N4 ch. $\frac{1}{2}$:$\frac{1}{2}$ Beni-Nejkirkh, Balatonfüred, 1959, Game 37) 9 ... N-B3 (9 ... B-KN5 10 P-KR3 B-R4 11 P-KN4±) 10 N-N5 Q-B3 11 0-0 (Rellstab-Vidmar, Bled, 1950) 11 ... B-KB4=.

(2) 7 0-0 N×N (or 7 ... B×N 8 P×B B-N5=) 8 P×N B×P 9 R-N1 N-B3? (after 9 ... N-Q2 Black can defend himself) 10 N-N5 P-KR3 11 N-K4 B-Q5 12 Q-R5 N-R4 13 B-KN5 Q-K1 14 N-B6 ch. 1 : 0 (Kapetzky-Engert, Leipzig, 1942, Game 38).

5 N-Q5 N×N 6 B×N P-B3 7 B-N3 P-Q4=.

5 ...	N-B3

Black has at least two other sound lines, **5 ... P-B3 6 P-Q3** (6 P-Q4 P×P 7 Q×P B×N∓) 6 ... P-Q4 7 B-N3 P-QR4 8 P-QR3 B×N=, or **5 ... P-Q3 6 P-Q3,** and now 6 ... B×N, or 6...P-B3 developing the queen's knight at Q2, a good line for positional players, for it is quite logical for Black to make a close game.

5 ... B×N is not good, 6 QP×B P-Q3 7 B-KN5 P-KR3 8 B-R4 B-N5 9 P-KR3±.

6 P-Q3

6 N-Q5 N×N 7 B×N P-Q3 8 P-B3 B-R4 9 P-Q3 (9 B×N P×B 10 Q-R4 B-N3 11 Q×BP B-N5∓) 9 ... B-KN5 10 P-KR3 B-Q2 11 B-N5 Q-K1= (Ed. Lasker-Marshall, New York, 1924).

6 ...	B×N
7 P×B	P-Q4

7 ... P-Q3 8 B-KN5 P-KR3 9 B-R4 Q-K2 10 R-K1 N-QR4, and Black's game is too passive.

8 P×P	N×P
9 R-K1	

9 Q–K1 R–K1 **10 N–N5** B–B4 **11 R–N1** "would favour White somewhat", says Alekhine. Instead Black should defend by playing 9 . . . N–N3!

9 . . .	B–N5
10 B–Q2	

10 P–KR3 N×P **11 Q–Q2** B×N **12 Q×N** B–Q4∓.

10 . . .	Q–Q3
11 R–N1	

After **11 Q–K2** QR–K1 Black has a fine game.

11 . . .	N–N3
12 B–QN5	QR–K1
13 B×N	P×B
14 P–B4	

See Diagram 59.

59

These moves were played in a game Bernstein–Alekhine, match, Paris, 1934. Black equalizes by **14 . . . B×N,** for if 15 Q×B N×P.

Game 39   Rohacek–Shefc, Trenčianske Teplice, 1949. 1 P–K4 P–K4 2 N–KB3 N–KB3 3 N–B3 B–N5 4 B–B4 N–B3 5 N–Q5 B–R4 6 P–B3 0–0 7 P–Q3 P–KR3 8 P–QR4 B–N3 9 P–QN4 P–R3 10 N×B P×N 11 Q–N3 Q–B2 12 P–R3 P–Q3 13 P–N4? B–K3! 14 P–KN5 B×B 15 Q×B P–N4 16 Q–R2 RP×P 17 B×P N–K2 18 B×N Q×P ch 19 K–K2 P×B 20 KR–N1 ch K–R2 21 QR–QB1 Q×P 22 R–B7 P–Q4 23 N–R4 P×KP 24 R×N P×P ch 25 K–Q1 Q×N 26 R×P ch K–R1 27 R(B7)–N7 Q–R4 ch 28 K–K1 QR–B1 29 Q–Q2 and Black mates in 2. If, in the game 14 B×B P×B 15 Q×P ch K–R1, White cannot meet Black's quadruple knight threats, N×KNP, N×KP, N×QNP, and N–Q5—a pretty theme, this.

Chapter 10

The Barcza Opening

1 P–K4	**P–K4**
2 N–KB3	**N–KB3**
3 P–Q3	

White plays the Old Indian with colours reversed, which is really a Philidor's Defence with colours reversed; or if White fianchettoes his KB, a King's Indian with colours reversed.

The idea is not new. The opening 1 P–K4 P–K4 2 P–Q3 was brought from India to England by Cochrane and V. Green. Green played it at London 1862. It was promptly dubbed the Indian Opening, and became father, in name, of all today's Indian openings. When Hanham played it at New York, 1889, and subsequently, he knew what he was doing although he did not do it very well. The idea did not catch on. Now it has at last become respectable and is known as Barcza's Opening.

White does not attack. Instead he constructs a solid centre, one that is proof against counter-attack. After establishing this "defensive centre" he is free to manoeuvre on the wings. In general, therefore, Black should not develop his bishop "outside the pawn-chain", i.e. at QB4 or KN5. By attacking such exposed pieces White will gain time, and a target, for a wing attack.

If, however, White plays 1 P–K4 P–K4 2 P–Q3, Black may, if he wants to, play 2 ... B–B4, because he can follow with a flank pawn-attack on White's centre, 3 N–KB3 P–Q3 4 B–K2 P–B4! 5 P–B3 N–KB3 6 QN–Q2 0–0 7 0–0 N–B3 (Barcza–Mikenas, Budapest, 1955). White may attack on the queen's side (P–QN4), but Black has sufficient counter-pressure on the king's side.

3 ...	**N–B3**

Black prepares ... P–Q4 establishing a modest centre. Instead he may play a close game, 3 ... P–Q3 4 P–KN3 P–KN3 5 B–N2 B–N2 6 0–0 0–0 7 P–B3 (7 R–K1 P–KR3 8 P–KR3 N–B3 9 P–B3 N–R2 10 QN–Q2 P–B4 11 P–QN4 P–QR3 12 B–N2 P–B5 with chances for both sides, Csom–Chernikov, Lipetsk, 1968) 7 ... QN–Q2 8 P–QR4 P–QR4 9 R–K1 P–N3 10 N–R3 B–N2= (Pilnik–Trifunovich, Beverwijk, 1963).

4 B–K2

The King's Indian Attack is becoming more popular, but is not particularly to be feared by Black: **4 P–KN3 P–Q4** (4 ... B–B4? 5 B–N2 P–Q3 6 P–B3 0–0 7 P–QN4±, Vasyukov–Radulov, Varna, 1964, or 6 0–0 P–Q3 7 P–B3 B–N3 8 QN–Q2 Q–Q2 9 Q–K2 P–KR3 10 N–B4 0–0 11 P–QR4 P–R3 12 N×B±, Balashov–Mikenas, Vilna, 1966) **5 QN–Q2** and now (1) 5 ... P–KN3 6 B–N2 B–N2 7 0–0 0–0 8 P–B3 P–QR4! a key move to reduce White's Q-side prospects, 9 R–K1 P×P 10 P×P N–Q2 11 Q–K2 P–N3 12 N–B4 B–QR3 13 B–B1 Q–B3= (Evans–Olafsson, Dallas, 1957), or (2) 5 ... B–K2 6 B–N2 0–0 7 0–0 B–KN5 (to provoke a weakening of the fianchetto position) 8 P–KR3 B–K3 (8...B–R4 puts the bishop out of play, and makes it a target for a subsequent pawn advance) 9 R–K1 P×P 10 P×P P–KR3 11 P–B3 Q–Q2= (Janoshevich–Bertok, Ljubljana, 1952).

4 QN–Q2 P–Q4 5 P–B3 B–KN5 (pointless) 6 P–KR3 B–R4? 7 Q–N3± (Benkő–Brady, St. Louis, 1960).

4 ...	P–Q4

4 ... B–B4? 5 0–0 P–Q3 6 P–B3 B–N3 7 Q–B2 B–KN5 8 P–QN4±. In spite of its modern look, this sequence of moves was played in the game Hanham–Gossip, New York, 1889!

5 QN–Q2	B–K2

Black has at least two other good moves here:

5 ... P–KN3, introduced in the game Tartakover–Bogoljubov, London, 1922, which continued 6 P–B3 B–N2 7 Q–B2 (7 P–QN4 0–0! 8 B–N2 N–KR4 9 P–N3 B–R6 10 B–B1 B×B 11 K×B Q–Q2∓, Csom–Polgár, Hungarian Championship, 1966, or 7 0–0 P–QR4! 8 R–K1 0–0=, Grunfeld) 7 ... 0–0 with level prospects. Tartakover incorrectly regrouped 8 N–B1 P–N3! 9 N–N3 and after 9 ... B–N2 Black gradually gained the upper hand.

5 ... P–KR3 6 P–B3 B–K3 7 Q–R4 B–Q3 8 N–B1 0–0 9 N–N3 N–Q2 10 Q–B2 B–K2= (Hanham–Lasker, New York, 1900). A solid line typical of Lasker's style.

Predictably **5 ... B–QB4** is inferior, 6 P–B3 P×P 7 P×P P–QR4 8 0–0 0–0 9 Q–B2 Q–K2 (9 ... R–K1 10 N–B4 Q–K2 11 B–KN5 Q–B1 12 N–K3 B–K2 13 B–N5 B–Q2 14 KR–Q1± Keres–Allan, Vancouver, 1975) 10 N–B4 with some pressure for White (Pachman–Nezhmetdinov, Bucharest, 1954).

6 0–0	

6 P–B3 P–QR4 7 Q–B2 0–0 8 N–B1 R–K1 9 N–N3 P–KN3 10 0–0 Q–Q3 11 P–N3 B–B1 12 B–N2 B–N2= (Csom–Lengyel, Hungarian Championship, 1966).

6 ...	0–0
7 P–B3	B–K3

7 ... P–QR4 restraining White on the Q-side is also good, 8 Q–B2 R–K1 (better than 8 ... B–KN5 9 R–K1 P–KR3 10 P–QN3 R–K1 11 B–N2 B–KB1 12 P–QR3±, Pachman–Minev, Marianske Lazne, 1954) 9 R–K1 B–B1 10 N–B1 P–KR3 11 B–Q1 P–QN3 12 N–N3 B–R3 13 B–K2 P–N3= (Barcza–Pogáts, Hungarian Championship, 1959).

7 ... **P-KR3** is sound, 8 P-QN4 B-Q3 9 B-N2 R-K1 10 Q-B2 N-K2 11 KR-K1 N-N3 12 P-N3= (Ney-Klavins, Riga, 1952).

8 Q-B2

See Diagram 60.

60

If **8 P-QN4** P-QR3 9 B-N2 Q-Q2 10 R-K1 N-K1 11 P-QR3 P-B3= (Pachman-Sliwa, Budapest, 1954).

The following examples show satisfactory play for Black:

8 ... P-KR3 9 R-K1 N-Q2 10 N-B1 P-B4, see Game 40. Black loosens his game a little, but gets an aggressive position.

8 ... N-Q2 9 P-QN4 P-QR3 10 P-QR3 P-B3 11 B-N2 K-R1 12 KR-Q1 Q-K1= (Kozomara-Milich, Jugoslav Championship, 1957).

8 ... Q-Q2 9 P-QN4 P-QR3 10 B-N2 B-Q3 11 KR-K1 QR-Q1= (Filip-Opochensky, Prague, 1953).

Game 40   Bogatyrchuk-Kan, Moscow, 1925. 1 P-K4 P-K4 2 N-KB3 N-KB3 3 P-Q3 N-B3 4 B-K2 P-Q4 5 QN-Q2 B-K2 6 0-0 0-0 7 P-B3 P-KR3 8 Q-B2 B-K3 9 R-K1 N-Q2 10 N-B1 P-B4 11 P×BP B×P 12 N-N3 B-N3 13 B-K3 B-B3 14 Q-N3 N-N3 15 P-QR4 B-B2 16 B-B5 KR-K1 17 P-R5 N-Q2 18 Q×NP? R-K3 19 B-R3 R-N1 20 Q-R6 N-Q5 21 Q×RP N-B7 22 P-N4 Q-QB1 23 B-Q1 N×QR 24 B-R4 N-N3! 25 P×N R(K3)×P 26 R×N R-R1 27 B-Q7 Q-Q1 28 Q×R Q×Q 29 B-N2 R-R3. 0 : 1 24 Q-K3 would have been better for White.

Although, for convenient arrangement, the main line of the Barcza Variation shows the development of Black's KB at K2, which is perfectly sound, there is much to be said for the king's fianchetto as played by Bogolyubov. Black should also bear in mind the possibility of fianchettoing his QB, as is shown in several variations. Finally, Black should note the move ... P-QR4, which played in time may nip in the bud White's attack on the wing.

Chapter 11

The Bishop's Opening

1 P–K4	P–K4
2 N–KB3	N–KB3
3 B–B4	

First analysed from the move order 2 B–B4 N–KB3 3 N–KB3 by Ponziani (1769). It is now considered a weak move.

| 3 ... | N×P |
| 4 N–B3 | |

See Diagram 61.

61

S. S. Boden first published an analysis of this gambit move in 1851, and it first occurs in serious play in the Staunton–Horwitz match played in the same year.

4 Q–K2 is objectively best, but offers no prospect of an opening initiative, 4 ... P–Q4 5 N×P (5 B–N3 Q–N4 6 N×P Q×NP 7 R–B1 N–QB3! 8 P–QB3—to stop 8 ... N–Q5— 8 ... N–B4 9 P–Q4 Q–K5 ch 10 Q–K2 Q×Q ch 11 K×Q N×B 12 N×R N×R 13 R–N1 B–KB4 14 N–Q2 0–0–0 15 N–B3 R–K1 ch +, Posen–Berlin, correspondence, 1839) 5 ... B–K3 (or 5 ... B–QB4 6 P–Q3 and now 6 ... P×B 7 Q×N 0–0 8 Q×BP Q–K2 9 P–Q4=, or 6 ... B×P ch 7 K–B1! B–N3 8 B–N3 Q–K2 9 B×P Q×N=) 6 P–Q3 (6 B–N3 Q–N4 7 Q–N5 ch P–QB3 8 Q×NP Q×NP 9 R–B1 B–KR6∓ in view of 10 Q×KBP ch K–Q1 11 B–B4 P×B 12 Q×BP Q×R ch 13 Q×Q B×Q 14 N–B7 ch K–K1 15 N×R B–KR6 trapping the knight) 6 ... N×P 7 N×P K×N 8 Q×N ch Q–B3 9 Q×Q ch P×Q 10 B–N3 N–B3 11 N–B3 N–Q5=.

* 4. N×P P–Q4 5. BN3

4 P–Q3 N–KB3 (4 ... N–Q3 5 B–N3 P–K5 6 Q–K2 Q–K2 7 P×P Q×P 8 B×P ch somewhat favours White) 5 N×P P–Q4 6 B–N3 (6 Q–K2 B–K2) 6 ... B–Q3 7 P–Q4 0–0 8 0–0 P–B4 9 P–QB3 N–B3 10 N×N P×N with a good game for Black. If now 11 P×P (11 B–KN5 is better) 11 ... B×P 12 B–N5 Q–Q3∓. In this line 4 ... N–B4 5 N×P P–Q4 is also good for Black.

4 N×P loses material, 4 ... Q–K2 (4 ... P–Q4 5 Q–K2⇄) 5 Q–R5! (5 P–Q4 P–Q3 6 B×P ch K–Q1 7 0–0 P×N 8 P×P ch B–Q2 9 B–Q5 N–B4∓, Jaenisch, 1842; if 10 P–QN4 P–B3, or if 10 P–KB4 K–B1) 5 ... P–KN3 6 B×P ch K–Q1 (or 6 ... Q×B 7 N×Q P×Q 8 N×R B–N2∓) 7 B×NP N–KB3 8 Q–K2 P×B 9 N×P Q×Q ch 10 K×Q R–N1 and the three pawns, all well back, are not as good as the piece.

See Diagram 61

4 ...   **N×N**

Theory holds that Black can get the better game by taking and holding the gambit pawn; but the evidence is not conclusive, for many attacking and defensive ideas have yet to be tried out and evaluated.

If Black doesn't like defensive play he can safely decline the gambit. The safe ways of declining are:

4 ... N–QB3, best, and the reason why the gambit is so rarely offered. (1) 5 N×N P–Q4 6 B–Q3 P×N 7 B×P B–Q3 8 P–Q4 (8 B×N ch P×B 9 P–Q4 P–K5, or 8 0–0 N–K2 intending P–KB4) 8 ... P×P 9 B×N ch (9 N×P 0–0∓, and if 10 N×N Q–R5! or 10 B–K3 Q–R5! Tarrasch–Lasker, Berlin, 1916) 9 ... P×B 10 Q×P 0–0 11 0–0 P–B4 (11 ... R–K1 12 P–QN3 P–QB4 13 Q–B3 R–K3 14 B–N2 R–N3 15 N–K5 B×N 16 Q×B B–R6 is a strong alternative, Cafferty–Schonherr, correspondence, 1962–3) 12 Q–B3 B–N2 and Black's bishops give him the superior game, e.g. 13 P–QN3 Q–Q2 14 B–N2 P–B3 15 QR–Q1 Q–B4 16 Q–B4 ch K–R1 (Tartakover–Bogoljubov, Pistyan, 1922). (2) 5 B×P ch K×B 6 N×N P–Q4∓, Black has the stronger centre, if 7 KN–N5 ch? K–K1; if 7 QN–N5 ch K–N1; and if 7 N–N3 P–K5. (3) 5 0–0 N×N 6 QP×N Q–K2! 7 N–N5 N–Q1∓. Black has avoided the weakening P–KB3 of the main line of the gambit, and can continue P–QB3 and P–Q4, while 8 P–B4? loses a piece).

4 ... N–KB3 is solid, 5 N×P P–Q4 6 B–N3 (or 6 Q–K2 B–K2 7 B–N3 0–0 8 P–Q4 P–B4=) 6 ... B–Q3 (or 6 ... B–K2, but not 6 ... P–B4 7 P–Q4 N–B3 8 B–N5, and now 8 ... B–K3 9 B×N Q×B 10 N×QP B×N 11 B×B N×N 12 P×N Q×KP ch 13 K–B1±, or 8 ... N×P 9 N×QP B–K3 10 B×N P×B 11 Q×N+) 7 P–Q4 P–B3 8 0–0 (or 8 Q–K2 0–0 9 B–N5 R–K1 10 0–0–0 QN–Q2 11 P–B4=, Keres) 8 ... QN–Q2 9 B–N5 0–0 10 P–B4 Q–N3=, see Game 44.

4 ... P–Q4, less complicated, but dull, 5 B×P N–KB3= (not 5 ... N×N 6 QP×N± since both B×P ch and N–N5 are threatened, Hemingway–Boxall, Hastings, 1953).

4 ... N–Q3 is not to be recommended, 5 B–N3 (better than 5 N×P N×B 6 N×N P–Q4) 5 ... P–K5 (after 5 ... N–B3 6 0–0 White also has the better chances) 6 Q–K2± according to Sozin. If 6...Q–K2 7 N–Q4 Q–K4 8 Q–K3.

4 ... N–B4? 5 N×P+.

5 QP×N   **P–KB3**

Black can even now decline the gambit by **5 ... P–QB3** 6 N×P P–Q4 7 0–0 B–Q3 (7 ... P×B 8 Q×Q ch K×Q 9 N×KBP ch K–K1 10 N×R B–K2 11 R–K1 K–B1 12 R–K4±) 8 R–K1 B–K3 9 B–Q3 N–Q2=.

Other moves are less satisfactory: **5 ... B–K2** 6 N×P 0–0 7 Q–R5 Q–K1 (7 ... P–Q4 8 B–Q3±) 8 0–0 P–Q3 9 N–B3 (9 N×P? R×N 10 R–K1 N–B3 11 B–KN5 Q–B1 +) 9 ... N–Q2 10 R–K1± (Wertheim–Wilson, Yale–Columbia, 1955); **5 ... P–Q3, 5 ... B–QB4** and **5 ... N–B3** are all weak and are met by 6 N–N5 +.

6 0–0

See Diagram 62.

62

By **6 N–R4** White commits himself rather too soon to one line of attack, 6 ... P–KN3 (6 ... Q–K2 7 N–B5 Q–B4 8 B–N3, and if 8 ... P–K5 9 N–N3 P–B4 10 B–K3 Q–R4 11 P–B3±) 7 P–B4 Q–K2 (7 ... P–B3? 8 P–B5 P–Q4 9 P×P P×B 10 Q–R5 K–Q2 11 P–N7 B×P 12 B–R6 or 12 Q–N4 ch +; if 10 ... K–K2 11 P×P Q–K1 12 N–N6 ch K–K3 13 B–K3 B–N2 14 0–0 +) 8 P–B5 Q–N2 (8 ... P–KN4 9 Q–R5 ch K–Q1 10 N–N6 Q–K1 11 B–K2±) 9 0–0 P–Q3 with the better game for Black—see Line 4.

Black has a prolonged defensive task to face. He should try to maintain an unbroken pawn front. The key to White's attack is control of the diagonal from his QR2 to KN8. Black usually wants to castle on the K-side and must therefore try to block this diagonal. He may play ... B–K3, or ... QN–B3–Q1–KB2, or ... P–Q4. After this last manoeuvre, however, his extended pawn centre may come under attack.

White, on the other hand, must try to break the opposing pawn-mass, sometimes by violent sacrifice, more often by long siege. If Black advances his pawn centre too soon, it will be more susceptible to attack.

In most examples from past play White has attacked on the king's side by N–KR4, and against this sound defences have been established. Instead, or as well, White should attack in the centre and on the queen's side, by moves such as R–K1, N–Q4, P–QN4, P–QR4, etc. Attacks of this kind have not yet been well tried out.

In the position of Diagram 62 White threatens 7 N×P, and Black has a choice of four sound defensive moves, 6 ... Q–K2, 6 ... P–KN3, 6 ... N–B3, and 6 ... P–Q3. He often ends up by playing them all. It is not at present possible to say which of these moves is best. Other moves lose rapidly: **6 ... B–B4?** 7 N×P +; **6 ... B–K2?** 7 B–KR6 +; **6 ... P–B3?** 7 N×P P–Q4 8 Q–R5 ch K–K2 9 Q–B7 ch K–Q3 10 N–N6 P×N 11 B–B4 ch K–B4 12 B–B7 Q–Q2 13 B–Q3 +.

LINE 1 (*Continue from Diagram 62*)

       6 ...   **Q–K2**

Introduced by T. W. Barnes, in the game quoted.

       7 R–K1

See Diagram 63.

63

7 N–R4 is not effective, 7 ... P–KN3 (better than 7 ... P–Q3 8 Q–R5 ch K–Q1 9 P–B4 B–K3 10 B×B Q×B 11 P×P QP×P 12 N–N6 B–B4 ch 13 K–R1 R–K1 14 Q×RP=, Morphy–Barnes, London, 1859) 8 R–K1 (or 8 B–K3 P–Q3∓) 8 ... N–B3 9 Q–Q5 (9 P–QN4 P–Q3∓) 9 ... N–Q1 10 P–QN4 P–Q3 11 Q–B3 B–N2 12 P–N5 B–K3+ (van Steenis–O'Kelly, Beverwijk, 1946).

From the position of Diagram 63 Black has the following possibilities:

7 ... P–Q3, the natural move, threatening to oppose bishops on K3, **8 N–Q4,** and now: (1) 8 ... P–B3 9 P–QN4 P–Q4 10 B–N3 B–Q2 11 P–QR4 Q–Q3 12 Q–B3 B–K2 13 P–N5 (Kinder–Jackson, correspondence, 1916), White can attack Black's extended centre, with about level chances—the game was drawn. (2) 8 ... P–QB4 9 N–K2 B–K3, Black keeps his pawn for the time being, but becomes very weak on the light-coloured squares. (3) 8 ... P–KN3 9 P–B4 B–N2 10 Q–B3 K–Q1 (10 ... P–B3 is perhaps better, but White keeps the attack by 11 P×P) 11 P–QN3 P–B3 12 B–R3 K–B2 13 QR–Q1 R–Q1 14 Q–Q3 B–N5 15 R–Q2 Q–Q2 16 P–R3 B–B4 17 N×B± (Edinburgh–Glasgow, correspondence, 1898). Here 10 P–QN4 P–B3 11 B–N3 P–Q4 12 P–QB4 also keeps the attack.

In answer to 7 ... **P–Q3** White may play **8 B–B4,** and now (1) 8 ... N–B3 9 N–Q4 N–Q1 10 B–KN3 P–QB4∓. (2) 8 ... B–K3 9 B×P QP×B 10 N×P P×N 11 R×P B×B 12 R×Q ch B×Q 13 Q–N4 N–B3=.

7 ... N–B3 8 N–Q4 N×N 9 P×N P–Q3 10 P×P QP×P 11 Q–B3 P–B3 12 Q–QN3 P–QN4 13 B–N8 P–N3 14 P–KB4 P–K5 15 B–Q2 B–KB4 16 B–R5 Q–KN2 17 Q–QB3 R–B1 18 B–N3+, a charming piece of geometry with the queen and bishops, played in Stockholm in 1867.

7 ... P–KN3—see Line 2.

7 ... **P–B3** is not good for Black, (1) **8 N×P** (Keres, 1952) **8 ... P×N 9 Q–R5 ch P–N3 10 Q×KP,** and now 10 ... Q×Q 11 R×Q ch K–Q1 12 B–N5 ch K–B2 13 B–B6 P–Q4 14 B×R P×B 15 R–K8±, or 10 ... P–Q4 11 Q×Q ch B×Q 12 B–KN5 0–0 13 B×B P×B 14 B×R K×B 15 QR–Q1 N–Q2 16 P–KN4±. A positional sacrifice. Black cannot develop without further loss. (2) **8 R×P** a combinative sacrifice (W. T. Pierce, 1877), hardly less effective for White, **8 ... P×R 9 B–KN5 Q–Q3** (9...Q–B4 comes to the same thing after 10 Q–K2 B–K2 11 P–QN4 Q–Q3 12 R–Q1; if here 10 ... P–Q4? 11 N×P, and now 11 ... B–K2 12 Q–R5 ch P–N3 13 N×NP P×N 14 Q×R ch K–Q2 15 Q–N7 K–Q1 16 Q–B8 ch K–Q2 17 Q–B7 K–Q1 18 R–K1 +, or 11 ... B–K3 12 N–N6 K–Q2 13 R–K1 P×N 14 Q×B ch K–B2 15 B–B4 ch K–N3 16 B–Q3 +, or 11 ... Q–Q3 12 B–Q3 +. Finally, if 10 ... P–KR3 11 P–QN4 Q×B 12 Q×Q P×B 13 N×KP P–Q4 14 Q–K2 R–R3 15 N–N6 ch K–B2 16 R–K1 +.) **10 Q–K2 B–K2** (10 ... P–QN4 11 R–Q1 P×B 12 R×Q B×R 13 N×P B×N 14 Q×B ch K–B2 15 Q–K7 ch K–N3 16 P–KR4+) **11 R–Q1 Q×R ch** (11 ... Q–B2? 12 N×P+) **12 Q×Q,** and now 12 ... B×B 13 N×B P–Q4 14 B–N3±, or 12 ... P–Q4 13 N×P B–KB4 14 Q–K2 B–K5 15 B×B K×B 16 Q–N4±.

LINE 2 (*Continue from Diagram 62*)

6 ...	P–KN3
7 R–K1	

Better than **7 N–R4** Q–K2, see Line 1.

7 ...	P–Q3

See Diagram 64.

64

After this move, and the following two alternatives White maintains sufficient attack for his pawn:

7 ... **Q–K2** 8 P–QN4 (or 8 N–Q4 B–N2 9 P–QN4, and not 9 P–B4 P–B3 10 P×P P×P 11 B–N3 P–Q4 12 P–B4 0–0 13 P×P Q–B4 +) 8 ... N–B3 (or 8 ... P–B3 9 N–Q4 P–Q4 10 B–N3 B–N2 11 P–QB4) 9 N–Q4.

7 ... **N–B3** 8 P–QN4 (8 B–KN5 P–Q3 9 B–N5 Q–K2∓, or 8 Q–Q5 Q–K2 9 N–Q4 N×N 10 P×N P–B3 11 Q–B3 B–N2∓, or 8 N–Q4 P–Q4∓) 8 ... B–N2 9 P–QR4 (9 N–Q4 P–Q4 10 B–N3 N–K2∓) 9 ... Q–K2 10 N–Q4.

7 ... B–N2 is inferior, 8 B–KN5 P×B 9 N×KP+.

8 P–QN4 is best here, probably transposing to one of the above variations.

8 B–B4 B–N2 (8 ... B–N5 9 N×P!) 9 Q–Q2 Q–K2 10 N–Q4 B–Q2 11 P–QN4 N–B3 12 Q–K2 0–0–0 (simpler 12 ... N–Q1 13 B–KN3 N–B2 14 P–B4 0–0∓) 13 B–QR6 N–N1 14 N–N5 N×B 15 N×RP ch K–N1 16 B–K3 P–KB4 17 KR–N1 P–B5 18 P–N5 N–B4 19 B×N P×B? (19 ... Q–K1 20 P–N6 P×B 21 P×P ch K×P 22 Q–B4 B–KB1+) 20 N–B6 ch B×N 21 P×B Q–K3 and White mates in 4 (Hartlaub–E. von Schmidt, Freiburg, 1889, Game 41).

8 B–KN5 P×B 9 N×KP P×N 10 R×P ch B–K2 11 Q–K2 N–B3+.

8 N–N5 P×N 9 R×P ch P×R 10 B–B7 ch K×B 11 Q×Q N–B3 12 Q×P ch B–K2 13 B×P R–Q1+.

LINE 3 (*Continue from Diagram 62*)

6 ...	N–B3

Played by Horwitz in 1851 (possibly the stem-game) and now recommended as best by the textbooks.

7 N–R4

The usual continuation. The centre attack **7 R–K1** is to be considered, if 7 ... P–Q3 8 P–QN4 (8 N–Q4 P–Q4 9 B–N3 B–QB4) 8 ... Q–K2 9 N–Q4 N×N 10 P×N B–K3 11 Q–B3.

7 ...	P–KN3
8 P–B4	P–B4

The point of Black's 6th move, if now 9 N×BP P–Q4+.

9 N–B3	P–K5
10 N–N5	B–B4 ch
11 K–R1	Q–B3

See Diagram 65.

65

11 ... Q–K2 12 P–QN4 (Estrin prefers 12 B–B7 ch K–B1 13 P–QN4, so that if 13 ... B–Q3 14 B–N3 N–Q1 15 B–K3, when the threats of Q–Q4 and B–Q4 are hard to meet, e.g. 15 ... N–K3 16 N×KP P×N 17 P–B5 with a very strong attack, Murka–Sakhnenko, correspondence, 1963) **12 ... B–N3** and now (1) 13 B–B7 ch K–B1 14 B–N2 Q–B3 15 B–Q5 P–KR3 16 N–B7+ (Zinn–Muhring, Zittau, 1956–7), (2) 13 P–QR4 P–QR3 14 B–R3 N–Q1∓, or 13 P–QR4 P–QR4? 14 B–B7 ch K–B1 15 B–N3 (15 P–N5? N–Q1 16 B–N3 P–Q3 17 B–N2 B–B4+, Ursell–Pachman, Southsea, 1949) 15 ... P–Q3 (15 ... P×P 16 P×P N×P? 17 B–N2 winning the exchange) 16 N–B7 R–N1 17 P–N5 N–N1 18 B–R3 B–B4 19 B×B P×B 20 Q–Q5 R–N2 21 N–N5 P–R3 22 N×P+.

This position somewhat favours Black.

12 Q–Q5 (12 P–QN4 first may be an improvement) **12 ... Q–K2** (12 ... P–Q3! 13 P–QN4 B–N3 14 N×RP Q–K2 15 N–N5 N–Q1∓, or here 14 ... Q–R5) 13 P–QN4 B–N3 14 P–N5 N–Q1 (14 ... N–R4!) 15 B–R3 P–Q3 16 QR–K1+ (Jerabek–Becker, correspondence, 1913).

12 B–B7 ch K–K2 13 B–Q5 P–Q3 14 R–K1 K–B1 15 P–KN4 N–K2 16 P×P N×B+ (Marco–Schlechter, Berlin, 1897).

LINE 4 (*Continue from Diagram 62*)

      6 ...   **P–Q3**

Black must know this line, for White can force it as indicated in the note to White's 6th move earlier in the chapter.

      7 N–R4

Either **7 R–K1,** or **7 P–QN4** Q–K2 8 N–Q4 could well be tried here, but failing definite practical proof to the contrary it must be assumed that the advantage still rests with Black.

      7 ...   **P–KN3**
      8 P–B4   **Q–K2**

See Diagram 66.

    66

Black prepares to defend his king's side, which is in some danger as the following brevities show:

8 ... N–B3 9 P–B5 N–K2 10 P×P P×P 11 R×P R×N 12 B–B7 ch K–Q2 13 B–N5 R–R2 14 Q–N4 ch K–B3 15 Q–B4 ch K–Q2 16 QR–KB1. 1 : 0 (played at Vienna, 1871, Game 42).

8 ... P–KB4 9 N×BP B×N 10 Q–Q5 B–K2 11 P×P N–B3 12 R×B N×P 13 R×N P×R 14 Q–B7 ch K–Q2 15 B–KN5. 1 : 0 (Spitzer–Szén, Pest, 1857, Game 43).

Black has the advantage:

9 P×P QP×P 10 Q–K2 N–B3 11 P–QN4 B–N2 12 B–K3 B–K3 13 B–N5 B–Q2 14 B–B5 Q–K3 15 N–B5 B–KB1 16 B–B4 B×B ch 17 P×B Q×N∓ (Consultants–Chigorin, Kharkov, 1884).

9 P–B5 (to prevent Black opposing bishops) 9 ... Q–N2 (this position can arise by transposition if, as noted earlier, White plays 6 N–R4 P–KN3 7 P–B4 Q–K2 8 P–B5 Q–N2 9 0–0 P–Q3) 10 B–K3 N–B3 11 Q–B3 B–K2 12 P–QN4 N–Q1 13 B–N3 P–B3 14 Q–N3 P–KN4 15 QR–K1 N–B2 16 N–B3 B–Q2 17 Q–B2 P–N3 18 P–KR4 P–KR3 19 Q–K2, and, at last, 19 ... 0–0+ (Meyer–Schlemm, correspondence, 1899). Here, 10 P–QN4 is better; if now 10 ... N–B3, see Game 45.

9 P–B5 P–KN4? 10 Q–R5 ch K–Q1 11 B×P P×B 12 P–B6 Q–K1 13 Q×NP + (Chigorin–Shabsky, St. Petersburg, 1904).

Nowadays the Bishop's Variation is for the most part played with a view to offering Boden's Gambit.

If you are Black you can choose a defence just to your liking: if you like defensive play accept the pawn, but beware of surprise attacks; if you like attacking play decline by 4 ... N–QB3, and in the hands of an active player the two bishops will outweigh the disadvantage of the doubled pawns; if you like solid manoeuvring the decline by 4 ... N–KB3; finally, if you want peace return the pawn by 4 ... N×N 5 QP×N P–QB3.

Game 44   van Steenis–Spielmann, Utrecht, 1936. 1 P–K4 P–K4 2 N–KB3 N–KB3 3 B–B4 N×P 4 N–B3 N–KB3 5 N×P P–Q4 6 B–N3 B–Q3 7 P–Q4 P–B3 8 0–0 0–0 9 B–N5 QN–Q2 10 P–B4 Q–N3 11 N–R4 Q–B2 12 P–B4! P×P 13 B–B2 P–N4 14 N–QB3 N–Q4 15 Q–R5 P–KB4 16 QR–K1 N(Q2)–B3 17 Q–R3 N×N 18 P×N N–K5 19 R×N! P×R 20 P–N4 B×N 21 B×P! P–KR3 22 QP×B Q–Q2 23 B–B5 R×B! 24 P×R P×B (better 24 ... Q×P) 25 P×P P–N3 26 P–K6 Q–K2 27 P–B6 (better 27 Q–R6=) 27 ... B×P! 28 Q–R6 Q–B2 29 R–B4 B–B4 30 R–R4 Q–Q2 31 Q–R8 ch K–B2 32 R–R7 ch K–K3 33 Q×R and Black has a forced mate in 14! A magnificent cut and thrust game. The finish is a masterpiece of calculation: 33 ... Q–Q8 ch 34 K–B2 Q–Q7 ch 35 K–B3 Q×BP ch 36 K–B2 Q–Q5 ch! 37 K–B3 B–K5 ch 38 K–K2 B–Q6 ch 39 K–B3 Q–K5 ch 40 K–B2 Q–K7 ch 41 K–N3 Q–K8 ch 42 K–R3 B–B4 ch 43 K–N2 B–K5 ch 44 K–R3 Q–K6 ch 45 K–R4 Q–B7 ch 46 K–R3 B–B4 mate.

Game 45   Hartlaub–Schories, Hamburg, 1922. 1 P–K4 P–K4 2 N–KB3 N–KB3 3 B–B4 N×P 4 N–B3 N×N 5 QP×N P–KB3 6 0–0 N–B3 7 N–R4 P–KN3 8 P–B4 Q–K2 9 P–QN4 P–Q3 10 P–B5 Q–N2 11 P–R4 P–KN4? 12 Q–R5 ch K–Q1 13 N–B3 P–KR3 14 P–N5 N–K2, now White has a winning combination, sacrificing both rooks, 15 N×KP! QP×N 16 R–Q1 ch N–Q4 17 R×N ch B–Q3 18 B–R3 K–K2 19 R–B5! P–B3 20 R–Q1 R–Q1 21 R×B! R×R 22 R×P! P×R 23 Q–Q1. 1 : 0.

Chapter 12

Philidor's Defence

THIS defence was favoured at times by Alekhine and Nimzowitsch, and was recommended in the late 1960s by Larsen. The normal move order 1 P–K4 P–K4 2 N–KB3 P–Q3 is based upon Philidor's idea that the BP's should not have their potential mobility limited by N–KB3 or N–QB3. In fact in his first edition of the epoch-making *L'Analyse* the Frenchman went so far as to consider 2 N–KB3 an error, preferring 2 B–B4. In later editions of the work he modified this view, but still held that 2 ... P–Q3 was the right answer to 2 N–KB3.

For supporters of the Petroff the possibility of playing Philidor's Defence arises from the move order 1 P–K4 P–K4 2 N–KB3 N–KB3 3 P–Q4 P–Q3. The advantage of the Philidor, apart from variety's sake, is that Black has the option of conducting a close positional struggle in the classical lines in which he avoids giving up the centre by KP×QP, while in some variations (notably 4 P×P and 4 N–B3 P×P) a lively open game results.

It is a matter of speculation whether Petrosian, with his liking for close manoeuvring, would have chosen this path in his 1969 world title match with Spassky if the latter had met the Petroff by 3 P–Q4 instead of 3 N×P as actually played.

THE HANHAM VARIATION

See Diagram 67.

67

| 4 N–B3 | QN–Q2 |
| 5 B–QB4 | |

The most usual move and the most aggressive, since White obtains tactical chances against KB7.

The slow **5 P–KN3** is met by 5 . . . B–K2 6 B–N2 0–0 7 0–0 P–B3 8 P–N3 R–K1 9 B–N2 B–B1 10 Q–Q2 Q–B2 11 QR–Q1 P–QN4 (Tartakover–Kostich, Teplice Sanov, 1922), or 5 . . . P–KN3 6 B–N2 B–N2 7 0–0 0–0= (Polugaevsky).

       5 . . .   **B–K2**

       6 0–0

See Diagram 68.

68

(1) **6 B×P ch?** K×B 7 N–N5 ch K–N1 8 N–K6 Q–K1 9 N×BP Q–N3 10 N×R Q×NP 11 R–B1 P×P! 12 Q–K2 P×N 13 Q–B4 ch P–Q4 14 Q×B ch K–B2 ∓ (A. Rabinovich–Ilyin-Zhenevsky, Moscow, 1922)—see illustrative game.

(2) **6 N–KN5 0–0 7 B×P ch?** R×B 8 N–K6 Q–K1 9 N×BP Q–Q1 10 N×R (10 N–K6? is not a draw by repetition as the queen gains its freedom by 10 . . . Q–N3+) 10 . . . P–QN4 (10 . . . Q–R4 11 B–Q2 P×P 12 N–Q5 Q–B4 is also playable) 11 N×P (11 P×P QN×P∓) 11 . . . Q–R4 ch 12 N–B3 N×P 13 0–0 N×N∓.

(3) **6 P×P P×P** (6 . . . QN×P 7 B–K2 N–N3 8 P–KR3 0–0 9 B–K3 P–B3 with a sound position of the sort that Nimzowitsch liked to defend, Larsen–Barendregt, Beverwijk, 1959) 7 B×P ch (7 N–KN5 0–0 8 B×P ch R×B 9 N–K6 Q–K1 10 N×BP Q–Q1 11 N×R P–QN4 12 N–Q5 B–Q3! 13 B–N5 B–N2 14 Q–Q2 B×N/R 15 0–0–0 B–B1 (Brashinsky–Heuer, U.S.S.R., 1965) 7 . . . K×B 8 N–N5 ch K–N1 (8 . . . K–N3 is a bold but risky attempt to win. After 9 P–KR4 P–KR4 10 P–B4 P×P 11 N–K2 B–Q3 12 P–K5 N×P 13 N×P ch K–R3 14 N–B7 ch N×N 15 N–K6 ch K–R2 Black gets more than enough compensation for his queen; or if 12 B×P N–K4∓, but such excursions with the king are not to everyone's taste) 9 N–K6 Q–K1 10 N×BP Q–N3 11 N×R Q×NP! 12 R–B1 N–B4 13 Q–K2 (not 13 P–B3 N–N5! Konovalov–Mordkovich, Kazakhstan, 1957) 13 . . . B–R6 14 B–K3 Q×R ch 15 Q×Q B×Q 16 K×B K–B2 (Kan–Riumin, Moscow, 1931). After 17 N–B7 KN×P White has insufficient advantage to win, as confirmed in Hoogendorn–Milner-Barry, Hastings, 1966–7.

       6 . . .   **P–B3**

6 . . . 0–0 often transposes. One independent line is Pickett's recent idea of piece regrouping, 7 Q–K2 (7 P–QR4 P–B3 8 P–R5 P–KR3 9 B–R2 R–K1 10 P×P P×P 11 Q–K2 B–B1 12 R–Q1 Q–B2 13 N–R4 and Black has a solid position, Stein–Petrosian, Moscow, 1971) 7 . . . P–B3 8 B–N3 P–QR4 9 P–KR3 Q–K1 (the start of an original plan to transfer the passively placed KB to Q1 and then to QB2 or QN3, while the queen holds the centre, and

gives extra protection to the tender spot KB2) 10 R–Q1 B–Q1 11 P×P P×P 12 B–K3 Q–K2 13 N–R4 P–KN3 14 B–R6 R–K1 15 Q–B3 N–B1 16 B–N5 K–N2 17 Q–K3 N–K3 18 B–R6 ch K–R1 19 N–B3 B–B2 with a slow manoeuvring game, akin to that in the closed Ruy Lopez (Poutianen–Najdorf, Nice, 1974).

7 P–QR4

To restrain the Q-side pawns. As Nimzowitsch showed Black gets good counter-chances if he can advance safely with P–QN4.

| 7 ... | 0–0 |
| 8 Q–K2 | |

8 P–QN3 P–KR3 9 B–N2 Q–B2=.
8 R–K1 P–KR3 9 P–R3 Q–B2 10 P×P P×P 11 N–R4 N–B4 12 N–B5 B–K3 13 B×B N×B 14 Q–B3 K–R2 15 B–K3 N–N1 16 P–R4 P–KN3 17 N×B Q×N 18 P–KR5= (Keres–Penrose, Hastings, 1957–8).

8 ...	P–KR3
9 B–N3	Q–B2
10 P–R3	

So far Alekhine–Marco, Stockholm, 1912. Black can continue, as Alekhine recommended 10 ... P–QN3, or 10 ... N–R2 (Euwe), or finally 10 ... P×P 11 N×P N–B4 with a more open game.

Black must be warned against opening the position too early (for example, 6 ... 0–0 7 P–QR4 P–B3 8 Q–K2 P×P 9 N×P N×P? 10 N×N P–Q4 11 N–B5! P×B 12 B–R6! N–B3 13 N(4)–N3 B×N 14 N×B P×B 15 N×B ch±, Tseshkovsky–Lutikov, Alma-Ata, 1969). Provided he avoids such early exposure to a swift attack Black gets into a middle game with a great deal of material left on the board, which provides great scope for both sides.

THE SOKOLSKY VARIATION.

(*Continue from Diagram 67*)

| 4 P×P | N×P |
| 5 QN–Q2 | |

White opens the position early. Sokolsky suggested in the late 1930s that this should give White the advantage, but the few modern examples do not confirm this. Another attempt to exploit the exposed knight is 5 Q–Q5 N–B4 (Polugaevsky suggests 5 ... P–KB4) 6 B–KN5 (6 N–N5 B–K3 7 N×B P×N 8 Q–B3 QN–Q2 9 P×P B×P 10 N–B3 Q–R5=, L. Steiner–Alekhine, Podrebady, 1936) 6 ... Q–Q2 7 N–B3 N–K3 8 P×P Q×P=, or 8 0–0–0 P–QB3 9 Q–Q2 P–Q4 10 B–Q3 B–N5=.

| 5 ... | N×N |

5 . . . B–B4 6 Q–K2 P–Q4 7 N–Q4 B–N3 8 Q–N5± (Sokolsky).

5 . . . N–B4 6 N–B4 P–Q4 7 B–N5 (7 N–K3 B–K3 8 P–B4 also looks good for White) 7 . . . B–K2 (7 . . . P–KB3 8 P×P P×P 9 KN–K5+, or 7 . . . Q–Q2 8 N–K3 P–QB3 9 N–Q4±) 8 B×B Q×B, and now 9 Q×P B–K3 10 Q–Q2 with some compensation for the pawn, or 9 N–K3 P–QB3 10 P–B4±.

6 B×N	**B–K2**
7 B–B3	

See Diagram 69.

69

7 P×P Q×P 8 B–B3 0–0 9 Q×Q B×Q 10 0–0–0 B–KN5 11 B–K2 R–K1 12 KR–K1 N–B3= (Boleslavsky–Keres, U.S.S.R., Team Championship, Moscow, 1962).

7 B–Q3 N–B3 8 Q–K2 B–K3 9 0–0–0 P×P 10 N×P Q–Q4 11 N–B4 N–Q5 12 Q–K5 Q×Q 13 N×Q 0–0 (Klovan–Heuer, U.S.S.R., 1962).

7 . . .	**0–0**
8 B–Q3	**N–B3**
9 Q–K2	**N×P**
10 N×N	**P×N**
11 0–0–0	**B–N4 ch**
12 K–N1	**Q–K2**

Black has little to fear once he closes the K-file by B–K3. Then he can play for further exchanges. On the whole the conclusion must be that Sokolsky's Variation is rather tame for White. The modern tendency goes against such early simplification.

THE COUNTER-ATTACK VARIATION
(Continue from Diagram 67)

4 N–B3	**P×P**

Often played in earlier times this surrender of the centre looks passive. However, in the last decade it has been linked with a definite counter-attacking plan which, though risky, has brought Black some success. The plan is recommended by Larsen and Antoshin and has been successful in Britain in the hands of J. E. Littlewood. The idea is to advance the

Q-side pawns to achieve the formation of pawns at QR3, QN4, QB4 and Q3. The KB is developed at K2, or more dynamically at KN2. The QR sometimes comes into play via QR2. Black suffers from a backwards QP, but as a number of modern opening systems have demonstrated (notably the King's Indian Defence and the ... P–K4 variations of the Sicilian Defence) such a weakness is not decisive if counter-chances are generated in other parts of the board.

5 N×P

5 Q×P B–K2 (5 ... N–B3 6 B–QN5 B–Q2 is the old way of playing it transposing to a Steinitz Defence to the Ruy Lopez. After 7 B×N the more dynamic recapture is 7 ... P×B, but it is a passive line) 6 B–KN5 0–0 7 0–0–0 N–B3 (now the queen is forced to move) 8 Q–Q2 P–KR3 (Polugaevsky suggests 8 ... B–K3 9 N–Q4 N×N 10 Q×N P–B4 11 Q–Q2 Q–R4=) 9 B–KB4 R–K1 10 P–KR3 B–KB1 11 B–Q3 N–K4 12 N×N P×N= (Llorens–Koltanovsky, match, 1935).

5 ...   B–K2

5 ... P–KN3 looks more dynamic, but lacks practical trials, 6 B–KN5 (6 B–QB4 B–N2 7 0–0 0–0 8 B–KN5 P–KR3 9 B–R4 N–B3 10 N×N P×N 11 P–B4! (11 Q–B3? P–KN4 12 B–N3 N–N5±, Kavalek–Larsen, San Juan, 1969) 11 ... Q–K1 with complicated play, (Larsen); or 6 B–KB4 B–N2 7 Q–Q2 0–0 8 0–0–0 R–K1 9 P–B3 N–B3 10 N×N P×N 11 P–K5 N–Q4, equally tense, and unclear, Tal–Larsen, Eersel, 1969) 6 ... B–N2 7 Q–Q2 P–KR3! (not 7 ... 0–0 8 0–0–0 R–K1 9 P–B3 N–B3 10 N×N P×N 11 P–KR4 with good attacking chances, Tompa–Hardicsay, Budapest, 1972) 8 B–KB4 P–KN4 9 B–N3 N–R4 10 B–K2 N×B 11 RP×N N–B3! 12 B–N5 B–Q2 13 QN–K2 Q–B3 14 0–0 0–0–0 (Hennings–Radulov, Siegen, 1970) and Black has good chances, though he soon went wrong and lost.

It should be noted that Larsen (and following his example J. E. Littlewood) prefer to play the straight Philidor 2 ... P–Q3 and follow up with the move order 3 ... P×P 4 N×P P–KN3. This has the advantage of not blocking the long black diagonal. Black retains the option of KN–K2, and with his pressure on White's Q4 sometimes induces the reply N×N after Black's N–QB3. The open QN file is then an extra trump for Black (see illustrative game Hazai–Sax). Unfortunately such a move order is not possible when Black has played into the Philidor via the Petroff.

6 B–K2

See Diagram 70.

70

(1) **6 P–KN3** 0–0 7 B–N2 B–N5 8 Q–Q2! N–B3 9 P–KR3 B–Q2 10 KN–K2 R–K1 11 P–N3 with a space advantage (Spassky–Kholmov, Rostov, 1972), or 6 ... P–Q4!? 7 P–K5 N–N5 (7 ... N–K5 8 N×N P×N 9 B–N2 Q–Q4 10 0–0 N–B3! 11 N×N Q×N 12 R–K1 B–KB4 13 Q–K2 0–0–0 =, according to I. Zaitsev) 8 P–K6 N–KB3 9 P×P ch K×P 10 B–N2 R–K1 11 0–0 P–B3 12 B–B4 N–R3 and White has achieved very little (Kagan–Cobo, Lugano, 1968), or in this 8 N–B3 B–QB4 9 Q×P B×P ch 10 K–K2 B–N3 11 P–KR3 N–R3 12 Q×Q ch K×Q 13 B–N5 ch with slight advantage to White (Palatnik–Kholmov, Rostov, 1972).

(2) **6 B–QB4** 0–0 7 B–N3 (7 0–0 N×P 8 N×N P–Q4 9 B–Q3 P×N 10 BxP N–Q2 11 P–QB3 N–B4 12 B–B2 N–K3 = (Jimenez–Antoshin, Moscow, 1964) 7 ... N–R3 8 0–0 N–B4 9 Q–B3 N×B = (Westerinen–S. Garcia, Lugano, 1968).

(3) **6 B–KB4** 0–0 7 Q–Q2 P–QR3 8 0–0–0 P–QN4 (this counter-attack seems best; 8 ... P–Q4 9 P×P N×P 10 N–B5±) 9 P–B3 P–N5 10 N–Q5 N×N 11 P×N P–QR4 12 B–B4 B–N2 13 N–B5 N–Q2 14 N×B ch Q×N 15 KR–K1 Q–Q1 16 B–KN5 P–KB3 17 B–K3 N–K4 = (Kholmov–Antoshin, Havana, 1968).

(4) **6 P–B3** 0–0 7 B–K3 P–Q4! 8 P–K5 P–B4 9 P×N B×P 10 KN–N5 P–Q5 11 N–K4 P×B 12 Q×Q B×Q 13 N×BP B–N3∓ (Damjanovich–S. Garcia, Havana, 1968).

6 ...   **0–0**

6 ... P–QR3 7 P–B4 P–B4 8 N–N3 (Bárczay–Fernandez, Havana, 1971) and now 8 ... B–K3, or 8 ... 0–0 with good fighting chances,

7 0–0   **P–QR3**

7 ... N–QB3 is playable, **8 N×N P×N 9 P–QN3** (Leonhardt–Nimzowitsch, San Sebastian, 1912) and now 9 ... N–Q2 10 B–N2 B–B3 = (Keres). The text is the introduction to the sharp system widely employed by Antoshin, and by the Cuban players to whom he was trainer in the late 1960s.

8 B–KB4

8 B–B3 R–K1 9 P–QN3 QN–Q2 10 P–N3 B–B1 11 B–QN2 P–KN3 12 B–N2 N–B4 13 R–K1 B–N2 14 Q–Q2 B–Q2 = (Liberzon–Antoshin, Spartakiad, 1967).

8 P–QR4 P–B4 9 N–B3 N–B3 10 P–R3 N–QN5 11 B–KN5 B–K3 12 Q–B1 P–Q4 =, Sakharov–Antoshin, Kiev, 1967.

8 ...   **P–B4**
9 N–B3

9 N–B5 B×N (9 ... N×P 10 N–R6 ch or 10 N×B ch Q×N 11 N–Q5! is the sort of premature freeing line Black should avoid) 10 P×B P–Q4 and if 11 B–B3 P–Q5 12 B×P? R–R2 +, or 11 N–K4 N–Q4.

9 N–N3 P–QN4= since White's knights are targets for the advancing pawns, while B–KB3 is always safely met by R–R2.

9 ...		B–K3
10 N–KN5		N–B3
11 N×B		P×N
12 B–B4		Q–B1
13 N–QR4		N×P!

Black's centre pawns and open KB file give him adequate counter-chances in this tense position.

(1) 14 N–N6 Q–Q1 15 B×P ch K–R1 16 N–Q5 (16 N×R? R×B+) 16 ... N–Q5 (16 ... B–N4 looks even better) 17 B–R3 and Black has reasonable chances (Ragozin–Antoshin, Leningrad, 1956).

(2) 14 Q–N4 P–Q4 15 N–N6 N–B3! 16 Q–R3 Q–Q1 17 N×R P–K4! 18 Q–K6 ch K–R1 19 B×KP P×B∓ (Dementiev–Antoshin, U.S.S.R. Championship, 1970).

Game 48   A. Rabinovich–Ilyin-Zhenevsky, Moscow, 1922. 1 P–K4 P–K4 2 N–KB3 P–Q3 3 P–Q4 N–KB3 4 N–B3 QN–Q2 5 B–QB4 B–K2 6 B×P ch? K×B 7 N–N5 ch K–N1 8 N–K6 Q–K1 9 N×BP Q–N3 10 N×R Q×NP 11 R–B1 P×P 12 Q–K2 (12 Q×P N–K4!) 12 ... P×N 13 Q–B4 ch P–Q4 14 Q×B ch K–B2 15 Q×P (15 Q×R BP×P 16 B×P B–N5 ch 17 P–QB3 Q×KP ch 18 K–Q2 N–K4 forces mate) 15 ... Q×KP ch 16 B–K3 R–QN1 17 Q×RP P×P 18 K–Q2 Q–QN5 ch 19 P–QB3 N–K5 ch 20 K–K2 N×P ch 21 K–B3 Q–K5 ch 22 K–N3 N–K7 ch 23 K–R3 Q–B6 mate.

Game 49   Hazai–Sax, Budapest, 1971. 1 P–K4 P–K4 2 N–KB3 P–Q3 3 P–Q4 P×P 4 N×P P–KN3 5 N–QB3 B–N2 6 B–KB4 N–QB3 7 N×N P×N 8 B–QB4 (8 Q–Q2 R–N1 9 0–0–0 is better) 8 ... R–N1 9 Q–B1 P–Q4! 10 P×P R–N5 11 B–N3 (11 B–Q3 safeguards the king better) 11 ... Q–K2 ch 12 B–K3 B–QR3! 13 Q–Q2 R–Q5 14 Q–B1 N–B3 15 P–B3 B–R3 16 K–B2 N–N5 ch 17 P×N Q–B3 ch 18 K–N1 (not 18 K–K1 Q–K4 19 N–Q1 B×B 20 N×B R–K5; the game was published in many sources with the claim that Black wins by force in this position, but after 18 K–N3 Q–K4 ch 19 K–B3! Q–B3 ch 20 K–N3 there is only a draw by perpetual check) 18 ... R–Q8 ch! 0 : 1.

PART II

Other King's Pawn Openings

1 P-K4 P-K4

Chapter 1

The Four Knights Opening

(1 P–K4 P–K4 2 N–KB3 N–KB3 3 N–B3 N–B3)

THE MAIN VARIATION

4 B–N5

For 4 P–Q4 see the Scotch Variation. For 4 B–B4 N×P see Petroff's Defence, Chapter 11.

4 ...	**B–N5**

We call this the Main Variation for no better reason than its being the oldest established. It has a reputation of being too sound, since it leads to a solid manoeuvring game with a draw as the likeliest outcome. For the livelier Rubinstein Variation 4...N–Q5 see the next section of the chapter.

5 0–0	**0–0**
6 P–Q3	

6 B×N QP×B 7 P–Q3 (7 N×P B×N 8 QP×B N×P=) 7 ... B–Q3 (7 ... Q–K2 and 7 ... R–K1 are also good) 8 B–N5 P–KR3 9 B–R4 P–B4 with a good game for Black. If 10 N–Q5? P–KN4∓ (Winter–Capablanca, Hastings, 1919).

6 ...	**P–Q3**
7 B–N5	

See Diagram 71.

71

If **7 N–K2** N–K2 8 P–B3 B–R4 9 N–N3 P–B3 10 B–R4 N–N3 11 P–Q4 and now, 11 ... R–K1 12 B–N3 P–KR3=, or 11 ... P–Q4, skating on thin ice, but offering chances for both sides, e.g. 12 P×QP P–K5 13 N–K5 P×P=.

7 B×N P×B 8 N–K2 R–K1 9 N–N3 P–Q4=.

From the position of Diagram 71 Black has more than one satisfactory continuation.

7 ... B×N 8 P×B Q–K2 9 R–K1 N–Q1 (Metger's move, and the one greatly favoured in modern practice) **10 P–Q4** and now:

(1) **10 ... B–N5** 11 P–KR3 (11 B–KB1 N–K3 12 B–B1 B×N 13 P×B N–R4∓) 11 ... B–R4 12 P–N4 B–N3 13 P–Q5 (13 N–R4 P–KR3 14 B–QB4 B–R2) 13 ... P–B3 14 B–KB1 (14 B–Q3 P×P 15 P×P R–B1 16 P–B4 P–K5∓) 14 ... R–B1 15 P–B4 P–QN3.

(2) **10 ... N–K3** 11 B–QB1 R–Q1 (11 ... P–B4 12 P×KP P×P 13 B–QB4 R–Q1 14 B–Q5 P–B5 or 14 ... N–B2 is also good) 12 B–B1 (12 N–R4 P–KN3 13 P–N3 P–Q4=) 12 ... P–B4 (12 ... N–Q2 13 P–N3 KN–B1 is also good) 13 P–Q5 N–B2=.

In the above variations Black gets at least an equal game with good chances of attack on White's weak Q-side pawns.

7 ... N–K2 is riskier, since the price for keeping the KB is the break-up of Black's K-side after 8 B×N P×B 9 N–KR4 N–N3 10 N×N RP×N 11 P–B4, though White's attacking chances are not to be feared after 11 ... B–B4 ch 12 K–R1 K–N2.

THE RUBINSTEIN VARIATION

(1 P–K4 P–K4 2 N–KB3 N–KB3 3 N–B3 N–B3 4 B–N5 N–Q5)

Black offers a pawn for a strong counter-attack, or else he rapidly equalizes. Masters consider that the pawn offer is satisfactory for Black, but analysis has not conclusively shown this to be so.

The defence is sound enough, however, for if he chooses Black can withdraw his offer (after 5 B–R4 or 5 B–B4) by playing 5 ... N×N ch with about level chances.

See Diagram 72.

72

5 B–R4

The most critical variation. After **5 B–B4** B–B4 6 N×P Q–K2 7 N–B3 (7 N–Q3 P–Q4∓) 7 ... P–Q4 8 N×QP (8 N×N P×B±) 8 ... Q×P ch 9 N–K3 B–KN5 10 B–K2 N×B 11 Q×N 0–0–0 12 P–Q3 Q–K3 13 0–0 N–Q4 14 R–K1 N–B5 Black has at the very least sufficient attack to compensate for the pawn.

It is bad for White to take the pawn at once, **5 N×P** Q–K2 6 P–B4 (6 N–B3 N×B 7 N×N Q×P ch 8 Q–K2 Q×Q ch 9 K×Q N–Q4 with the better long-term prospects in view of the two bishops) 6 ... N×B 7 N×N P–Q3 8 N–KB3 Q×P ch 9 K–B2 N–N5 ch 10 K–N1 (10 K–N3 Q–N3, and now 11 Q–K2 ch K–Q1 12 R–K1 B–Q2∓, or 11 N–R4 Q–R4 12 P–KR3 Q×QN 13 P×N P–N4∓, or here 12 N×P ch K–Q1 13 P–KR3 N–B3 14 N×R Q×N ch!+) 10...Q–B3 11 Q–K2 ch B–K2 12 P–KR3 Q–N3 ch 13 P–Q4 N–B3 with a good game for Black. *14. KR2 BQ2 MCO*

5 0–0 N×B 6 N×N P–B3 7 N–B3 P–Q3 8 P–Q4 Q–B2 and Black has the bishop-pair.

5 B–K2 N×N ch 6 B×N B–B4 7 P–Q3 P–Q3=.

5 N×N P×N 6 P–K5 P×N 7 P×N Q×P! (accepting the gambit by 7 ... P×QP ch 8 B×P Q×P gives White a strong initiative) 8 QP×P Q–K4 ch 9 Q–K2=, a grandmaster draw variation. This is one reason why Black may choose not to play Rubinstein's Variation.

5 ...	**B–B4**
6 N×P ∗	**0–0**
7 N–Q3	

∗ *6. 00 00 7 PQ3 PQ3 8. N×N B×N 9. BKN5 PB3 10. GQ2 PKR3= (BAGIROV · SHAMKOVICH '61)*

If 7 N–B3, or 7 P–Q3 then 7...P–Q4!

7 ...	**B–N3**

See Diagram 73.

73

We give some of the possible continuations:

8 0–0 P–Q4 9 N×P N×KP (9 ... N×N 10 P×N Q–R5 11 K–R1 B–N5 12 P–KB3 B×P?! 13 P×B N–B4 14 P–N3 Q–R6 15 R–B2 B×R turned out successfully in Hadzhi-petrov–Minev, Bulgarian Championship, 1960, but in view of the improvement 14 P–N4 Black seems well advised to continue prosaically with 10 ... Q×P 11 N–B4 Q–KN4 12 P–Q3 B–N5 with excellent chances) 10 N–B3 N–KB3 with approximately equal chances.

8 P–K5 N–K1 9 0–0 P–Q3 10 P×P N–KB3 11 P–Q7 (11 P×P Q–Q3) 11 ... B×P 12 B×B Q×B 13 N–K1 QR–K1 14 P–Q3 N–N5 15 P–KR3 P–KB4! with a strong attack, or 15 N–B3 N×N ch 16 Q×N N×BP 17 N–Q5 Q×N and Black forces perpetual check.

8 N–B4 P–Q4 9 P–Q3 (9 KN×P N×N 10 N×N Q–R5 11 0–0 B–N5+)9 ... B–N5 10 P–B3 N–R4! 11 N×N (11 P×B Q–R5 ch 12 P–N3 N×NP 13 N–N2 Q–B3) 11 ... B×N 12 N×P P–QB3 13 N×B P×N 14 B–N3 Q–R5 ch 15 K–B1 (15 P–N3 Q–R6) 15 ... N×B 16 BP×N P–KB4 with at least enough attack for the two pawns.

THE SCOTCH VARIATION

(1 P–K4 P–K4 2 N–KB3 N–KB3 3 N–B3 N–B3 4 P–Q4)

4 ...   P×P

See Diagram 74.

74

5 N×P

5 N–Q5, the Belgrade Gambit, was in vogue for a time, but it is no longer thought to be effective, especially as the element of novelty or surprise has disappeared. If Black accepts the gambit White gets promising chances in the complications arising from 5...N×P 6 Q–K2 P–B4 7 N–N5 P–Q6 8 P×P N–Q5. Black has two sound ways of declining:

(1) **5 ... N–QN5** 6 B–QB4 (6 N×N ch Q×N 7 P–QR3 N–B3 8 B–KN5 Q–N3 9 B–Q3 P–Q3, or 6 N×QP N×KP 7 N–N5 P–QB3 8 N×N B×N ch 9 P–B3 Q–B3∓) 6 ... QN×N 7 P×N B–N5 ch 8 B–Q2 Q–K2 ch 9 Q–K2 B×B ch=.

(2) **5 ... B–K2,** simple and solid, 6 N×P (6 B–KB4 P–Q3 7 N×QP KN×N 8 P×N N×N 9 Q×N B–B3=) 6...KN×N 7 P×N N×N 8 Q×N 0–0= (Padevsky–Smyslov, Moscow, 1956). *6. B-QN5 PQ3 7. N×P BQ2 8.0-0 KN×N 9. P×N N×N 10. B×B Q×B 11. Q×N 0-0=(SEFE- Szabo '49)*

5 ...   B–N5
6 N×N

6 B–KN5 P–KR3 is very satisfactory for Black.

6 ...   NP×N
7 B–Q3

7 B–Q2 0–0 8 B–Q3 P–Q4 9 P–B3 P×P 10 N×P N×N 11 P×N B–QB4 (Alekhine–Alexander, Margate, 1937), Black stands well.
7 Q–Q4 Q–K2 8 P–B3 P–B4 9 Q–B2 0–0∓.

7 ...   P–Q4
8 P×P

8 P–K5 N–N5 9 0–0 0–0 10 B–KB4 P–B3∓.
8 0–0 B×N 9 P×B P×P 10 B–R3 P×B 11 Q–K1 ch B–K3 12 P–KB4 K–Q2 +.

8 ...   **P×P**

If seeking a draw, Black may play **8 ... Q–K2 ch** 9 Q–K2 P×P. *10. 0-0 Q×Q 11. N×Q P-B4*
12. P-QB3 B-R4 13. B-KB4 B-N3± (SPIELMAN · BOGOLIUBOV '22)

9 0–0

Here White may seek easy equality by **9 B–N5 ch** B–Q2 10 B×B ch.

9 ...   **0–0**
10 B–KN5   **B–K3**

Considered best because Black is now free to advance his QBP.

See Diagram 75.

75

10 ... P–B3 is a good alternative, 11 Q–B3 (11 N–K2 P–KR3) 11 ... B–Q3 (or 11 ...
B–K2 12 QR–K1 R–K1 13 P–KR3 B–K3=) 12 B×N (12 B–B5 B–K4 13 KR–K1 Q–Q3)
12 ... Q×B 13 Q×Q P×Q 14 N–K2 B–K3= (Czerniak–Unzicker, Moscow, 1956).
  In the position of Diagram 75 Black has a small theoretical advantage, an extra pawn in
the centre, which often gives him a slight edge. There follow some examples from play:
  11 Q–B3 B–K2 12 QR–K1 (12 P–KR3 R–N1 13 P–QN3 P–B4∓) 12 ... R–N1 13 N–Q1
(Ekstrom–Euwe, Hastings, 1945–6) 13 ... P–B4.
  11 N–K2 P–KR3 12 B–R4 B–Q3, and now: 13 N–Q4 P–B4 14 N–B5 B×N 15 B×B
B–K4 16 P–QB3 R–N1 17 P–KB4 B–B2 18 P–QN3 Q–Q3 19 Q–B3 KR–K1 20 QR–Q1
P–Q5 (Alexander–Unzicker, Amsterdam, 1954), or 13 P–KB4 B–B4 ch 14 K–R1 B–KN5
15 P–KR3 B×N 16 Q×B R–K1 (Alexander–Smyslov, London, 1954).
  11 N–N5, a recent idea, 11 ... P–B4 12 P–QB3 (12 P–QR3 B–R4 13 P–QN4 B–N3 14 P×P
B×P∓, Parma–Trifunovich, Yugoslav Championship, 1960) 12 ... B–R4 13 Q–R4 B–N3
14 Q–R4 P–KR3 15 B×P P×B 16 Q×P P–B5 17 Q–N5 ch. ½ : ½ Ivkov–Gligorich, Buenos
Aires, 1960, Game 46.
  If **11 P–B4** P–B3 12 P–B5 B–Q2 White has merely weakened his pawns; and if **11 B×N**
Q×B 12 N×P? B×N 13 Q–R5 KR–Q1 +.

Chapter 2

The Vienna Opening

(1 P–K4 P–K4 2 N–QB3)

Line 1

2 ...	**N–KB3**
3 B–B4	

For 3 P–B4, the Vienna Gambit, see Line 2.

3 ...	**N×P**

This move is the simplest, breaking White's centre. If, however, you do not like the variations which follow, then you may safely play **3 ... N–B3 4 P–Q3** (4 P–B4 N×P 5 N–B3 N–Q3±) **4 ... B–N5 5 N–K2** (5 B–KN5 P–KR3 6 B×N B×N ch 7 P×B Q×B 8 N–K2 P–Q3 9 Q–Q2, or 9 0–0, then 9 ... P–KN4∓ with a firm grip on the black squares; or 5 B–Q2 0–0 6 KN–K2 P–Q3 7 0–0 B–K3=, since if 8 P–B4 B×B 9 P×B P×P; or 5 N–B3 P–Q3 6 B–KN5 B–K3=) **5 ... P–Q4 6 P×P N×P 7 B×N** (7 0–0 B–K3) **7 ... Q×B 8 0–0 Q–Q1** (or 8 ... Q–R4 9 P–QR3 0–0 10 B–K3 B×N 11 N×B N–Q5=) **9 P–B4 P×P 10 B×P 0–0 11 N–K4 B–K2=**.

4 Q–R5	**N–Q3**
5 B–N3	

White may simplify here by **5 Q×KP ch** Q–K2 6 Q×Q ch B×Q 7 B–N3 N–B4 8 N–B3 P–QB3 9 0–0 P–Q4 10 R–K1 0–0=.

5 ...	**B–K2**

Black may also play **5...N–B3,** the most aggressive move, which involves sacrificing at least the exchange in return for a very strong attack. Practical play has shown the sacrifice to be very strong in over the board play, but in view of the doubts expressed by a few theoreticians the line may be less suitable for correspondence play, since new ideas for each side are regularly being found. Play continues 6 N–N5 P–KN3 7 Q–B3 P–B4 8 Q–Q5 Q–K2 9 N×P ch K–Q1 10 N×R P–N3 11 P–Q3 B–QN2 with excellent practical chances.

6 N–B3

6 Q×P 0–0 7 P–Q4 N–B3 8 Q–B4 P–QN4 9 N–B3 B–N2∓.

6 ...	**N–B3**
7 N×P	

7 P–Q3 P–KN3 8 Q–R3 N–B4 9 P–N4 KN–Q5 10 B–R6 B–B1 and White has inadequate compensation for the pawn (Alekhine).

7 P–KR4 P–KN3! (Larsen), but not 7 . . . 0–0 8 N–KN5 P–KR3 9 Q–N6 B×N 10 P×B Q×P 11 Q×Q P×Q 12 P–Q3 or 12 N–Q5 with good play for White in both cases.

7 ...	**0–0**
8 N–Q5	**N–Q5**
9 0–0	**N×B**
10 RP×N	**N–K1**
11 P–Q4	**P–Q3**

According to Alekhine it is level.

LINE 2 (*after* **1 P–K4 P–K4 2 N–QB3**)

2 ...	**N–KB3**
3 P–B4	

The Vienna Gambit. Another idea stemming from L. Paulsen is **3 P–KN3,** and now 3 . . . P–Q4 4 P×P N×P 5 B–N2 B–K3 6 N–B3 N–QB3 7 0–0 B–K2 8 R–K1 B–B3 9 N–K4 0–0 10 P–Q3 B–K2 11 P–QR3 N–N3 12 P–QN4 B–N5 13 P–B3 P–QR3= (Smyslov–Polugayevsky, U.S.S.R. Championship, 1961), or 3 . . . B–B4 4 B–N2 0–0 5 P–Q3 R–K1 6 KN–K2 P–B3 7 0–0 P–Q4 8 P×P N×P 9 K–R1 B–KN5 10 P–KR3 B–K3 11 N–K4 B–K2= (Portisch–Toran, Malaga, 1961).

3 ...	**P–Q4**
4 P×KP	

4 P×QP N×P 5 N×N Q×N 6 P×P N–B3 7 N–B3 B–KN5 8 B–K2 N×P=.

4 P–Q3 P×BP 5 B×P (5 P–K5 P–Q5) 5 . . . B–QN5 6 P×P N×P 7 B–Q2 B×N 8 P×B 0–0 9 N–B3 R–K1 ch 10 B–K2 Q–K2 11 P–B4 (Spielmann–Lasker, St. Petersburg, 1909) 11 . . . N–KB3 12 B–N5 B–N5∓.

4 ...	**N×P**

See Diagram 76.

76

With an open KB file and a pawn at K5 White hopes for a K-side attack. Nowadays masters consider that Black gains full equality by active counter-play in the centre.

5 P–Q3, it is probably best for White to deal at once with Black's advanced knight, 5 ... N×N, simplest and best, 6 P×N B–K2 (Black can simplify if he chooses by 6 ... P–Q5 7 N–B3 N–B3! 8 P×P B–N5 ch=, or 8 B–K2 B–QB4 9 0–0 0–0 10 K–R1 P×P 11 Q–K1 N–Q5=) 7 N–B3 0–0 8 P–Q4 P–KB3 9 B–Q3 P×P 10 N×P, and now 10 ... B–KB4 11 0–0 B×B 12 R×R ch B×R 13 Q×B N–Q2 14 B–B4 N×N= (Fine); or 10 ... Q–K1 11 Q–K2 N–Q2 12 N–B3 B–Q3 with good play for Black (Flórián–Lilienthal, Moscow, 1949).

5 N–B3 B–K2 (5 ... B–KN5 6 Q–K2 N–N4 7 P–Q3 B–K2 is playable) 6 P–Q4 (6 Q–K2 P–KB4 7 P–Q3 N–B4 8 P–Q4? N–K5∓, or 8 P–KN3 P–Q5 9 N–Q1 N–K3 10 B–N2 0–0 11 N–B2 N–B3=) 6 ... B–QN5! (or 6 ... 0–0 7 B–Q3 P–KB4 8 P×P e.p. B×P 9 0–0 N–B3) 7 Q–Q3 (the sacrifice 7 B–Q3 N×N 8 P×N is not clear. If instead 7 B–Q2 P–QB4 8 P×P B×N 9 P×B Q–R4=, or 8 N×N P×N 9 B×B P×B 10 N–N1 N–B3∓, Ivashin–Borisenko, Kuibyshev, 1948) 7 ... P–QB4 8 P×P, and now 8 ... N–QB3 (Alekhine) or 8 ... N×P 9 Q–K3 N–B3 10 B–QN5 N–K3 11 P–QR3 B–R4 12 P–QN4 B–N3 13 Q–Q3 0–0 14 Q×P (Spielmann–Marshall, New York, 1927) 14 ... B–Q2∓.

5 N×N P×N 6 P–Q4 P×P e.p. 7 B×P N–B3 8 N–B3 B–K2 9 B–Q2 B–K3∓.

5 Q–K2? N–QB3! 6 N×N? N–Q5 7 Q–Q1 (7 Q–Q3 P×N 8 Q×P B–KB4+) 7 ... P×N∓

5 Q–B3 N–QB3 (the simpler move, but 5 ... P–KB4 is also sound, 6 P×P e.p. N×P 7 P–Q4 B–K2 and ... 0–0, or 6 P–Q3 N×N 7 P×N P–Q5 8 Q–N3 N–B3 9 B–K2 B–K3 10 B–B3 Q–Q2!) 6 B–N5 (6 N×N N–Q5) 6 ... N×N 7 NP×N Q–R5 ch 8 P–N3 Q–K5 ch 9 Q×Q P×Q 10 B×N ch P×B 11 N–K2 B–K2, Black's bishops give him the better endgame. If 12 R–B1 0–0 13 R–B4 P–B3∓.

Chapter 3

The Scotch Opening

(1 P–K4 P–K4 2 P–Q4 P×P 3 N–KB3 N–QB3)

BY AND large 3 ... N–QB3 transposing to the Scotch Opening gives Black the widest choice of favourable possibilities. He could instead play 3 ... N–KB3—see Petroff's Defence, Normal Variation of the Modern Attack. Or he could play 3 ... B–B4 4 N×P N–KB3 5 N–QB3 P–Q4 6 P×P 0–0=. Even the anti-positional 3 ... P–QB4 seems feasible provided Black meets 4 P–B3 by 4 ... P–Q4, and 4 B–QB4 by 4 ... N–KB3 intending an early ... P–Q4.

See Diagram 77.

77

LINE 1 (*Continue from Diagram 77*)

4 N×P	**N–KB3**
5 N×N	

For 5 N–QB3 see the Four Knights Opening.

5 ...	**NP×N**

Play now divides into two main lines:
6 B–Q3 P–Q4 7 N–Q2 (for the time being White avoids undoubling Black's pawns. 7 P×P is playable, leading to a fairly level game. 7 P–K5 is not good, 7 ... N–N5 8 0–0

B–QB4∓, for now 9 B–KB4 P–B3 10 P×P 0–0!, or 9 Q–K2 Q–R5 10 P–KR3 P–KR4!, or 9 P–KR3 N×KP 10 R–K1 Q–B3 11 Q–K2 0–0∓) 7 ... B–QB4 8 0–0 0–0 9 Q–B3 *12.Q×N Q×P 13.KR1 B×P!* (9 P–KR3 R–K1 10 Q–B3 N–Q2=) 9 ... N–N5 10 P×P Q–Q3 11 Q–N3 Q×Q 12 P×Q P×P 13 N–N3 B–N3 with a good game for Black.

6 P–K5, this looks aggressive, but the pawn becomes an object of attack, **6 ... Q–K2 7 Q–K2 N–Q4 8 P–QB4** (8 N–Q2 B–N2 9 N–N3 0–0–0 10 P–QB4 N–N3 11 B–Q2 R–K1 12 P–B4 P–B3=) 8 ... B–R3 9 N–Q2 (9 Q–K4 N–N3) 9 ... N–N3 (9 ... N–N5 10 N–B3 P–QB4 11 P–QR3 N–B3 12 B–Q2 Q–K3 13 B–B3 is also good) 10 P–QN3 P–N3 11 N–K4? (11 B–N2 B–N2 12 0–0–0 0–0–0 13 P–B4 KR–K1 14 Q–B2 leaves White in less trouble on the K-file) 11 ... 0–0–0 12 B–N2 B–KN2 13 P–B4 KR–K1 14 Q–Q2 P–Q3 15 P–QB5?! B×B 16 K×B (16 P×N P×KP 17 P×RP R×Q+) 16 ... P×KP with great complications in Black's favour. *15.QR5 BN2 16.0-0-0 P×P 17.BQ3 KN1 18 NB5= (LUTIKOV–NEZHMETDINOV '52*

LINE 2 (*Continue from Diagram 77*)

        4 P–B3   **P×P**

There is no reason why Black should not accept the pawn. However, 4 ... P–Q4 is also a good move—see Centre Game, Chapter 4.

        5 B–QB4   **N–B3**

Taking more pawns is risky, 5 ... P×P 6 B×P B–N5 ch 7 N–B3 N–B3 8 Q–B2! (8 P–K5 P–Q4 9 P×N Q×P! 10 0–0 B×N 11 B×B Q×B 12 Q–K2 B–K3∓, Stein–Spassky, Tallinn, 1959) 8 ... P–Q3 9 0–0–0 B×N 10 Q×B B–K3 11 KR–K1 with great pressure along the centre files.

        6 N×P   **B–N5**
        7 0–0

7 P–K5 P–Q4 8 B–N3 N–K5 9 0–0 B×N 10 B×P B–B4 11 P×B N×QBP 12 B×N ch P×B 13 Q–K1 N–Q4=, or here 8 P×N P×B 9 Q×Q ch N×Q 10 P×P B×N ch 11 P×B R–KN1 12 B–R6 N–K3 13 0–0–0 N×P=.

        7 ...   **B×N**
        8 P×B   **P–Q3**

See Diagram 78.

     78

Here Black may play instead **8 . . . 0–0** 9 B–R3 (9 Q–B2 P–Q3 10 P–K5 N×P 11 N×N P×N 12 B–R3 R–K1=) 9 . . . R–K1 10 Q–N3 P–Q4=.

Examples from play:

9 B–R3 B–N5 10 B–N5 (10 Q–N3 N–QR4 11 B×P ch K–B1 12 Q–R4 B×N 13 P×B K×B 14 Q×N R–K1∓, Alekhine) 10 . . . 0–0 11 B×N P×B 12 P–K5 N–Q4∓ (Penrose–Smyslov, Munich, 1958).

9 P–K5 N×P 10 N×N P×N 11 Q–N3 (11 Q×Q ch K×Q 12 B×P K–K2 13 B–N3 B–K3∓, Yukhtman–Furman, U.S.S.R. Championship, 1959) 11 . . . Q–K2 12 B–R3 P–B4 13 Q–N5 ch N–Q2 14 QR–K1 0–0 15 P–B4 P–QR3 16 Q–N3 P–K5 17 R–K3 R–K1∓ (Penrose–Unzicker, Leipzig, 1960).

LINE 3 (*Continue from Diagram 77*)

4 B–QB4	**B–B4**

It is a question of taste and fashion whether Black plays the text or 4 . . . N–B3, given in the first edition at this point.

Arguably 4 . . . B–B4 is slightly preferable to avoid the line 5 P–K5 P–Q4 6 B–QN5 N–K5 7 N×P which has brought White some success in recent years.

4 . . . B–N5 ch is not to be recommended, 5 P–B3 P×P 6 0–0 (6 P×P B–R4 7 0–0 P–Q3 8 Q–N3 Q–Q2 9 P–K5 is also good) 6 . . . P–Q3 (6 . . . P×P 7 B×P N–B3 8 P–QR3 B–QB4 9 N–N5 with great pressure, or 6 . . . Q–B3 7 P–K5±) 7 P–QR3 B–R4 8 P–QN4 B–N3 9 Q–N3±.

5 P–B3

5 0–0 P–Q3 (5 . . . N–B3 leads to the famous Max Lange attack dating back to 1854. The complex variations arising after 6 P–K5 P–Q4 7 P×N P×B 8 R–K1 ch B–K3 9 N–N5 Q–Q4 10 N–QB3 Q–B4 11 QN–K4 0–0–0! 12 P–KN4 Q–K4 were long thought to give Black at least an even game, but the recent improvement 13 N×QB P×N 14 B–N5 casts some doubt on this) 6 P–B3 B–KN5! (a good counter-attacking line ignored in most modern reference works) 7 Q–N3 B×N! (7 . . . N–QR4 8 Q–R4 ch P–B3 9 P×P B×N 10 P×B B×P 11 B×P ch=) 8 B×P ch K–B1 9 B×N (9 P×B N–K4) 9 . . . R×B 10 P×B P–KN4! and it is Black who has the attack, e.g. 11 Q–Q1 Q–Q2 12 P–N4 B–N3 13 B–N2 P–Q6 14 Q×P N–K4 15 Q–K2 Q–R6 16 N–Q2 P–N5+ (Kolisch–Anderssen, Paris, 1860), or 11 Q–K6 N–K4 12 Q–B5 ch K–N2∓ (Reiner–Steinitz, Vienna, 1860).

5 . . .	**N–B3**

The soundest, transposing to a line of the Giuoco Piano which masters have long given up playing for White.

6 P×P

6 0–0 N×P 7 P×P P–Q4! 8 P×B P×B 9 Q×Q ch (9 Q–K2 Q–Q6∓) 9 . . . K×Q 10 R–Q1 ch B–Q2 11 B–K3 K–B1=.

6 P–K5 P–Q4 **7 B–QN5** N–K5 **8 P×P** (8 N×P B–Q2) 8 ... B–N3 **9 0–0** 0–0 **10 N–B3** B–N5=.

6 ...	**B–N5 ch**
7 B–Q2	

The Moller Attack **7 N–B3** seems ineffective, 7 ... N×P 8 0–0 B×N 9 P–Q5 B–B3 10 R–K1 N–K2 11 R×N P–Q3 12 B–N5 (12 P–KN4 0–0 13 P–N5 B–K4 14 N×B P×N 15 R×P N–N3∓) 12 ... B×B 13 N×B and now the long-established 13 ... 0–0 14 N×RP K×N 15 Q–R5 ch K–N1 16 R–R4 P–KB4 17 Q–R7 ch K–B2 18 R–R6 R–KN1 19 R–K1 leading to an early draw by perpetual check can be improved upon by 13 ... P–KR3 14 B–N5 ch (14 Q–K2 P×N 15 QR–K1 B–K3! 16 P×B P–KB3∓) 14 ... B–Q2 15 Q–K2 B×B 16 Q×B ch Q–Q2 17 Q–K2 (17 Q×P 0–0 18 QR–K1 N–N3 19 N–B3 KR–N1∓) 17...K–B1 and White has too little for his pawn, e.g. 18 N×P? K×N 19 R–K1 N–N1 20 P–B4 ~~N–B3~~ 21 R–K7 R–K1 + (Bárczay–Portisch, Budapest, 1969) or 18 N–B3 N×P∓.

(handwritten: 6 17...P–B3)

(handwritten: K–B1!)

7 ...	**B×B ch**
8 N×B	**P–Q4**

White also has very little after **8 ... N×KP 9 N×N** P–Q4 **10 Q–K2** 0–0 **11 0–0–0** B–N5 **12 P–KR3** B×N **13 P×B** P×B **14 Q×P** Q–R5 (Mednis–Fischer, New York, 1963).

8 P×P	**KN×P**
9 Q–N3	

See Diagram 79.

79

White has some pressure, but Black can neutralize it and then hope to exploit his sounder pawn structure.

10 ... QN–K2 11 0–0 0–0 12 KR–K1 P–QB3 13 P–QR4 Q–N3=.

10 ... N–R4 (Tarrasch's recommendation which has hardly ever been tried. The queen is driven from its best post, and unless White is prepared to accept a draw by repetition he must fall in with Black's wishes) 11 Q–R4 ch N–QB3! 12 Q–N3 N–R4 13 Q–R4 ch N–QB3 14 N–K5 0–0! 15 N×N Q–K1 ch! 16 B–K2 P×N with free play for Black, while White cannot easily castle. 16 ... N–B5 looks even stronger, which implies that White must give up castling straight away in answer to 15 ... Q–K1 ch.

Chapter 4

The Centre Opening

(1 P–K4 P–K4 2 P–Q4 P×P)

LINE 1

       3 Q×P

This is the Centre Game, practically abandoned in master chess for decades. There are some recent suggestions to strengthen White's play, but if correctly countered all lines tend to react in Black's favour.

       3 ...   **N–QB3**
       4 Q–K3

W. Paulsen's move, which gave the Centre Game a short lease of life in the 1880s. According to modern ideas the queen should not be too exposed in the middle of the board, so by analogy with the Centre Counter (1 P–K4 P–Q4 2 P×P Q×P 3 N–QB3 Q–QR4) **4 Q–R4** is suggested as objectively better. Then 4 ... P–Q4 may be premature in view of 5 B–QN5 B–Q2 6 P×P N–N5 7 N–QB3, or 5 N–QB3! (Harding). Pachmann's 4 ... B–B4 5 N–KB3 KN–K2 6 N–B3 0–0 can be met by 7 B–KN5 P–KR3 (7 ... B–QN5 8 Q–N3) 8 B–R4 P–Q3 9 0–0–0 Q–K1 10 N–Q5± (Sokotow–Szewczyk, correspondence, 1968–70). We suggest **4 ... N–B3** 5 B–KN5 (5 N–QB3 B–N5 6 B–Q2 0–0 7 0–0–0 R–K1 8 B–Q3 P–Q3=) 5 ... B–K2 6 N–QB3 P–Q4!=.

    4 Q–B4 N–B3 5 N–QB3 P–Q4=.

       4 ...   **N–B3**

See Diagram 80.

80

Most other moves give White some attacking chances, whereas now White has very little indeed.

5 P–K5, the point here, as shown by Berger, is that this move does not gain the advantage for White, 5 ... N–KN5, and now (1) 6 Q–K4 P–Q4 7 P×P e.p. ch B–K3 8 B–QR6 (8 P×P· Q×P with a lead in development. The spectacular 8 ... Q–Q8 ch is also possible) 8 ... Q×P 9 B×P Q–N5 ch 10 Q×Q N×Q 11 N–QR3 R–QN1 12 B–K4 B–QB4∓ (Levin–Beylin, U.S.S.R., 1949). (2) 6 Q–K2 P–Q3 7 P–KB3 (7 P×P ch B–K3 8 P×P Q×P∓, or 7 P–KR3 KN×KP 8 P–KB4 N–Q5 9 Q–K4 P–QB4 10 N–R3 Q–R5 ch +) 7 ... N–R3 8 P×P ch B–K3, and now 9 B×N Q–R5 ch∓, or 9 P×P Q×P 10 B×N N–Q5 +.

5 N–QB3, and now (1) 5 ... B–N5 6 B–Q2 0–0 7 0–0–0 R–K1 8 B–B4 (8 P–B3 P–Q4 9 Q–B2 P×P∓, or 8 Q–N3 R×P 9 B–KN5 B×N 10 Q×B P–KR3 11 P–B3 R–K1 12 B–R4 P–Q3∓, Gliksman–Fuderer, Zagreb, 1959, or 9 B–Q3 R–N5 10 Q–R3 P–Q3∓) 8 ... P–Q3 (better than 8 ... N–QR4 9 B–Q3 P–Q4 10 P–K5 P–Q5 11 Q–N3 P×N 12 B–KN5) 9 N–B3 (9 P–B3 N–K4 10 B–N3 B–K3 11 P–N4 P–B3 12 P–N5 KN–Q2∓, or 9 N–R3 N–QR4 10 B–Q3 P–Q4 11 Q–N3 P×P∓) 9 ... B–K3 10 B×B R×B 11 N–KN5 R–K1 12 P–B4 P–KR3 13 P–KR4 Q–B1 14 Q–B3 K–B1 15 N–Q5 N×N∓ (Tartakover–Reshevsky, Stockholm, 1937). (2) 5 ... B–K2 6 B–B4 0–0 (or 6 ... N–QN5 7 Q–K2 P–Q4) 7 B–Q2 (7 KN–K2 N–KN5 8 Q–Q2 B–B4 9 N–Q1 Q–K2 10 P–KB3 Q–R5 ch 11 P–N3 KN–K4 12 P×Q N×P ch 13 K–B1 P–Q4 14 K–N2 N×Q 15 B×P B–KN5∓, Troianescu–Spassky, Budapest, 1958) 7 ... P–Q3 8 0–0–0 B–K3 9 B×B P×B 10 Q–R3 Q–Q2 11 KN–K2 P–K4 12 Q×Q N×Q=.

5 B–Q2 B–K2 (5 ... B–N5 is playable, for 6 N–QB3 transposes to the preceding paragraph, and 6 P–QB3 B–K2 rather favours Black) 6 N–QB3 P–Q4 7 P×P N×P 8 N×N Q×N 9 N–K2 B–KN5 10 N–B4 Q–Q2 11 P–KB3 0–0–0 12 0–0–0 B–KB4∓.

5 B–K2 Q–K2 6 N–QB3 P–Q4 7 P×P N–QN5 8 B–Q3 KN×P 9 N×N N×N 10 Q×Q ch B×Q∓ (Mason–Schlechter, Paris, 1900).

LINE 2 **(1 P–K4 P–K4 2 P–Q4 P×P)**

3 P–QB3

Played several times by Severin From, of Denmark, at Paris, 1867. His handling of it was far from dynamic, but since then it has been called the Danish Gambit. Black must play exactly, since in the hands of an attacking player it can be a formidable weapon.

3...   P–Q4

Declining the gambit is the simplest course. An alternative of a more combative kind is 3 ... **Q–K2**, favoured by Chigorin. Play continues 4 P×P (4 P–B3 P–Q4! or 4 Q–K2 N–KB3 5 N–Q2 P–Q4 6 P–K5 P–Q6∓, or 4 Q×P P–KB4=, or 4 B–Q3 P–Q4∓) 4 ... Q×P ch 5 B–K3 (5 B–K2 Q×NP 6 B–B3 Q–N3 7 N–B3 B–N5 8 N–K2 N–K2∓) 5 ... N–KB3 6 N–KB3 B–N5 ch 7 N–B3 0–0∓.

4 KP×P	Q×P
5 P×P	N–QB3
6 N–KB3	

This position could also have arisen from the sequence 1 P–K4 P–K4 2 P–Q4 P×P 3 N–KB3 N–QB3 4 P–B3 P–Q4 (see the note in Line 2 of the Scotch Opening) 5 KP×P Q×P 6 P×P.

6...	**B–N5**

6...N–B3 7 N–B3 B–QN5 8 B–K2 N–K5 is a good equalizing line, 9 B–Q2 B×N 10 P×B N×B 11 Q×N 0–0 12 0–0 Q–Q3 13 QR–N1 P–QN3 14 B–Q3 P–KR3 15 KR–K1 B–Q2 16 R–K3 QR–K1= (Klovan–Averbakh, U.S.S.R., 1969).

7 B–K2

See Diagram 81.

81

Black now has the following options:

7 ... B–N5 ch 8 N–B3 QB×N 9 B×B Q–B5 10 B–K3 (10 B×N ch P×B 11 Q–K2 ch=, Black has a satisfactory endgame, providing that he does not carelessly exchange minor pieces, or 10 Q–N3 Q×Q 11 P×Q N×P 12 B×P with complications in which Black can hold his own, 12 ... N–B7 ch 13 K–K2 N×R 14 B×R N×P 15 B–B6 ch K–Q1 16 R–Q1 ch K–B1 17 N–Q5 B–B4=, Ljubojevich–Stein, Yugoslavia–U.S.S.R., 1972) 10 ... B×N ch (usually bad, but here Black has a definite purpose) 11 P×B Q×P ch 12 K–B1 Q–B5 ch 13 K–N1 KN–K2 14 R–B1 Q×RP 15 R–R1 Q–B5 16 R–B1 Q–R7 ½ : ½ (Marshall–Capablanca, Lake Hopatcong, 1926, Game 50). These moves cannot be improved upon, so it is evident that Black has a forced draw.

7 ... N–B3 8 N–B3 Q–QR4 9 B–K3 B–Q3 and now 10 B–Q2 is an awkward move to meet.

7 ... 0–0–0 8 B–K3 N–B3 9 N–B3 (9 P–KR3 B–N5 ch 10 N–B3 B×N 11 B×B Q–B5∓) 9 ... Q–QR4 10 0–0 B–QB4 (10 ... K–N1 11 P–QR3 N–Q4 is to be considered) 11 P–QR3 (recommended by Keres. If 11 Q–N3 B×P 12 N×B N×N 13 B×B ch N×B 14 Q×P KR–B1 15 Q–K7 **Q–K4**=) 11 ... B–N3 12 N–QN5 B×N 13 P×B N×P 14 N×N R×N! (14 ... Q–K4 15 P–B4!) 15 B×R R–Q1. White has won the exchange, or Black has sacrificed it. The chances are about even.

Chapter 5

The King's Gambit

(1 P–K4 P–K4 2 P–KB4 P×P)

You are advised to accept the King's Gambit, because this offers a wide choice of reasonable defences, though there is the recent imaginative **2 ... Q–R5 ch 3 P–KN3 Q–K2 4 P×P P–Q3!** 5 P×P Q×P ch 6 Q–K2 Q×Q ch=, or 4 N–KB3 P×P 5 N–B3 P–Q4 6 N×P Q×P ch 7 Q–K2 Q×Q ch 8 B×Q B–Q3=.

THE KNIGHT'S GAMBIT (3 N–KB3)

See Diagram 82.

82

LINE 1 (*Continue from Diagram 82*)

    3 ...   **B–K2**

This is the line for Black to play if he wants to equalize rapidly.

    4 B–B4

    4 N–B3 N–KB3 (the check is not good, 4 ... B–R5 ch 5 K–K2 P–Q4 6 N×P N–KB3 7 N×N ch Q×N 8 P–K5 Q–K2 9 P–Q4 0–0 10 P–KN3 B–N4 11 P×P±, Prins–Zuidema, tie-match, Dutch Championship, 1965) and now (1) 5 P–K5 N–N5 6 P–Q4 (6 P–KR3 B–R5 ch) 6 ... N–K6 7 B×N P×B 8 B–B4 P–Q3 9 0–0 0–0 10 Q–Q3 N–B3 11 P×P (Spassky–

* 5...PQ3 6.PQ4 BN5= MCO12

138

Kholmov, Moscow, 1964) 11 ... B×P 12 Q×P B–K2=. (2) 5 P–Q4 P–Q4 6 B–Q3 (6 P–K5 N–K5 7 B×P P–QB4 8 B–N5 ch B–Q2=) 6 ... P×P 7 N×P N–Q4=, or here 7 ... N–B3 8 B×P 0–0 9 P–B3 N×N 10 B×N B–R5 ch!= (Lukin–Faibisovich, Leningrad, 1967).

4 ...	**N–KB3**
5 P–K5	

5 N–B3 N×P! 6 B×P ch (6 N–K5 N–N4 7 P–Q4 P–Q3 8 N–Q3 P–B6∓) 6 ... K×B. 7 N–K5 ch K–N1 8 N×N P–Q3 9 N–KB3 P–Q4 10 N–B2 N–B3 with good play for Black. **5 Q–K2** P–Q4 6 P×P N×P 7 N–B3 B–K3=.

5 ...	**N–N5**

White can get no real advantage:

6 N–B3 P–Q3 7 P×P (7 P–Q4 P×P 8 P×P Q×Q ch 9 N×Q B–KB4=) 7 ... Q×P= (Euwe), or 7 ... B×P 8 Q–K2 ch Q–K2 9 Q×Q ch K×Q 10 P–Q4 R–K1 11 0–0 P–KR3=.

6 P–Q4 P–Q4 7 B–N3? (7 B–Q3 B–R5 ch 8 K–K2 N–B7 9 Q–K1 N×B∓) 7 ... B–R5 ch 8 K–B1 P–QN3+ (Kramer–Euwe, match, 1941).

6 0–0 N–QB3 7 P–Q4 P–Q4 8 P×P e.p.? (8 B–K2 N–K6=) 8 ... B×P 9 N–B3 (9 R–K1 ch K–B1) 9 ... 0–0∓ (Keres–Alatortsev, U.S.S.R. Championship, 1960).

6 Q–K2 0–0 7 P–Q4 P–Q3 8 QB×P P×P 9 P×P N–QB3 10 N–B3 N–Q5=.

LINE 2 (*Continue from Diagram 82*)

3 ...	**P–Q4**

This classical answer leads to interesting middlegames with chances for both sides.

4 P×P	**N–KB3**

See Diagram 83.

83

There are two main lines here:

5 N–B3 N×P 6 N×N Q×N 7 P–Q4 B–K2 8 P–B4 (Korchnoy recommends the unclear 8 B–K2 P–KN4 9 0–0 with some attacking chances for White, but Black has no need to be greedy and should equalize by 8 ... P–QB4) **8 ... Q–K5 ch,** and now (1) 9 B–K2 N–B3

10 0–0 B–KB4 11 R–K1 0–0–0=. (2) 9 K–B2 B–KB4 10 P–B5 (10 B–K2 N–B3 11 R–K1 0–0–0 12 B–B1 Q–B7∓) 10 ... N–B3 11 B–N5 Q–Q4 12 R–K1 B–K5 13 Q–K2 P–B4 14 B×P 0–0–0 15 QR–Q1 B–B3 16 B×N Q×B 17 B–K5 KR–K1 18 B×B P×B with good play for Black.

5 B–N5 ch, the sternest test of this line, 5 ... P–B3 (enterprising; the safe 5 ... B–Q2 is less clear after 6 B–B4) **6 P×P P×P** (the time-honoured move; Spassky's innovation 6 ... N×P, originated in a simultaneous game against him, continues 7 P–Q3 B–Q3 8 0–0! 0–0 9 QN–Q2 B–KN5 10 N–B4 with White for choice) **7 B–B4** (Pachman recommends the untested 7 B–K2 B–Q3 8 P–QN3 0–0 9 N–R3) 7 ... N–Q4 8 N–B3! (8 P–Q4 B–Q3 9 0–0 0–0 10 N–B3 N×N 11 P×N B–KN5∓, Bronstein–Botvinnik, U.S.S.R. Championship, or 8 0–0 B–Q3 9 N–B3 B–K3 10 N–K4 B–B2 11 B–N3 0–0 12 P–Q4 N–Q2 13 P–B4 N–K6=, Tal–Haubt, Prague, 1960) 8 ... N×N 9 NP×N B–Q3 10 Q–K2 ch Q–K2 11 Q×Q ch K×Q=.

Finally, if **5 B–B4** B–Q3; or if 5 P–B4 P–B3 6 P–Q4 B–N5 ch 7 N–B3 P×P 8 B×P 0–0 9 **B**–K2 P×P 10 B×P N–Q4!∓ (Korchnoy).

Game 51   Bronstein–Botvinnik, Moscow, 1952. 1 P–K4 P–K4 2 P–KB4 P×P 3 N–KB3 P–Q4 4 P×P N–KB3 5 B–N5 ch P–B3 6 P×P P×P 7 B–B4 N–Q4 8 P–Q4 **B**–Q3 9 0–0 0–0 10 N–B3 N×N 11 NP×N B–N5 12 Q–Q3 N–Q2 13 P–N3 N–N3! 14 B–N3 P–B4 15 P–B4 Q–B3 16 N–K5 B×N 17 P×B Q×P 18 B×P Q–R4 19 KR–K1 KR–K1 20 P–QR4 B–K7 21 Q–QB3 N–Q2! 22 P–R5 N–B3 23 B–R4 R–K3 24 K–N2? N–K5 25 Q–R3 P–N4. 0 : 1 after the bishop retreats comes R–KB3. 24 Q–Q2 would have prolonged the resistance.

THE BISHOP'S AND OTHER GAMBITS

LINE 1 (*The Bishop's Gambit*; 1 P–K4 P–K4 2 P–KB4 P×P 3 B–B4)

3 ...	N–KB3

The best move, and the chief reason why the Bishop's Gambit is no longer considered effective for White.

3 ... **P–Q4** leads to simplifying equality, **4 B×P** (4 P×P Q–R5 ch 5 K–B1 B–Q3 6 N–KB3 Q–R4 7 N–B3 N–K2 8 P–Q4 0–0 9 N–K4 N×P=) **4 ... N–KB3** (4 ... Q–R5 ch 5 K–B1 is also sound for Black, 5 ... N–KB3 6 N–QB3 B–QN5=, or 5 ... B–Q3 6 P–Q4 N–K2 7 N–QB3 P–KB3 8 N–B3 Q–R4 9 B–B4 P–B3=) **5 N–QB3 B–QN5 6 N–B3** (6 KN–K2 B×N 7 NP×B N×B 8 P×N Q–R5 ch 9 K–B1 B–N5 10 Q–K1 Q×Q ch 11 K×Q P–B6∓, or 6 Q–B3 0–0 7 KN–K2 R–K1∓) **6 ... B×N 7 QP×B P–B3=.**

4 N–QB3	

If **4 P–K5** P–Q4. If **4 P–Q4** N×P. If **4 P–Q3** P–Q4. If **4 Q–K2** P–Q4 5 P×P ch B–K2 6 N–KB3 0–0= (Gheorghiu–Portisch, Amsterdam, 1970)

4 ...	P–B3
5 Q–B3	

White appears to have nothing better than this somewhat artificial move. If **5 B–N3** P–Q4 6 P×P P×P 7 P–Q4 B–Q3∓; or if **5 N–B3** P–QN4 6 B–N3 P–N5 7 N–QR4 N×P+; or if **5 Q–K2** P–Q4 6 P×P ch B–K2 and now 7 P×P N×P 8 N–B3 0–0 9 0–0 B–B4 ch 10 K–R1 B–KN5∓, or 7 P–Q4 0–0 8 N–B3 P×P 9 B–Q3 B–Q3 10 0–0 N–B3∓ (Milev–Barcza, Bucharest, 1953); or if **5 P–Q4** B–N5 6 Q–B3 P–Q4 7 P×P 0–0 8 N–K2 P×P 9 B–Q3 B–N5 10 Q×BP B×KN∓ or 6. P·K5 N·K5 7. Q·B3 P·Q4! 8. P·PeP 0-0 9. N–K2 Q–R5ch 10. P·N3 P×P 11. P×P Q–N5 12. Q×Q B×Q 13. B·Q3 R–K1∓ (Sokolski)

5 ...	P–Q4
6 P×P	B–Q3

See Diagram 84.

84

White cannot gain any opening advantage.

7 KN–K2 0–0 8 0–0 (8 N×P B–KN5 9 Q–B2 B×N 10 Q×B R–K1 ch∓) 8...B–KN5 9 Q–B2 P×P (9 ... P–QN4 is also good) 10 B–N3 N–B3, or 10 ... P–B6 with good prospects for Black.

7 P–Q4 0–0 8 B×P B–KN5 9 Q–N3 R–K1 ch 10 K–B1 B×B 11 Q×KB P×P 12 B–Q3 N–B3∓.

7 P–Q3 B–KN5 8 Q–B2 0–0 9 B×P R–K1 ch 10 K–B1 (10 K–Q2 B–N5 11 P–Q6 P–QN4 12 B–QN3 B×P 13 B×B Q×B∓) 10...B×B 11 Q×B P×P 12 N×P N×N 13 B×N Q×B 14 Q×B N–B3 15 N–B3 Q–QB4=.

LINE 2 (*The Lesser Bishop's Gambit*: 1 P–K4 P–K4 2 P–KB4 P×P 3 B–K2)

3 ...	P–Q4

Even simpler perhaps is **3 ... N–K2** 4 P–Q4 (4 N–QB3 P–Q4 5 P×P N×P 6 N×N Q×N 7 N–B3=) 4 ... P–Q4 5 P×P N×P 6 N–KB3 B–N5 ch 7 P–B3 B–K2 8 0–0 0–0 9 P–B4 N–K6 with a fine game for Black (Tartakover–Alekhine, New York, 1924).

4 P×P	N–KB3
5 P–B4	

For **5 P–Q4** N×P, see above note.

5 ...	P–B3
6 P–Q4	B–N5 ch

See Diagram 85.

85

From White's point of view the sedate Line 2 is better than the complex Line 1, since he can now equalize without any trouble.

7 B–Q2 B×B ch 8 Q×B P×P 9 N–KB3 N–B3=. Play might continue 10 0–0 P×P 11 B×P 0–0 12 N–B3 B–N5 13 QR–Q1 Q–N3.

7 K–B1 P×P 8 P×P (Alekhine commends 8 P–B5 0–0 9 B×P N–K5 as being better for White) 8 ... P×P 9 B×N (naïve to say the least) 9 ... N–Q4!∓ (Tartakover–Capablanca, New York, 1924).

7 N–B3 P×P (7 ... N–K5! says Alekhine) 8 B×P (8 N–B3 P×P 9 QB×P 0–0 10 0–0 B×N 11 P×B B–K3∓) 8 ... P×P 9 B×P 0–0 10 KN–K2 B–N5 11 0–0 QN–Q2 12 Q–N3 B×QN (Tartakover–Bogolyubov, New York, 1924). White has, perhaps, a slight edge.

LINE 3 (*The Keres Gambit:* 1 P–K4 P–K4 2 P–KB4 P×P 3 N–QB3)

As in the previous two lines White provokes Black into ... Q–R5 ch, but this time the disruption in White's game outweighs the drawbacks to bringing out the queen early.

3...	Q–R5 ch
4 K–K2	P–Q4
5 N×P	

See Diagram 86.

86

White's king has been displaced in the hope of obtaining a strong centre. Black sacrifices his QP so as to obtain an attack against White's king. There can follow:

5 ... B–N5 ch 6 N–B3 N–QB3 (fainter hearts will prefer 6 ... B–Q3 7 P–Q4 N–QB3

8 P–K5 0–0–0 9 B×P! KN–K2 10 P–B4, Spassky–Furman, Tallinn, 1959, and now 10 . . . B–N5∓, or **7**. . .N–K2**8** N×N Q×N**9** P–K5 P–KB3∓) 7 N×P ch K–Q1 8 N×R N–Q5 ch 9 K–Q3 Q–B3 10 P–B4 N–K2 11 P–K5 KN–B3∓ (J. E. Littlewood). If here 10 P–K5 B–B4 ch 11 K–B3 (11 K×N Q–K2+) 11...Q–K2 12 P–QN3 B×P, or 12 P–QR3 B×P 13 Q–K1 Q–B4 ch 14 B–B4 P–QN4∓ (Fuller). See also Game 52.

LINE 4 *(The Breyer Gambit:* 1 P–K4 P–K4 2 P–KB4 P×P 3 Q–B3)

An attempt by a leading hypermodern to play the King's Gambit in a more positional way, laying stress on the open KB file, rather than on straightforward development. If Black now checks White answers P–KN3 opening files on the K-side.

3 . . .	N–QB3

3 . . . P–Q4 4 P×P B–Q3 (4 . . . N–KB3 5 N–B3 B–N5 6 Q×P B–Q3 7 Q–K3 ch B–K2 8 B–B4±, Planinc–Gligorich, Pula, 1968) 5 B–N5 ch N–Q2=.

4 P–B3	

After **4 N–K2** or **4 Q×P**, then 4 . . . P–Q4.

4 . . .	N–B3
5 P–Q4	P–Q4
6 P–K5	N–K5
7 B×P	

7 B–N5 Q–R5 ch 8 K–B1 P–KN4∓.

7 . . .	P–B3

Or 7 . . . B–K2 8 N–Q2 (8 B–Q3 P–B4 9 P×P e.p. B×P 10 N–K2= is correct) 8 . . . P–B4 9 P×P e.p. N×KBP 10 B–Q3 0–0 11 N–K2? (11 N–R3 B–KN5 12 Q–K3 Q–Q2 13 0–0 QR–K1∓, Spielmann–Grunfeld, Baden-Baden, 1925) 11 . . . B–KN5, see Game 53.

8 B–QN5	

After **8 B–Q3** P×P 9 B×N P×KB 10 Q×P B–K2, Black's position is worth more than the pawn.

8 . . .	B–K2
9 P×P	B×P
10 N–Q2	

10 N–K2 0–0 11 0–0 P–KN4±.

91 . . .	N×N

After 11 K×N (best) 11...0–0 Black has a very satisfactory game.

Game 52   Lein–Terentyev, U.S.S.R. Championship Preliminaries, 1966. 1 P–K4 P–K4 2 P–KB4 P×P 3 N–QB3 Q–R5 ch 4 K–K2 P–Q4 5 N×P B–N5 ch 6 N–B3 N–QB3 7 N×P ch K–Q1 8 N–Q5 P–B4 9 P–K5 N×P 10 N–B3 B–N5 11 P–Q4 N×N 12 P×N B×N 13 B–N2 N–B3 14 K–Q3 N–K5 15 Q–B1 Q–B3 16 P×KB Q–R3 ch 17 P–B4 R–QB1 18 B×P Q×P ch 19 K–K3 Q×BP. 0 : 1.

Game 53   Drimer–Unzicker, Hastings, 1969–70. 1 P–K4 P–K4 2 P–KB4 P×P 3 Q–B3 N–QB3 4 P–B3 N–B3 5 P–Q4 P–Q4 6 P–K5 N–K5 7 B×P B–K2 8 N–Q2 P–B4 9 P×P e.p. N×KBP 10 B–Q3 0–0 11 N–K2 B–KN5 12 Q–B2? N–KR4! 13 P–KN3 N×B 14 P×N B–R5 15 N–KN3 Q–K2 ch 16 K–B1 B–R6 ch 17 K–N1 Q–Q3 18 P–B5 N–K2 19 Q–K3 N×P 20 B×N B×B 21 R–K1 B–R6 22 Q–K5 Q–KN3 23 Q×QP ch K–R1 24 R–K3 Q–B7 25 N(3)–B1 B–B7 mate.

THE KING'S GAMBIT DECLINED

If Black wishes to dictate the course of events in the King's Gambit he will decline it. We recommend as a good defence 2...N–KB3. Black avoids many complications, and can hope to equalize by straightforward play.

3 P×P

3 N–KB3 N×P 4 P×P is merely a transposition. If **4 P–Q3 N–B4 5 P×P P–Q4** (5 ... P–Q3 6 P–Q4) 6 P–Q4 N–K5 (6 ... N–K3 intending an early P–QB4 looks safer, 7 B–Q3 P–QB4 8 P–B3 N–B3=, Showalter–Pollock, New York, 1889, or 7 P–B4 P–QB3) 7 B–Q3 B–K2 8 0–0 0–0 9 P–B4 (Bronstein–Kostro, Tbilisi, 1970) 9 ... P–QB3 10 Q–B2 B–KB4 11 N–B3 N–R3! or 11 KN–Q2 N×N 12 R×B N×P with good equalizing chances.

3 N–QB3 P–Q4 transposes to the Vienna Opening, Chapter 2, Line 2.

3 ...	**N×P**
4 N–KB3	**N–N4**

See Diagram 87.

87

The key move in the defence, despite its bad appearance due to the loss of tempi. Black plays to remove the defending knight so that he can force ...Q–R5 ch. This simplifies the position by exchanges. **4 ... P–Q4 5 P–Q3** transposes to the previous note.

5 P–Q4

Steinitz preferred **5 P–B3** P–Q3 (5 ... N×N ch 6 Q×N Q–N4 7 B–K2! Q×KP 8 0–0 Q–K2 9 P–Q4 with excellent attacking chances after 10 Q–N3 and then B–N5 or B–R5, Chigorin–Bernstein, Kiev, 1903) 6 P–Q4 (6 P×P? B×P 7 P–Q4 Q–K2 ch 8 K–B2 N–K5 ch 9 K–N1 0–0 10 B–Q3 P–KB4 11 P–B4 P–B4!∓, Steinitz–Barbour, Philadelphia, 1883; or 6 N×N Q×N 7 P–Q4 Q–R5 ch forcing the king to move) 6 ... N×N ch 7 Q×N Q–R5 ch 8 P–KN3 Q–N5 9 Q×Q B×Q 10 B–N2 P–B3= (Ravinsky).

5 B–N5 (the introduction to a piece sacrifice suggested by the Australian Hay. Obviously not 5 B–B4? N×N ch 6 Q×N Q–R5 ch +) 5 ... P–QR3 (or 5 ... P–QB3 creating an extra weakness at Q3) 6 0–0! P×B 7 P–Q4 N–K3 (7 ... N×N ch 8 Q×N Q–K2 9 N–B3, then N–Q5, or N–K4 with a powerful attack) 8 P–Q5 B–B4 ch 9 K–R1 0–0 10 N–B3! with good attacking chances. Black's correct response to 5 B–N5 is 5 ... B–B4 6 P–B3 (6 P–Q4 loses the QP) 6 ... N×N ch 7 Q×N P–QR3 8 P–Q4 (8 B–K2 Q–N4) 8 ... P×B 9 P×B Q–R5 ch! 10 P–KN3 Q–QB5∓. Black still prevents castling, and threatens to take the QBP or QRP.

5 ...	N×N ch
6 Q×N	Q–R5 ch
7 Q–B2	

7 P–KN3 Q×QP is a bad gambit, since White has no aggressive square on which to develop his KB.

7 ...	Q×Q ch
8 K×Q	P–Q3

8 ... N–B3 9 P–B3! (9 B–K3 P–Q3 10 P×P B×P 11 N–B3 B–KB4 12 R–B1 P–QR3 13 B–K2 0–0 with easy equality, Bronstein–Bernstein, Paris, 1954) 9 ... P–Q3 10 P×P B×P 11 N–Q2 B–K3 12 N–K4 B–K2 13 N–N5 B×N 14 B×B P–KR3 15 B–KR4 P–KN4 16 B–N3 0–0 17 B–N5 with some pressure (Fischer–Wade, Vinkovci, 1968).

9 B–KB4	N–B3
10 B–QN5	B–Q2
11 B×N	B×B
12 P×P	B×P

Black may try to exploit his two bishops either by **12 ... P×P** 13 R–K1 ch K–Q1 14 N–B3 P–Q4, or by the gambit line **12 ... 0–0–0** 13 P–Q5! (13 P×P R×P 14 B–K3 B–B4 threatening 15 ... R–KB5 ch, or here 14 ... R–QN5 15 P–QN3 R–N5 16 R–N1 B–Q3 17 P–N3 B–K4 with excellent prospects) 13 ... B×P 14 P×P (14 N–B3 P–QB3=) 14 ... B–B4 ch 15 K–N3 R–Q2 with good chances.

13 B×B	P×B
14 N–B3	

Korchnoy thinks that White has some endgame advantage, but it seems very slight after 14 ... 0–0–0.

Chapter 6

The Bishop's Opening

(1 P–K4 P–K4 2 B–B4)

2 ...	N–KB3

Although known since 1561 (Lopez) this is called the Berlin Defence because it was played in a famous correspondence game, Posen–Berlin, 1839; since when the opening fell out of favour (see Part 1, Chapter 11 for the opening moves of the game).

The opening was revived in 1964 by Larsen who played it in the Interzonal Tournament and the following year against Portisch in his Candidates Match. The opening has had a great deal of attention devoted to it in Britain culminating in the publication of T. D. Harding's monograph on the subject in 1973. Black equalizes without much difficulty.

3 P–Q3

3 P–Q4 P×P (3 ... P–Q4 is playable, 4 QP×P P×B 5 Q×Q ch K×Q 6 P×N P×P 7 N–QB3 P–B3 with two bishops in an open position, or 4 KP×P P–K5 intending ... QN–Q2–N3 with unclear consequences) 4 N–KB3—see Petroff's Defence.

3 P–B4 N×P (Harding recommends 3 ... P–Q4 4 KP×P P–K5 transposing to a variation of the Falkbeer Counter Gambit considered good for Black, but Larsen continues 5 P–Q3 B–KN5 6 N–K2 B–QB4 7 P–Q4 with slight advantage to White) 4 P–Q3 (4 Q–B3 P–Q4 5 P×P Q–R5 ch 6 P–KN3 N×P 7 P×N Q×B=) 4 ... N–Q3 5 B–N3 N–B3 (or 5 ... P–K5 6 P×P N×P 7 B×P ch K×B 8 Q–Q5 ch K–K1 9 Q×N ch Q–K2 with slight advantage to Black in view of his bishops, Larsen) 6 N–KB3 P×P 7 B×P B–K2 8 0–0 0–0 9 N–B3 N–B4 10 P–Q4∓.

3 ...	P–B3

See Diagram 88.

88

3 ... **N–B3** is sound if less enterprising, 4 P–B4 (4 N–QB3 transposing to the Vienna is better) 4 ... P×P 5 B×P P–Q4 6 P×P N×P 7 B–Q2 B–QB4∓, Spielmann–Chigorin, Nuremberg, 1906, or 7 B×N Q×B 8 N–KB3 B–KN5 9 0–0 0–0–0∓ (Alapin–Chigorin, St. Petersburg, 1881).

3 ... **P–Q4** is premature as the KP comes under pressure, 4 P×P N×P 5 N–KB3 N–QB3 6 0–0 B–KN5 7 R–K1 B–K2 8 P–KR3, and if 8 ... B×N 9 Q×B N–Q5 10 Q–N4+ (Larsen–Berger, Amsterdam, 1964).

Black cannot be prevented from forming a pawn centre, gaining time by attacking White's KB.

4 N–KB3 P–Q4 5 P×P (5 B–N3 B–N5 ch 6 P–B3 B–Q3 7 B–N5 P×P 8 P×P Q–K2=) 5 ... P×P 6 B–N3 (6 B–N5 ch B–Q2 7 B×B ch QN×B 8 0–0 B–Q3=, Schnitzler–L. Paulsen, Berlin, 1867) 6 ... B–N5 ch (to block White's QB3 square) 7 P–B3 B–Q3 8 B–N5 B–K3 9 P–Q4 P–K5 10 N–K5, and Black has fully equalized; 10 ... QN–Q2 11 P–KB4 P×P e.p. 12 N×PB3 Q–B2 (Adams–Steiner, St. Louis, 1941).

4 Q–K2 (an artificial attempt to prevent Black's central advance) 4 ... B–K2 (4 ... P–Q4 is still possible as a gambit, 5 P×P P×P 6 Q×P ch B–K2 7 B–N5 ch B–Q2 with some compensation for the pawn) 5 P–B4 (5 N–KB3 0–0 6 B–N3 P–Q4 7 0–0 B–KN5 8 P–KR3 B–R4=, Ubivala–Gulko, Batumi, 1969) 5 ... P–Q4 6 P×QP (6 BP×P N×P) 6 ... P×BP 7 B×P (for 7 N–KB3 see Game 54) 7 ... 0–0 8 QN–Q2 (8 P×P N×P 9 N–QB3 N–Q5 10 Q–Q2 B–QN5 11 P–QR3 R–K1 ch 12 K–B1 B–R4 13 P–QN4 B–N3 14 N–R4 N–R4+, Adams–Levin, Ventnor City, 1941) 8 ... P×P 9 B–N3 P–QR4∓ (Alekhine).

Game 54   Barrett–Hooper, Surrey Championship, 1955. 1 P–K4 P–K4 2 B–B4 N–KB3 3 P–Q3 P–B3 4 Q–K2 B–K2 5 P–B4 P–Q4 6 P×QP P×BP 7 N–KB3 N×P 8 0–0 0–0 9 B×N P×B 10 B×P N–B3 11 N–B3 B–K3 12 K–R1 R–B1 13 Q–B2 B–B3 14 QR–K1 N–N5 15 N–K5 N×BP 16 R–K2 N–N5 17 Q×P B–B4 18 P–Q4 B×N 19 R×B N–B3 20 Q×P N×R 21 B×N B–Q6 22 R–Q1 P–B3 23 B–N3 B–B5 24 P–N3 R–KB2 25 Q–N4 B–R3 26 N–R4 R–B7 27 P–QR3 R–N2 28 Q–K1 R–K2 29 Q–N1? R(K2)–K7 30 N–B5 B–B1 31 R–K1 Q–K1 32 R×R Q×R 33 P–R3 B×P. 0 : 1.

Another variation to be mentioned in passing is **1 P–K4 P–K4 2 N–K2** (Alapin's Opening). White intends to open the KB file without facing the risks of a King's Gambit. 2 ... N–KB3 3 P–KB4 P×P (or 3 ... P–Q4 4 BP×P N×P 5 P–Q3 N–B4 6 P–Q4 N–K3 or 6 ... N–K5=, while 3 ... P–Q3 is quite sound) 4 N×P (4 P–K5 N–R4 5 P–KN3 P–Q3∓) 4 ... P–Q4 (not 4 ... N×P 5 Q–K2 Q–K2 6 N–Q5+) 5 N×P N×N 6 P×N Q×P 7 N–B3 Q–K4 ch 8 Q–K2 (8 B–K2 N–B3 with good play) 8 ... Q×Q ch 9 B×Q=.

Index of Games

(The heavy type indicates the player having white. The numbers refer to game numbers.)

Alapin – **Tarrasch**   31
Alekhine – Levitsky   9
Alexander – **Matanovich**   34
Alexander – **Schmid**   29
Andersen – **Desler**   23
Andersen – **Norman-Hansen**   24
Bardeleben – Hartlaub   5
Bardeleben – **Wolf**   15
Barrett – Hooper   54
Batik – **Duhrssen**   18
Beni – Nejkirch   37
Bhend – **Schmid**   12
Bisguier – **Evans**   30
Bisguier – **Browne**   13
Black – Schroeder   16
Bogatyrchuk – Kan   40
Botvinnik – **Bronstein**   51
Breazu – **Pavlov**   2
Bronstein – Botvinnik   51
Bronstein – **Trifunovich**   27
Browne – Bisguier   13
Capablanca – **Marshall**   50
Chalupetsky – **Ed. Lasker**   37
Dely – Malich   10
Desler – Andersen   23
Drimer – Unzicker   53
Duhrssen – Batik   18
Engert – **Kapetzky**   38
Evans – Bisguier   30
Fischer – German   6
Fuderer – Kostich   35
Gehl – Marshall   33
German – **Fischer**   6
Gligorich – **Ivkov**   46
Gunsberg – Weiss   19
Gusakov – **Zhilin**   4
Hartlaub – Bardeleben   5
Hartlaub – Schmidt   41
Hartlaub – Schories   45
Hazai – Sax   49
Hooper – **Barrett**   54
Hooper – **O. Penrose**   14
Hulak – **Sax**   36
Ilyin-Zhenevsky – **Rabinovich**   48
Ivkov – Gligorich   46
Janowski – Marshall   22
Kan – **Bogatyrchuk**   40

Kapetzky – Engert   38
Karpov – Korchnoy   20
Khmielevsky – **Kugayevsky**   17
Korchnoy – **Karpov**   20
Kostich – **Fuderer**   35
Krause – Nielsen   25
Kugayevsky – Khmielevsky   17
Ed. Lasker – Chalupetsky   37
Lein – Terentiev   52
Levitsky – **Alekhine**   9
Lilienthal – **Sokolsky**   11
Mackenzie – Mason   32
Malich – **Dely**   10
Maróczy – Showalter   8
Marshall – Capablanca   50
Marshall – **Gehl**   33
Marshall – **Janowski**   22
Marshall – **Nimzowitsch**   28
Mason – **Mackenzie**   32
Mason – **Schlechter**   26
Matanovich – Alexander   34
Nejkirch – **Beni**   37
Nielsen – **Krause**   25
Nimzowitsch – Marshall   28
Norman-Hansen – Anderssen   24
Olafsson – **Pilnik**   21
Pavlov – Breazu   2
Penrose O. – Hooper   14
Pilnik – Olafsson   21
Rabinovich – Ilyin-Zhenevsky   48
Rohachek – Shefc   39
Rossetto – **Spassky**   3
Rossetto – **Tal**   1
Rotlewi – **Tereschenko**   7
Sax – **Hazai**   49
Sax – Hulak   36
Schlechter – Mason   26
Schmid – Alexander   29
Schmid – Bhend   12
Schmidt – **Hartlaub**   41
Schories – **Hartlaub**   45
Schroeder – **Black**   16
Shefc – **Rohachek**   39
Showalter – **Maróczy**   8
Sokolsky – Lilienthal   11
Spassky – Rossetto   3
Spielmann – **Steenis**   44

Spitzer – Szén   43
Steenis – Spielmann   44
Szén – **Spitzer**   43
Tal – Rossetto   1
Tarrasch – Alapin   31
Terentiev – **Lein**   52

Tereschenko – Rotlewi   7
Trifunovich – Bronstein   27
Unzicker – **Drimer**   53
Weiss – **Gunsberg**   19
Wolf – Bardeleben   15
Zhilin – Gusakov   4

Addendum

The Petroff has maintained its reputation in recent years, notably as a solid drawing weapon in the new variation 1 P-K4 P-K4 2 N-KB3 N-KB3 3 N×P P-Q3 4 N-KB3 N×P 5 P-Q4 6 B-Q3 B-K2 7 0-0 N-B3 8 R-K1 and now Hübner's 1980 innovation 8... B-KB4. One may quote these high-level games in which Black came out of the opening with nothing to fear:

9 QN-Q2 N×N 10 Q×N (10 B×B N×Nch 11 P×N 0-0 is slightly better for Black) 10... B×B 11 Q×B 0-0 12 P-B3 and now 12... Q-Q2 (Adorjan-Hübner, Candidates Match, 1980), or 9 B-QN5 B-B3! (9... 0-0 10 B×N P×B 11 N-K5 gives White something to play for, as in Timman - Portisch, Moscow, 1981) 10 QN-Q2 (10 N-K5 B×N 11 P×B 0-0 looks about even) 10... 0-0 11 N-B1 N-K2 = (Karpov - Korchnoi, World championship, Merano, 1981).

December, 1981

Arrangement of Material

Part I Petroff's Defence 1 P-K4 P-K4 2 N-KB3 N-KB3

Chapter 1	3 P-Q4 P×P 4 P-K5			3
	4 B-QB4			23
	3 ... N×P			27
Chapter 2	3 N×P P-Q3 4 N-KB3	N×P 5 P-Q4		44
Chapter 3		5 Q-K2		67
Chapter 4		5 N-B3		76
Chapter 5		5 P-B4		81
Chapter 6		5 P-Q3		84
Chapter 7	4 N-B4			87
Chapter 8	4 N×P			91
	3 ... Q-K2			92
	3 ... N×P			93
Chapter 9	3 N-B3			97
Chapter 10	3 P-Q3			102
Chapter 11	3 B-B4			105
Chapter 12	3 P-Q4 P-Q3			113

Part II Other King's Pawn Openings 1 P-K4 P-K4

Chapter 1	2 N-KB3	N-KB3 3 N -B3 N-B3	123
Chapter 2	2 N-QB3		128
Chapter 3	2 P-Q4 P×P 3 N-KB3	N-QB3	130
Chapter 4	3 Q×P		135
Chapter 5	2 P-KB4		138
Chapter 6	2 B-B4		146